MAMMALS OF INDIANA

INDIANA NATURAL SCIENCE
Gillian Harris, editor

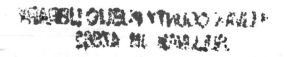

INDIANA UNIVERSITY PRESS
Bloomington and Indianapolis

MAMMALS

of

INDIANA

–A Field Guide–

JOHN O. WHITAKER, JR.

This book is a publication of

Indiana University Press
601 North Morton Street
Bloomington, Indiana
47404-3797 USA

www.iupress.indiana.edu

Telephone orders   800-842-6796
Fax orders   812-855-7931
Orders by e-mail   iuporder@indiana.edu

© 2010 by John O. Whitaker, Jr.

This book is printed on acid-free paper.

MANUFACTURED IN CHINA

Library of Congress Cataloging-in-Publication Data

Whitaker, John O.
  Mammals of Indiana : a field guide /
John O. Whitaker, Jr.
    p. cm. — (Indiana natural science)
  Includes bibliographical references and index.
  ISBN 978-0-253-22213-8 (pbk : alk. paper)
  1. Mammals—Indiana—Identification. I. Title.
  QL719.I6M865 2010
  599.09772—dc22
                                    2010004622

1 2 3 4 5   15 14 13 12 11 10

Contents

Preface and Acknowledgments

This is the first true field guide to the mammals of Indiana, one that can be put into one's pocket, taken into the field, and used to determine species of mammals seen. It can also be used in some cases to help decipher what mammal left its track, produced that feces, or made that burrow or cutting.

There are currently 59 mammal species living in Indiana excluding man, domestic animals, and accidentally introduced animals that have not managed to thrive. All of these will be considered in the main body of the text.

Eight of the species have been extirpated (i.e., are "extinct") in Indiana but still are present elsewhere. These species will be briefly described in an "in memoriam" section. Remains of some of these species may still be found—two separate sections of elk antlers were found in Parke County in 2002.

There have been other books on mammals of Indiana (Hahn 1909; Lyon 1936; Mumford 1969a; Mumford and Whitaker 1982; Whitaker and Mumford 2008). However, all of them were scientific treatises, bringing together much of what was known about the mammals of the state at the time they were written. This book includes keys to the skins and whole animals, keys to the skull, and range maps of Indiana mammals, as did some of the books above. But this book includes many more photographs of the animal, its skull, its habitat, and sometimes its tracks, den, burrow, and other signs such as cuttings.

I hope that this book will help you to learn about the mammals of our state and will help you to enjoy the Hoosier outdoors more fully.

I am indebted to all of the people who have worked previously on mammals of Indiana, beginning with Willard S. Blatchley, Walter L. Hahn, and Marcus W. Lyon, who compiled and presented much of the earlier work on Indiana mammals (1897, 1909, and 1936, respectively). Next my great thanks go to

Russell E. Mumford, who invited me to participate with him on studies of mammals of Indiana (Mumford and Whitaker 1982; Whitaker and Mumford 2008). My thanks also go to James B. Cope (deceased) for his stimulation, his knowledge, and our many discussions on bats (Whitaker et al. 2007). He is missed.

I am also indebted to numerous former students of Indiana State University and Purdue, far too numerous to mention here, but see acknowledgments in Mumford and Whitaker (1982) and Whitaker and Mumford (2008). A few of them most directly involved were David Rubin, Sherry Gummer, Tom French, Steven Ford, Gwilym Jones, David Pascal, Larry Schmeltz, Ted Terrel, Richard Tuszynski, Harmon P. Weeks, Dale Sparks, Brianne Walters, Leslie Rissler, Beth Vincent, and Jacques and Sherry Veilleux.

Also, I thank Linda Oblack of Indiana University Press for suggesting that I put this book together as the second in a series begun by my friend and colleague Marion Jackson with *101 Trees of Indiana* (2004). Jackson's book set the style and format for this book.

Indiana State University supplied funding, office space, equipment, and supplies for the project. Bill Brett and Charlie Amlaner have freely offered encouragement, help, and advice. Scott Johnson and Katie Smith, Indiana Department of Natural Resources (IDNR), and Scott and Lori Pruitt of the United States Fish and Wildlife Service have provided funding and help in many other ways. Laura Bakken typed the entire manuscript and made many helpful suggestions on this and preceding manuscripts. Linda Castor made the maps, took all of the skull photos, made many of the drawings, and helped get the photographs ready for publication.

If not indicated otherwise, photos are by the author.

I thank my parents and Robert E. Goodwin for nurturing my early interests in these areas, and William J. Hamilton, Jr., for guiding me through my graduate training. Finally, I thank my wife, Royce, and the rest of my family for putting up with much time spent on this and other projects. To my daughter Lynne, who has read and greatly improved the entire manuscript, I also give my thanks.

Indiana's State Mammal—a Proposal

Indiana has a state bird—the cardinal—and a state tree—the tulip tree—but no state mammal. We therefore propose for the state mammal the Indiana myotis. The Indiana myotis was one of only two species of mammal originally described from Indiana. The other is the prairie vole, described by Wagner from New Harmony, Indiana, in 1842.

The Indiana myotis was described from Wyandotte Cave by Gerritt S. Miller and Grover M. Allen in 1928. It is listed as endangered because its rangewide population has gone from about 880,000 in 1960 to about 380,000 today. Kentucky and Missouri used to have the largest populations, but the population has been decreasing for some time in those states, until today, when Indiana has more Indiana myotis than any other state.

Therefore, because it was described from Indiana, because it has its largest population here, and because it takes its name from our state, we propose that the Indiana myotis be named the state mammal.

In Memory of the Recently Extirpated Native Species

The mammalian fauna of Indiana is constantly changing, as is evidenced by the number of species that have become extirpated over the past 150 years. Other species may be extirpated in the future. For this reason, most states have compiled lists of endangered and threatened species. The Indiana endangered (in danger of extirpation) list currently includes the Indiana myotis, gray myotis, evening bat, swamp rabbit, Franklin's ground squirrel, Allegheny woodrat, and bobcat. The threatened species list is no longer recognized in Indiana (species that are likely to become endangered within the foreseeable future); it included only one species, the badger. Rafinesque's big-eared bat is currently very rare in Indiana and is of only accidental occurrence. The southeastern myotis wintered regularly in caves in south central Indiana but is now probably extirpated.

EXTIRPATED NATIVE SPECIES
(Dental formulas given below are described on pp. 26–27.)

Porcupine, *Erethizon dorsatum*. The porcupine is best known for its quills, which occur over most of the dorsal part of the body except for the face and inside of the legs. They are present on the underside of the tail. The quills are yellowish-white with black tips and range from about 1 to 4" in length. Though not as obvious as that of the skunk, the porcupine has a black and white warning pattern that tends to alert would-be predators. The total length of the porcupine is 36–40" (900–1,000 mm), tail 150 mm, hind foot 87–100 mm. Weight 15–25 lbs or more when fat. Skull: length 92–111 mm.

Dental formula:

$$I \ \frac{1}{1} \ \ C \ \frac{0}{0} \ \ P \ \frac{1}{1} \ \ M \ \frac{3}{3} \ = \ 20$$

Porcupines mate in late autumn. One young (occasionally two) is produced. The young are very large. Porcupines are born with eyes opened and fully haired, often with quills. The porcupine declined because of loss of forest and also because of killing by humans, as they, like bats and snakes, have an undeserved bad reputation. In reality, they are a very interesting species that reproduces very slowly. Most of the late records of this species in Indiana were in the 1800s.

Gray wolf, *Canis lupus*. There is confusion in the literature about the native species of *Canis* in Indiana involving the timber wolf, *Canis lupus*; red wolf, *Canis rufus*; and coyote, *Canis latrans*. The timber wolf was present at the time of settlement and disappeared by 1908. The coyote apparently was rare at the time of settlement but increased after disappearance of the gray wolf, especially since the 1980s. There is much more question about the Texas red wolf. It may simply have been a southern, smaller form of the gray wolf and may or may not have been in Indiana. Most workers today consider it to be a full species, although genetically it is similar to the gray wolf, the coyote, and the domestic dog. The gray wolf is very large, weighing about 100 lbs. Adult males measure about 1,300–1,800 mm, tail 400 mm, hind foot 240 mm. The main food of wolves was deer and other large species, which were hunted in packs. The gray wolf is now gone from the eastern United States except for areas in Minnesota, Wisconsin, and the upper peninsula of Michigan. Skull: 232–263 mm.

Dental formula:

$$I \ \frac{3}{3} \ C \ \frac{1}{1} \ P \ \frac{4}{4} \ M \ \frac{2}{3} \ = \ 42$$

Black bear, *Ursus americanus*. The black bear is about 5–6' long (1,500–1,800 cm) with a tail of 5" (125 mm), hind foot 7½" (185 mm), weight about 200–500 lbs (90–227 kg). The skull is about 10" (255 mm) long.

Dental formula:

$$I \ \frac{3}{3} \ C \ \frac{1}{1} \ P \ \frac{4}{4} \ M \ \frac{2}{3} \ = \ 42$$

The black bear is very dark brown or black. Black bears den in hollows in trees, under banks, under tree trunks, and in other such protected places. They remain in the den for most of the winter but do not truly hibernate. They produce one to four young (usually two) during their winter denning period. Bears are remarkable for their tiny size at birth, only about 200 grams and about 180 mm in length. Black bears feed on grasses and forbs in spring and fruits and mast in summer and fall. They will also eat berries of many kinds but especially blueberries, as well as mice, fish and other small animals, and of course honey. Despite their size, bears are good climbers. They leave ample signs where they are active—footprints, torn-up ground, torn-apart stumps and logs, and scratch marks on trees.

The black bear once ranged over essentially all of the eastern United States but currently occurs in northern Michigan and Wisconsin, from New England through New York down the Appalachians, and in several areas along the coast from North Carolina to Louisiana. The black bear originally occurred throughout Indiana but was nearly extirpated by about 1830, although there were a few records through 1888.

Fisher, *Martes pennanti*. The fisher is a dark-colored, elongate weasellike mammal, about the size of a fox, with an elongate, bushy, tapering tail. The male is considerably larger than the female. The total length of the male is about 3' (900 mm), tail about 14" (350 mm), hind foot about 4" (100 mm). The weight is about 8–12 lbs (3.6–5.5 kg).

Dental formula:

$$\text{I } \frac{3}{3} \text{ C } \frac{1}{1} \text{ P } \frac{4}{4} \text{ M } \frac{1}{2} = 38$$

The underparts are very dark and there are a few white spots on the throat. The fisher is primarily terrestrial but is arboreal, especially when harassed. It lives in conifer or mixed conifer-hardwood areas. Fishers use "maternity dens," and also use temporary dens while moving about their home ranges. Despite its name, it seldom feeds on fish. Rather it feeds primarily on rabbits, squirrels and other rodents, and even porcupines. Fishers kill porcupines by attacking their faces until they weaken the porcupine. Female fishers breed at 1 year and produce a litter at 2 years of age. The fisher was eliminated by overtrapping and loss of habitat over much of its U.S. range in the late 1800s and early 1900s. It still exists and has made a remarkable comeback in Wisconsin and in the Upper Peninsula of Michigan, and it has been doing well in New England and New York. In Indiana there are only a few records of its occurrence.

Mountain lion, *Puma concolor.* The mountain lion is easily distinguished from any other North American mammal by its large size, catlike form, and uniform coloration. Its length is about 7½' (2,300 mm) for male, 6½' (2,000 mm) for female. Total length is 59–108", tail 21–35", hind foot 8.5–11.5". Weight varies but averages about 150 lbs (79–227 kg). The skull length is about 200–250 mm.

Dental formula:

$$I \ \frac{3}{3} \quad C \ \frac{1}{1} \quad P \ \frac{3}{2} \quad M \ \frac{1}{1} \ = \ 30$$

The color of the mountain lion is yellowish-brown, lighter below; the ear is blackish on the outside. The tip of the tail is darkish-brown. Mountain lions are active year round and prey on a variety of food items, but especially deer. They hunt by stalking. Mating is in late autumn or early winter, and gestation is 13–14 weeks. The young, usually one to four, are born in late winter or early spring. The eyes open at about 10 days, and the young are weaned at about 3 or 4 months. They are spotted for the first 6 months. The mountain lion was gone from Indiana quite early, mostly by the 1830s, although there were a few later records, including one in Morgan County in 1851.

Wapiti or elk, *Cervus elaphus.* The elk formerly occurred over much of the United States and was found throughout Indiana. Males are much larger than females. Males have a total length of about 9', the tail is about 6', and the hind foot about 25". The weight is about 700 lbs. Females are about 7½' long, the tail is about 5', and the weight is about 500 lbs.

Dental formula:

$$I \ \frac{0}{3} \quad C \ \frac{1}{1} \quad P \ \frac{3}{3} \quad M \ \frac{3}{3} \ = \ 34$$

Mating of elk is in autumn when the antlers in the male are fully developed; they are used during the struggle for mates. Gestation is about 8½ months. Usually one white-spotted young is produced, which is able to stand up and walk within hours of birth. The last elk reports from Indiana were from Ripley County (1810), Wayne County (1811), Vigo County (1816), Allen County (1818), and Knox County (1830).

Bison, *Bison bison.* The bison or "buffalo," order Artiodactyla, is a member of the cow/African antelope family Bovidae.

Bison are characterized by their true horns, slightly larger in males; by their large heads; and by their massive size. Horns of bovids, consisting of a bony core covered with keratin fiber, are never shed. Males are much larger than females. Total length of males is about 11', the tail is 24", hind foot 24". The weight is about 1,800 lbs. Females are about 7' in length, with a tail length of 18" and hind foot 20". Female weight is about 1,000 lbs (Lyon 1936). Bison were the largest mammals in Indiana in historic times. There are no upper incisors or canines.

Dental formula:

$$\text{I} \quad \frac{0}{3} \quad \text{C} \quad \frac{0}{1} \quad \text{P} \quad \frac{3}{3} \quad \text{M} \quad \frac{3}{3} \quad = \quad 32$$

The bison was gregarious, occurring on the Great Plains by the millions. About the middle of the nineteenth century, a great slaughter for meat and hides began and continued until the animal was almost exterminated. One young (rarely twins) was produced. Bison were migratory, traveling between feeding grounds on well-beaten pathways or "traces" through the state. One of the best-known traces extended from the prairies of Illinois, crossing the Wabash River near Vincennes, then went to the southeast to the falls of the Ohio near Louisville, where it crossed to Ohio and went on to Big Bone Lick and the bluegrass region of Kentucky. Bison were not seen in the state after 1808.

Black rat, *Rattus rattus*. The black rat made it to Indiana early, at least to Indianapolis, but is believed to have been outcompeted by the Norway rat, *Rattus norvegicus*. Like the Norway rat, it is mainly found in buildings. It was last seen in Indiana about 1845.

Dental formula:

$$\text{I } \frac{1}{1} \quad \text{C } \frac{0}{0} \quad \text{P } \frac{0}{0} \quad \text{M } \frac{3}{3} \; = \; 16$$

MAMMALS OF INDIANA

SPECIES OF QUESTIONABLE RECENT OCCURRENCE

Eastern spotted skunk, *Spilogale putorius*. Mumford and Whitaker (1982) recorded the spotted skunk as extirpated in Indiana. However, as for the wolverine, the evidence for its recent occurrence is meager, and one would not expect it here on the basis of its recent range. Hall and Kelson (1959) and Hall (1981) include Indiana in its range only on the basis of two relatively shaky Indiana records. However, there is abundant fossil evidence indicating that this species was present at least in prehistoric times, as remains of at least 25 individuals were collected by Ron Richards of the Indiana State Museum from nine separate localities. Richards concluded that the spotted skunk was a rare inhabitant of at least southwestern Indiana in historic times but that it is now extirpated. We agree with this interpretation.

The spotted skunk is generally black but has four white stripes along the back, uninterrupted from the head to the middle of the back, and broken into patches or spots on the hindquarters. Males are larger than females. Total length is 463–610 mm in males, 403–544 in females. Tail is 193–280 mm in males, 165–210 in females, and the hind foot is 43–59 mm in males, 39–47 in females. Weight is 1–2.5 lbs in males, 0.8 to 1.25 in females. Skull length is 43–55 mm.

Dental formula:

$$\text{I } \frac{3}{3} \text{ C } \frac{1}{1} \text{ P } \frac{3}{3} \text{ M } \frac{1}{2} = 34$$

Red Wolf, *Canis rufus*. As indicated in the account of the gray wolf, there is question as to whether the red wolf is a distinct species and what its relationships are to the gray wolf and to the coyote.

Seminole Bat, *Lasiurus seminolus*. Three Seminole bats have appeared in Indiana in the last few years, all in the Evansville area. They are considered to be accidental species, as they appear to have come in with shipments of Spanish moss, *Tillandsia usneoides*.

Species List of Indiana Mammals

Species are arranged here phylogenetically by order, family, genus, and species, which is the same order that the species accounts appear in the book (other than for the extirpated species). By listing species phylogenetically, related (thus usually similar) species are generally grouped together, which facilitates species comparisons.

I = Introduced

	Order	Family	Sub Family	Species/Common Name	Pages
I	DIDELPHIMORPHIA	Didelphidae		*Didelphis virginiana* Kerr / Virginia Opossum	59–62
	SORICOMORPHA	Soricidae		*Sorex cinereus* Kerr / Masked Shrew	64–67
	SORICOMORPHA	Soricidae		*Sorex fumeus* Miller / Smoky Shrew	68–69
	SORICOMORPHA	Soricidae		*Sorex hoyi* (Baird) / Pygmy Shrew	70–72
	SORICOMORPHA	Soricidae		*Sorex longirostris* Bachman / Southeastern Shrew	73–75
	SORICOMORPHA	Soricidae		*Blarina brevicauda* (Say) / Northern Short-tailed Shrew	76–79
	SORICOMORPHA	Soricidae		*Cryptotis parva* (Say) / Least Shrew	80–81
	SORICOMORPHA	Talpidae		*Scalopus aquaticus* (Linnaeus) / Eastern Mole	82–85
	SORICOMORPHA	Talpidae		*Condylura cristata* (Linnaeus) / Star-nosed Mole	86–88

(continued)

I	Order	Family	Sub Family	Species / Common Name	Pages
	CHIROPTERA	Vespertilionidae		*Myotis lucifugus* (Le Conte) / Little Brown Myotis	92–95
	CHIROPTERA	Vespertilionidae		*Myotis austroriparius* (Rhoads) / Southeastern Myotis	96–97
	CHIROPTERA	Vespertilionidae		*Myotis grisescens* Howell / Gray Myotis	98–100
	CHIROPTERA	Vespertilionidae		*Myotis leibii* (Audubon and Bachman) / Eastern Small-footed Myotis	101–103
	CHIROPTERA	Vespertilionidae		*Myotis septentrionalis* (Trouessart) / Northern Myotis	104–105
	CHIROPTERA	Vespertilionidae		*Myotis sodalis* Miller and G. M. Allen / Indiana Myotis	106–109
	CHIROPTERA	Vespertilionidae		*Lasionycteris noctivagans* (Le Conte) / Silver-haired Bat	110–111
	CHIROPTERA	Vespertilionidae		*Perimyotis subflavus* (F. Cuvier) / Eastern Pipistrelle	112–114
	CHIROPTERA	Vespertilionidae		*Eptesicus fuscus* (Beauvois) / Big Brown Bat	115–117
	CHIROPTERA	Vespertilionidae		*Nycticeius humeralis* (Rafinesque) / Evening Bat	118–119
	CHIROPTERA	Vespertilionidae		*Lasiurus borealis* (Müller) / Red Bat	120–122
	CHIROPTERA	Vespertilionidae		*Lasiurus cinereus* (Palisot de Beauvois) / Hoary Bat	123–125
	CHIROPTERA	Vespertilionidae		*Corynorhinus rafinesquii* (Lesson) / Rafinesque's Big-eared Bat	126–127

Order	Family	Subfamily	Species / Common name	Pages
CINGULATA	Dasypodidae		*Dasypus novemcinctus* Linnaeus / Nine-banded Armadillo	129–132
LAGOMORPHA	Leporidae		*Sylvilagus floridanus* (J. A. Allen) / Eastern Cottontail	134–137
LAGOMORPHA	Leporidae		*Sylvilagus aquaticus* (Bachman) / Swamp Rabbit	138–141
RODENTIA	Sciuridae		*Tamias striatus* (Linnaeus) / Eastern Chipmunk	145–148
RODENTIA	Sciuridae		*Marmota monax* (Linnaeus) / Woodchuck	149–152
RODENTIA	Sciuridae		*Spermophilus tridecemlineatus* (Mitchill) / Thirteen-lined Ground Squirrel	153–156
RODENTIA	Sciuridae		*Spermophilus franklinii* (Sabine) / Franklin's Ground Squirrel	157–159
RODENTIA	Sciuridae		*Sciurus carolinensis* Gmelin / Gray Squirrel	160–163
RODENTIA	Sciuridae		*Sciurus niger* Linnaeus / Fox Squirrel	164–167
RODENTIA	Sciuridae		*Tamiasciurus hudsonicus* (Erxleben) / Red Squirrel	168–171
RODENTIA	Sciuridae		*Glaucomys volans* (Linnaeus) / Southern Flying Squirrel	172–174
RODENTIA	Geomyidae		*Geomys bursarius* (Shaw) / Plains Pocket Gopher	175–178
RODENTIA	Castoridae		*Castor canadensis* Kuhl / Beaver	179–185
RODENTIA	Cricetidae	Neotominae	*Reithrodontomys megalotis* (Baird) / Western Harvest Mouse	186–189
RODENTIA	Cricetidae	Neotominae	*Peromyscus maniculatus bairdii* (Wagner) / Prairie Deer Mouse	190–193

(continued)

I

INTRODUCTION: PURPOSE AND PLAN OF THE BOOK

The purpose of this book is to help people identify and learn something about mammals of Indiana, from the skin or skull, tracks, feces, or other sign. It covers all the mammals—59 species—known to occur in Indiana today or recently, along with some information on the species that have become clearly extirpated in the past two centuries.

This book is for the educator, the student, the conservationist, the amateur or professional naturalist, or anybody who is interested in the great outdoors. I hope that it proves useful.

What is a mammal? It is a vertebrate (backboned) animal with hair and one that feeds milk to its young. In this book we will include all the native and introduced mammals that occur naturally in the state. However, we have not included humans, dogs, cats, pigs, cows, horses, or other exotic or domesticated animals.

Distribution maps are provided with the counties marked in which a species has been seen or captured. In time, undoubtedly many more counties will be added to the maps. Many species have been relatively stable in their range, including most of the species of the state. Many occur throughout the state. Others have more limited ranges, such as the red squirrel and thirteen-lined ground squirrel in the northern part of the state, and Franklin's ground squirrel just in the northwest. The eastern wood rat occurs along the Ohio River bluffs of Harrison and Crawford counties and is in trouble there. Some species have been increasing their range; for example, the western harvest mouse, which moved into the state from Illinois in 1969 and spread into the whole northwest part of Indiana. The badger, though very uncommon, has increased its Indiana range nearly to the Ohio River. Also, the ranges and/or populations of some species have gotten larger, even to the point of becoming nuisances. This is true of the beaver and raccoon. The beaver and deer were completely gone from the state as of 1800, and the river otter as of 1942. All of these have been reintroduced (the otter in the 1990s by IDNR), and all are doing fine.

Photographs are included of each animal and its skull, and when possible other signs such as its lodge, tracks, feces, and cuttings.

We used the metric system for many of the standard measurements. Although this may be unfamiliar to some, you should be able to become familiar with the few we have used. To help in this, there are conversion scales and tables for comparison of the two systems in the back matter (see p. 289).

The book is presented in typical field book style, its size and shape allowing it to fit easily into a hip pocket, purse, or small pack.

INDIANA · AN OVERVIEW

THE INDIANA LANDSCAPE AND
MAJOR HABITATS

Indiana is about 275 miles from north to south (41° 50'—37° 40' north latitude), and about 175 miles east to west (88° 2'—84° 49' west longitude). The state encompasses 36,291 square miles. It is bordered on the south by the Ohio River, on the north by Lake Michigan in the northwest, and by the state of Michigan in the northeast. Ohio borders Indiana on the east and the Wabash River and Illinois on the west. The Wabash River forms much of the line between the two states in southwestern Indiana. Beginning in Ohio, the Wabash flows to the west across Indiana through Huntington, Wabash, Peru, and Logansport, then turns south through Lafayette, Terre Haute, and Vincennes and enters the Ohio River at the southwest corner of the state. The Wabash is the longest undammed river in the United States. The state averages about 700' above sea level and ranges from 1,257 at the highest point (Randolph County) to 313 at the lowest (Posey County).

Most of the state has been glaciated, much of it several times, except for a large triangular area in the southern portion of the state with its base along the south central portion of the Ohio River and its point near Bloomington. This is the rugged unglaciated hill country of southern Indiana and includes the cave or "karst" areas. Karst has most of its drainage underground in caves and usually contains numerous "sink holes" (holes from the surface into caves that may be open or may be filled with debris).

In the northwest part of the state are the Indiana Dunes, which have been preserved and resurrected thanks to the efforts of Illinois Senator Paul Douglas. Classic studies of succession were done in this area, including Cowles' 1899 study of plant succession and Shelford's (1912a,b) study of animal succession. Across northern Indiana are numerous lakes and potholes as well as earlier large marshes, the Great and Grand marshes. In the northwest, large black soil prairies existed prior to settlement. However, much of the state, especially in the north, now consists of vast farmlands where corn, soy-beans, and wheat are the primary crops on what was once forest or grasslands.

During presettlement years (prior to 1800), about 20 million acres (87%) of the 23,227,000 acres constituting the state were forest. About half the forest of the state contained beech-maple, 30 percent various oak-hickory combinations, and the other 7 percent variable. The remaining 13 percent were mostly in prairie, wetlands, and water.

Forested land had decreased to about 7 percent of the state by 1917 but since has increased to about 20 percent. Much of the reforestation has occurred in the southern half of the

NATURAL REGIONS OF INDIANA

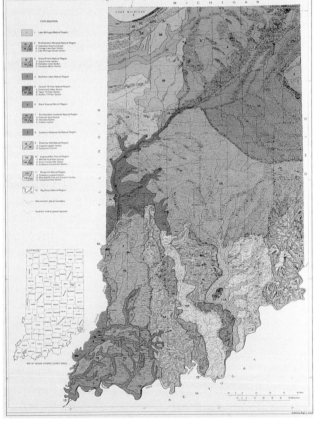

state, especially in the Hoosier National Forest and the rest of the unglaciated portion of south central Indiana. The many rivers in the state provide much bottomland habitat, and we are fortunate to have the major bluffs along the Ohio River, which provide habitat for the woodrat and a variety of other species.

There are 92 counties in the state, and Homoya et al. (1985) and Homoya (1985) divided the state into 12 natural regions. A natural region is a "unit" of the landscape with distinctive natural features. The natural regions are shown below; see Homoya et al. (1985) and Jackson (1997) for descriptions of the natural regions.

COUNTY MAP OF INDIANA

ECOLOGICAL RELATIONSHIPS OF MAMMALS

Indiana has a number of different major habitats, such as upland and bottomland forest; prairie and other grassland; marsh, swamp, and other wetlands; caves; and of course human-created habitats such as farmland and buildings. Most species are not restricted to one habitat but live in or move across other habitats.

Many of the larger species have fewer ties to habitats than smaller species. This may be at least in part because our state is fragmented into small patches of habitat, and the larger animals have home ranges larger than many of the fragments. For whatever reason, opossums, raccoons, cottontail rabbits, coyotes, eastern moles, New York weasels, and white-tailed deer are not related as closely to specific habitats. Among the foxes, the red fox is a species of more open country and the gray fox of more wooded habitat. The bluffs along the Ohio River in Harrison and Crawford counties are the home of the woodrat.

Upland Forest: All of the tree squirrels need trees and derive much of their food from trees—but they will venture from wooded areas on occasion. The gray, flying, and red squirrels are most dependent on trees, whereas the fox squirrel is often found in open woods and it often enters cultivated fields for corn and other crops. The white-footed mouse is one of the most common mammals of Indiana, and it is partial to wooded situations. The woodland vole is also most often found in woods. Bats that normally live in trees in summer are the Indiana myotis (under sloughing bark), northern bat (in woodpecker holes and cracks), pipistrelles (in tiny groups in clusters of leaves), and red and hoary bats (hang among the leaves of trees, although not always in woods). The pygmy shrew and smoky shrew, not discovered in Indiana until 1982, are confined to the wooded ravines of Indiana's south central unglaciated area.

Bottomland Forest: The only inhabitant really restricted to bottomland woods in Indiana is the swamp rabbit. It lives in southwest Indiana in areas with cane but also in other ground cover types, but today most of the 80 or so swamp rabbits left are found in Gibson County. Swamp rabbits are good swimmers and climbers but need high ground near their haunts as "refugia" during major floods. However, most of the "refugia" have been cleared and planted to crops, which is perhaps the major reason why the species has decreased precipitously.

Prairie: There are a few prairie forms. The pocket gopher and the Franklin's ground squirrel are confined to the prairie area of northwestern Indiana. The thirteen-lined ground squirrel, badger, and least weasel are other prairie forms, but they have spread far beyond the limits of the prairies of Indiana.

Other Grassland Forms: The prairie and meadow voles, meadow jumping mouse, which will enter bottomland woods in northern Indiana, bog lemming, least shrew, and western harvest mouse are common grassland inhabitants. Also, the masked shrew can be very abundant in grasslands, especially when the area is moist. The prairie vole is found in dry grasslands, the meadow vole in moist grasslands. The harvest mouse invaded Indiana in Newton County about 1969 and has been increasing its range in the northwest portion of the state ever since.

Wetlands and Aquatic Forms: The beaver, muskrat, and otter are our most aquatic species, followed by the mink and star-nosed mole. The star-nosed mole will enter water to seek food. The best way to determine that star-nosed moles are present is by the typical mole hills, but unlike the eastern mole, they are in muckland. Beaver and muskrats can best be found by their sign—large lodges in the case of the beaver (they use bank burrows along rivers) and much smaller houses in the case of muskrats (they often use bank burrows also). Cut trees and cut tree limbs and cuttings of cattails and other aquatic plants are signs of beaver and muskrats, respectively. Otters are known for their slides, but their feces full of fish scales may prove a more obvious character.

Farmlands: Many of the species of Indiana mammals often forage or hide in cultivated fields. However, the only species that are abundant in corn and soybean fields are the prairie deer mouse and the house mouse. The original habitat of the prairie deer mouse is not clear. It was probably not on the heavily vegetated prairies, as prairie deer mice seldom occur in permanent vegetative cover now. They were probably on poorly vegetated open areas, as today they are abundant in the cultivated fields—remaining there through plowing, planting, growing and harvesting, whether there is cover or not. They use the soil for cover. The house mouse is the other species that occupies this habitat, but only when plants such as foxtail and other grasses are abundant enough to form good ground cover. House mice relocate (some to buildings, but many to other grassy fields) when the crops are harvested or the field is planted.

Caves: Many species of mammals use caves occasionally, such as wood rats, white-footed mice, raccoons, and foxes, but bats are best known for their use of caves. Some people assume that most bats live in caves, and it is true that many bats of some species hibernate in caves. The Indiana myotis forms huge clusters in a very few caves. The little brown bat forms small clusters in a number of caves. The pipistrelle is solitary, but a few may be found in a large number of caves. Northern bats hibernate in caves and mines but are solitary in cracks and holes, therefore are very seldom where they can be seen. A few big brown bats hibernate in caves or mines but most hibernate in attics of heated buildings. Also, a very few silver-haired bats hibernate in Indiana caves. Except for some males and nonreproductive females, none of the above bats are "cave" bats except during hibernation. The only true "cave" bat in Indiana (occupying caves winter and summer) is the gray bat, and there is only one summer colony of this species in the state. It is in a quarry at Sellersburg in Clark County. It first appeared there about 1982 and the colony then contained about 400 bats, but it has continued to grow ever since until it now contains more than 6,000 bats. Being a true "cave bat" this species presumably hibernates in caves farther south but we do not know where as yet.

Buildings: Several species of mammals often live in buildings, including several kinds of bats. The main bats in buildings are big and little brown bats, but northern bats and pipistrelles occasionally have summer colonies there. Also, all evening bat colonies known from Indiana prior to 1993 were in buildings, but all we are aware of since 1993 have been in trees. Norway rats sometimes inhabit buildings, especially barns and feed storage areas where food is available as well as shelter. There are two kinds of mice that normally inhabit buildings in Indiana, the house mouse in open and cultivated situations and the white-footed mouse in wooded areas. Other species that can be pests in and about buildings are raccoons, flying squirrels, chipmunks, and sometimes woodchucks and skunks.

NAMING AND IDENTIFYING MAMMALS

HOW MAMMALS ARE NAMED

All mammals, and all organisms for that matter, have one valid scientific or Latin name. The purpose for this is that people will always know what species is being discussed. The scientific name consists of two parts, the generic name (genus, plural genera) and the trivial or species name. For example, the Indiana myotis is *Myotis sodalis* Miller and Allen, 1928. Gerrit S. Miller, Jr., and Grover M. Allen first recognized and described the Indiana myotis as a new species. It is closely related to *Myotis lucifugus,* thus is in the same genus. Miller and Allen named it *sodalis,* meaning "social," because it gathers in tight clusters during hibernation in winter. They could have named it for some characteristic of the bat, for the locality where they found it (Wyandotte Cave, or Indiana), or they could have named it to honor some other person. Also, they could have used any of many other names, provided the name was unique, that is, not previously used in that genus. I am often asked if I would name it after myself if I found a new species. No— that would not be in good taste and would be frowned upon. There are rules governing the assignment of scientific names to be sure that they are unique. Sometimes you will see the name of an author of a species in parentheses such as for the eastern woodrat, *Neotoma floridana* (Ord). The parentheses signify that when the species was originally described, it was delegated to a genus other than *Neotoma.* In contrast, Miller and Allen, 1928, above is not in parentheses because *M. sodalis* was originally described in the genus *Myotis.*

Lay people usually like to use "common names" rather than Latin names because they are usually easier to spell, pronounce, and remember. Sometimes scientific names are used as common names, for example, *Rhinoceros* and *Hippopotamus.* These usually do not bother people because they are familiar with them. It would be good if we could have just one set of names; however, that is not likely any time in the near future. Common names are nice for the reasons mentioned above. However, they have their problems in that people can not be sure they are talking about the same organism. For example, people in Indiana often refer to *Sciurus niger,* the fox squirrel, as a red squirrel. However, the true red squirrel is a smaller squirrel found in northern Indiana, *Tamiasciurus hudsonicus.* The chipmunk, *Tamias striatus,* is often called a ground squirrel. However, there are two true ground squirrels in Indiana, including the thirteen-lined ground squirrel, *Spermophilus tridecemlineatus,* which is often called a "gopher." Yet there is also a gopher in Indiana, the Plains pocket gopher, *Geomys bursarius,* which occurs in northwestern Indiana. To go farther afield, in the southeastern United States, "gopher" usually refers to a turtle, the gopher tortoise. In those areas, to find a pocket gopher, you need to ask for a "salamander," while salamanders are referred to as "lizards." You get the picture. You need to be very careful when using common names.

The mammals are all related to each other. Very similar species are placed in one genus, for example, there are six species of bats in the genus *Myotis* in this book. Closely related genera are placed together in families. All the bats in Indiana belong to one family, the Vespertilionidae, and all the families of bats are placed in one order, the Chiroptera, and all the orders of mammals, such as the Rodentia, Carnivora, Lagomorpha (rabbits) are placed together in the class Mammalia.

In a discussion of animal names, the words "classify" and "identify" are often confused, that is, "classify" is often used when one means "identify." I am often asked to classify something, which I can't do, at least not without a great deal of work. To classify something is to study it in relation to all its relatives, to describe it and give it a name or a new name if it needs it, and to fit it into the classification scheme. To "identify" something is usually what is meant by the question—to identify is to determine the proper name for something already within the classification scheme. However, many of the characteristics used to classify mammals are also the characteristics used to identify them. We will use taxonomic keys in this book to identify (not to classify) the various mammals of Indiana.

HOW MAMMALS ARE IDENTIFIED

Each "kind" or species of mammal is different from every other. They differ from each other genetically in the DNA they carry and also in the characteristics expressed by the DNA. Individuals within a species differ from each other, thus police departments can use DNA evidence to solve crimes and we can use DNA evidence to separate individuals of bats within a species. The differences are much greater between species than between individuals, so we can use DNA analysis to determine species. DNA analysis can also be used to classify; that is, DNA relationships can be used to build groups of organisms into an evolutionary system including species and also higher groups.

However, most of us do not have access to the high-priced equipment necessary to run DNA analysis on all those species we want to identify. Even if we did, we would not be able to use it to identify species in the field. Therefore, we use the characteristics of the animals to identify them, and we cluster the species into taxonomic keys using those characteristics. Here we will discuss some of the main characteristics used in identification of mammals. Usually we want to identify the whole animal, the stuffed skin, or the skull.

WHOLE ANIMAL

Standard measurements are normally taken in mm (1' = 25.4 mm). In the descriptions later in the book, units are understood to be mm or grams (for weight) unless otherwise noted.

They consist of the following:

Total Length: From tip of nose to tip of tail bone (not hairs).

Tail Length: From base of tail (bent upward at right angle to body) to tip of tail bone.

Hind Foot: From posterior of ankle to end of longest toenail.

Ear: From notch to tip of ear (not all workers measure this).

Weight: Usually in grams (1 ounce = 28.6 grams).

And in addition, the following measurements are included for bats:

Forearm Length (FA): Total length of the long bone of the wing.

Tragus (TR): Total length of ear lobe (vertical portion inside of the ear from notch to tip).

Wingspan (optional): From wingtip to wingtip.

Standard measurements are always written in order; for example: TL—181 T—76 HF—23 Ear—12 Wt.—21.0

Feet: Mammals may have hooves, but most have claws. The number of toes on front and hind feet can be counted; for example, 5-4 means that there are five toes on the front feet, four on the hind feet. Sometimes a thumb may be differentiated (opossum) or a toe may be represented by a nail only.

Wings of a Bat: The wings of a bat are modified forelimbs. They are formed of skin over the finger bones. The thumb of a bat is the claw on the front of the wing at the end of the forearms; the other four finger bones are the bones that support the wing.

Interfemoral Membrane of a Bat: This is the skin membrane that stretches between the hind legs, enveloping most of the tail, and it connects to the hind part of the wing membranes. Uropatagium is another name for the interfemoral membrane.

Calcar of Bat: A small cartilage protruding from the ankle into and helping to support the interfemoral membrane.

Patagium: The flattened skin between front and hind limbs of a flying squirrel.

THE SKULL AND TEETH

Teeth are much used in keys to various mammals. Mammalogists write a "tooth formula" to indicate the numbers of each kind of teeth as follows:

Incisors: The front teeth, those in the premaxillary bones of the upper jaw and in the anterior end of the mandible.

Canines: The single tooth, usually elongated and often pointed, situated behind the incisors and in front of the molariform teeth; that is, the first tooth in the maxillary bone.

Molariform Teeth (cheek teeth): The teeth behind the canines. They consist of the premolars (anterior ones) and the molars. It is often best to count them just as molariform teeth because it is not possible to distinguish premolars from molars just by looking at them. Technically they differ in that the premolars are preceded by milk or "baby" teeth, whereas the molars are not.

Dental Formula is written (for the dog) as

$$\text{I} \ \frac{3}{3} \quad \text{C} \ \frac{1}{1} \quad \text{P} \ \frac{4}{4} \quad \text{M} \ \frac{2}{3} \ = \ 42$$

although the letters I, C, P, and M for incisors, canines, premolars, and molars are often omitted. The tooth formula above indicates that there are 3 incisors in the upper and the lower jaw, 1 canine in each, 4 premolars in each, 2 molars in the upper jaw, and 3 in the lower. This all adds to 21 teeth per side × 2 sides = 42 teeth.

Or you could also combine molariform teeth (premolars and molars) and write it more simply as

$$\frac{3}{3} \quad \frac{1}{1} \quad \frac{6}{7} \ = \ 42$$

Unicuspids: In shrews, the 3–5 small teeth between the pair of large, two-cusped upper incisors and the large cheek teeth.

Other helpful terms for use of keys are arranged alphabetically below. Check the glossary of this book for more terms.

Anterior palatine foramina: The anterior two of the openings in the front of the bony palate.

Basal length of skull: From the anterior edge of the foramen magnum to the most anterior portion of the skull.

Bony palate: The bony roof of the mouth.

Diastema: A distinct gap or space between teeth where teeth have been lost through evolution; for example, between the incisors and the molariform teeth of rabbits and rodents (due to the loss of the canines), or in the front part of the jaws of the white-tailed deer (due to the absence of the upper incisors).

Fenestra: An opening.

Fenestrate: Filled with a labyrinth of small openings, here especially on the rostrum of a hare or rabbit.

Foramen: An opening.

Foramen magnum: The large opening at the base of the skull into which the spinal cord passes.

Infraorbital foramen: The opening on the side of the rostrum, just anterior to the orbit, that passes through the maxillary bone and into the orbit.

Interorbital constriction: The space dorsally between the orbits.

Orbit: The bony eye ring of the skull.

Palate: The roof of the mouth, which has an anterior bony and posterior soft part. The bony palate has two pairs of openings, the anterior and posterior palatine foramina.

Palatine: Of or pertaining to the palate.

Posterior palatine foramina: The posterior two of the openings in each side of the front of the bony palate.

Postorbital process: A projection of the frontal bone above and behind the orbit (eye socket).

Premaxillary bones or premaxilla: The anterior bones of the skull. The upper incisors are in the premaxillae.

Rostrum: The preorbital or snout part of the skull.

Sagittal ridge or crest: A raised, longitudinal ridge of bone on the braincase, serving as an attachment area for muscles.

Zygomatic arch: The arch of bone forming the lower and outside edge of the eye socket.

USE OF KEYS

Taxonomic keys to identify organisms are incorporated into this volume. Keys call on the user to make choices one after the other until an answer, hopefully the correct species, is determined. Keys are meant to help get an answer quickly. The alternative is to look through the descriptions of all of the possible species until you come to the right identification. Keys are of greatest use when trying to decide among a fairly large number of closely related species.

The value of keys is that you make only one choice at a time, choosing between two groups of characteristics. For example, if you have a bat in hand and go to the key to bats, you will find the first "couplet" as follows:

1. Interfemoral membrane with hairs above, either completely or on basal half 2
   Interfemoral membrane without hairs above...................4

You then make the choice about the hair on the interfemoral membrane and move on to the next choice; for example, if you decide the hair is present on the interfemoral membrane, you then go on to couplet #2, which reads as follows:

2. Interfemoral membrane with hair on basal half only ....
   ....*Lasionycteris noctivagans*, p. 110
   Interfemoral membrane fully haired 3

You then determine whether the hair is on the basal half or covers the entire membrane. If it covers the basal half and fits the rest of the couplet, then you have your answer, the silver-haired bat, *Lasionycteris noctivagans*. You then check the entire description to be sure the rest of the characteristics fit and you have helped confirm your answer.

If you determine that you have "keyed" to the wrong species, then try keying again, looking carefully for any place that you might have gone wrong. Common reasons for "going wrong" in the key are that you do not understand a characteristic, that the material to be identified is of poor quality, or that you try to go through the key too fast. Often we go wrong when we have "prejudged" what the species is and tend to make the key work in that direction. Using keys is a help or tool and is not fool-proof. Practice in use of the key is of great help. The more different species you have keyed, the better you understand the characteristics. It helps greatly to know some of the species as you use keys, and also it helps to practice by keying some "knowns" through to their correct answers.

IDENTIFICATION KEYS

KEY TO ORDERS OF MAMMALS OF INDIANA
USING SKINS OR WHOLE ANIMALS

1. Front limbs modified as wings (Fig. 1); thin interfemoral membrane (uropatagium) connecting hind limbs and tail....................................Bats, Order Chiroptera, p. 89
   No wings; uropatagium absent or not as described above 2

2. Toes terminating in hooves . . . Hoofed Mammals, Order Artiodactyla ....White-tailed Deer
   (*Odocoileus virginianus*), p. 281
   Toes terminating in claws..3

3. With well-developed armor of bony plates over much of the body....................................Nine-banded Armadillo
   (*Dasypus novemcinctus*), Order Cingulata, p. 129
   Animal not covered with armored plates............................4

4. Innermost toe of hind foot thumblike and without claw; female with abdominal pouch; ears thin and naked; tail round, naked, black at base, whitish on terminal half or more; fur grayish.............Virginia Opossum (*Didelphis virginiana*), Order Didelphimorphia, p. 59
   Not as above...5

5. Always five clawed toes on front foot (first toe sometimes reduced, high on inside of foot, and not touching ground when animal walks)...6
   Usually only four well-clawed toes on front foot (thumb may be present as small knob with nail); if five, then tail either naked and much flattened (laterally or dorsoventrally) or a short cottony tuft...7

6. Length of head and body less than 115 mm, or if more than 115 (in some moles) no ears visible and belly not white......... Shrews and Moles, Order Soricomorpha, p. 63
   Length of head and body more than 115 mm, ears visible ....Carnivores, Order Carnivora, p. 233

7. Ear longer than tail; hind foot with four claws covered with fur; soles of feet completely covered with dense fur; tail forming a cottony tuft ....Rabbits, Order Lagomorpha, p. 133

8. Ear shorter than tail; hind foot with five well-clawed toes; soles of feet not completely covered with dense fur; tail not a cottony tuft ....Rodents, Order Rodentia, p. 143

KEY TO SPECIES OF ORDER SORICOMORPHA

1. Forefeet greatly developed for burrowing, more than twice as wide as hind feet and turned outward; eyes not visible . . . Moles...2
Forefeet less than twice as wide as hind feet and not turned outward; eyes small but visible . . . Shrews 3

2. Tail more than 60 mm; 22 fleshy tentacles on snout ....
..........................Star-nosed Mole (*Condylura cristata*), p. 86
Tail short, generally not more than 45 mm; snout lacking tentacles ....Eastern Mole (*Scalopus aquaticus*), p. 82

3. Tail generally less than 28 mm and about 20 percent or less of the total length..4
Tail generally 27 mm or more and about 30–40 percent of the total length . . . *Sorex* 5

4. Color gray; total length 95 mm or more..............................
....................Short-tailed Shrew (*Blarina brevicauda*), p. 76
Color brownish; total length less than 95 mm ....
.... Least Shrew (*Cryptotis parva*), p. 80

5. Shrews brownish, total length 85–100 mm, weight about 3–5 grams 6
Shrews often grayer and either smaller (usually 2–3 grams) or larger (usually over 5 grams).............................7

6. Tail shorter, about 32–38 percent of total length; longest hairs at end of tail when unworn about 2–3 mm ....
.... Southeastern Shrew (*Sorex longirostris*), p. 73
Tail longer, about 35–46 percent of total length; longest hairs at end of tail when unworn about 4.5–6 mm............
....................................Masked Shrew (*Sorex cinereus*), p. 64

7. Shrews tiny. Total length under 90 mm; weight seldom much over 3 grams. This shrew is very similar to *Sorex*

cinereus and *S. longirostris* but is smaller. (The best character for separating this species from those two is in the unicuspid teeth, which can be seen by pulling back the upper lip. Unicuspids 3 and 5 are reduced giving the appearance of 3 unicuspid teeth in this species. There are four semi-equal in size with the fifth smaller but clearly visible in *Sorex cinereus* and *S. longirostris*.) ....
.... Pygmy Shrew (*Sorex hoyi*), p. 70
Shrews larger (5–9 grams), and usually over 100 mm total length .... Smoky Shrew (*Sorex fumeus*), p. 68

KEY TO SPECIES OF ORDER CHIROPTERA

1. Interfemoral membrane with hairs above, either completely or on basal half...2
   Interfemoral membrane without hairs above....................4

2. Interfemoral membrane with hairs on basal half; body color dark chocolate or blackish, with few silvery tipped hairs dorsally .... Silver-haired Bat
   (*Lasionycteris noctivagans*), p. 110
   Interfemoral membrane fully haired above; body coloration much paler, reddish or rich brown and grayish-mixed 3

3. Forearm more than 45 mm; dorsal hairs rich brown with tips obviously "frosted" with white.....................Hoary Bat
   (*Lasiurus cinereus*), p. 123
   Forearm less than 45 mm; body color usually brick red or yellowish-red; dorsal hairs lightly frosted or unfrosted .... Red Bat
   (*Lasiurus borealis*),* p. 120

4. Small, reddish bat (forearm 35 mm or less), with tricolored dorsal hairs (dark at base, pale in intermediate portion, dark tips); *or* brownish bat with very large ears (more than 30 mm long)...5
   Brownish or grayish bat; dorsal hairs not tricolor (or indistinctly so), ears much less than 30 mm long.............6

---

* Two seminole bats, *Lasiurus seminolus,* have been taken in Posey County, Indiana. They are considered as accidentals but one should be on the watch for that species. Seminole bats are very dark chestnut rather than bright brick red (males) or yellowish-red (females).

5. Small, reddish, with tricolor hair on back ....
.... Eastern Pipistrelle (*Perimyotis subflavus*), p. 112
Brownish, ears more than 30 mm long (considered as
accidental in Indiana)............... Rafinesque's Big-eared Bat
(*Corynorhinus rafinesquii*), p. 126

6. Forearm more than 41 mm long...7
Forearm not more than 41 mm long, usually shorter 8

7. Dorsal hairs uniform gray (sometimes brownish) from
base to tips...............Gray Myotis (*Myotis grisescens*), p. 98
Dorsal hairs dark at base, brown at tips ..... Big Brown Bat
(*Eptesicus fuscus*), p. 115

8. Tragus about 9 mm long, pointed, somewhat curved or
sickle-shaped (Fig. 2) ....Northern Myotis
(*Myotis septentrionalis*), p. 104
Tragus 4–7 mm long, rounded at tip (Figs. 3, 4) 9

9. Tragus about 4–5 mm long, blunt and curved (Fig. 3);
membranes, ears, and nose black (only one upper incisor
on each side)..... Evening Bat (*Nycticeius humeralis*), p. 118
Tragus about 6–7 mm long, not curved (Fig. 4);
membranes, ears, and nose not black 10

10. Calcar well keeled (Fig. 1), not easily seen in dried specimens; dorsal hair dull, dark pinkish-gray or (rarely)
brownish, some dorsal hairs may be faintly tricolor; the
hairs short and indistinct, not extending beyond nails.....
.... Indiana Myotis (*Myotis sodalis*), p. 106
Calcar not keeled, or indistinctly so; dorsal hairs not
tricolor, body some shade of brown, or grayish 11

11. Ventral hairs white-tipped; dorsal hairs appear woolly
(this species has apparently disappeared in Indiana).........
.... Southeastern Myotis (*Myotis austroriparius*), p. 96
Ventral hairs not white-tipped, but color varies considerably in this species; dorsal fur not woolly, the hairs
distinct and extending beyond nails....................................
.... Little Brown Myotis (*Myotis lucifugus*),* p. 92

---

* The Eastern small-footed bat has been found in Indiana too late to
be incorporated into the keys (see species account). It is smaller than
M. lucifugus and has a black mask.

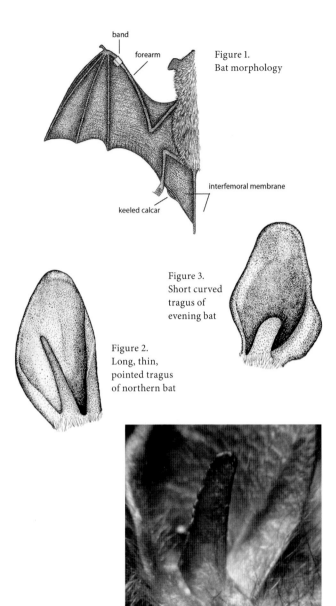

band

forearm

Figure 1.
Bat morphology

interfemoral membrane

keeled calcar

Figure 3.
Short curved
tragus of
evening bat

Figure 2.
Long, thin,
pointed tragus
of northern bat

Figure 4.
Long, blunt
tragus of little
brown bat

KEY TO SPECIES OF ORDER LAGOMORPHA

1. Nape rich cinnamon; hind foot about 90 mm; dorsum of hind foot white ....Eastern Cottontail (*Sylvilagus floridanus*), p. 134
    Nape not rich cinnamon; hind foot about 105 mm; dorsum of hind foot brown .... Swamp Rabbit (*Sylvilagus aquaticus*), p. 138

KEY TO SPECIES OF ORDER RODENTIA

1. Tail horizontally flattened, well furred or scaly 2
    Tail not flattened 10

2. Tail flat, broad, and scaly; hind feet well webbed ....
    ....Beaver (*Castor canadensis*), p. 179
    Tail densely furred; hind feet not webbed......................... 3

3. Tail short, less than one-fourth of total length; animals large, averaging 6–8 lbs.......................Woodchuck (*Marmota monax*), p. 149
    Tail more than half total length; animals smaller, weighing less than 4 lbs.. 4

4. Furred patagium present between front and hind legs, or else obvious stripes on dorsum 5
    No patagium, no dorsal stripes.. 7

5. Furred patagium between front and hind legs...................
    ....Southern Flying Squirrel (*Glaucomys volans*), p. 172
    No patagium 6

6. One pair of pale dorsolateral stripes.....................................
    .... Eastern Chipmunk (*Tamias striatus*), p. 145
    Several pale dorsal stripes.............. Thirteen-lined Ground Squirrel (*Spermophilus tridecemlineatus*), p. 153

7. Tail with relatively small amount of hair; ears relatively small; dorsal pattern of obscure spotting........... Franklin's Ground Squirrel (*Spermophilus franklinii*), p. 157
    Not as above; tail very bushy.. 8

8. Total length less than 400 mm.........................Red Squirrel (*Tamiasciurus hudsonicus*), p. 168
    Total length more than 400 mm... 9

9. Tail hairs yellow-tipped.................................... Fox Squirrel (*Sciurus niger*), p. 164

10. Hind legs very long and tail at least one and one-third times as long as head and body.. .... Meadow Jumping Mouse (*Zapus hudsonius*), p. 229

Tail shorter 11

11. Prominent fur-lined external cheek pouches......................
Plains Pocket Gopher (*Geomys bursarius*), p. 175

No external cheek pouches.. 12

12. Tail short, less than one-third the length of head and body; ears small... 13

Tail longer than one-third the length of the head and body... 16

13. Tail very short, about the length of the hind foot........... 14

Tail longer 15

14. Hairs very fine; incisors not grooved........ Woodland Vole (*Microtus pinetorum*), p. 210

Hairs grizzled; incisors lightly grooved................................
.... Southern Bog Lemming (*Synaptomys cooperi*), p. 218

15. Belly hairs silvery; tail usually more than twice the length of the hind foot.....................................Meadow Vole (*Microtus pennsylvanicus*), p. 203

Belly hairs usually buff-colored; tail usually about twice the length of the hind foot.................................Prairie Vole (*Microtus ochrogaster*), p. 207

16. Animal at least 285 mm in total length; tail naked and laterally compressed ....Muskrat (*Ondatra zibethicus*), p. 213

Animal smaller; tail not flattened dorsoventrally........... 17

17. Belly gray or brown; tail scaly and sparsely furred......... 18

Belly usually white (sometimes buffy in *Reithrodontomys*); tail furred 19

18. Total length less than 250 mm; tail less than 110 mm........
.... House Mouse (*Mus musculus*), p. 225

Total length more than 250 mm; tail more than 110 mm .... Norway Rat (*Rattus norvegicus*), p. 221

19. Size large, more than 250 mm total length ....
.... Allegheny Woodrat (*Neotoma magister*), p. 198

Size smaller, less than 220 mm total length.....................20

20. Eyes small; hind feet usually less than 17 mm; incisors grooved .... Western Harvest Mouse (*Reithrodontomys megalotis*), p. 186

Eyes prominent; hind feet usually 17 mm or more; incisors not grooved 21

21. Hind foot usually 17 or 18 mm; tail usually much less than one-half total length .... Prairie Deer Mouse (*Peromyscus maniculatus bairdii*), p. 190

Hind foot usually 19 mm or more; tail usually just under one-half of the total length .... White-footed Mouse (*Peromyscus leucopus*), p. 194

KEY TO SPECIES OF ORDER CARNIVORA

1. Tail bushy and ringed, or else animal catlike with very short tail (shorter than hind foot) 2

Not as above 3

2. Tail bushy and ringed; face with black mask .... Raccoon (*Procyon lotor*), p. 247

Animal catlike with very short tail (less than length of hind foot); cheek and throat hair tuft present .... Bobcat (*Lynx rufus*), p. 276

3. Animal doglike . . . Canidae 4

Animal not doglike 6

4. Size large, adult weight more than 20 lbs .... Coyote (*Canis latrans*),* p. 235

Size smaller, weight less than 20 lbs 5

5. General color reddish; tail tip white .... Red Fox (*Vulpes vulpes*), p. 239

General color grayish; tail tip black .... Gray Fox (*Urocyon cinereoargenteus*), p. 244

6. Color black and white, or else grayish-brown with a white longitudinal stripe on forehead 7

---

* The skull may be smaller, but otherwise the domestic dog also keys out here; it has a relatively shorter, broader rostrum. Measure the inside distance between the 2 anterior premolars, and divide this into the length of the molariform toothrow. In a coyote this ratio will generally be more than 3.66, in a dog it will generally be less than 3.00, and in a coyote-dog hybrid it will generally be 3.0–3.5.

Color brown, often with a black tail tip, or color sometimes white in winter 8

7. Color black and white, or occasionally solid black or nearly so..................................... Mephitidae: Striped Skunk
(*Mephitis mephitis*), p. 272
Color grayish brown with a white longitudinal stripe on forehead .... Badger (*Taxidea taxus*), p. 269

8. Tail black-tipped....................................Long-tailed Weasel
(*Mustela frenata*), p. 262
Tail not black tipped 9

9. Size small, less than 300 mm total length; tail about 1" long........................... Least Weasel (*Mustela nivalis*), p. 259
Size large, more than 300 mm total length; tail much more than 1" long.. 10

10. Feet broad and webbed, over 100 mm long. Large aquatic animal with thick tail...River Otter
(*Lontra canadensis*), p. 253
Hind feet less than 60 mm, tail with black tip, animal white or yellowish below, may be white in winter ....
.... Mink (*Mustela vison*), p. 266

KEY TO THE SKULLS OF MAMMALS OF INDIANA

1. Prominent, sharp-pointed canine teeth present in upper and lower jaws 2
Canines absent, or if present, not noticeably differing from adjacent teeth (in *Condylura* the third upper incisor looks like a canine, but canines are in the maxillary bones, incisors are in the premaxilla).................................4

2. Five incisors above and 4 below on each side ....
.... Virginia Opossum (*Didelphis virginiana*),
Order Didelphimorphia, p. 59
Incisors never more than 3 per side, above or below........3

3. Premaxillary bones and their corresponding upper incisors separated in front by a distinct gap; one or two incisors per side .... Order Chiroptera, p. 89
Premaxillary bones confluent, thus upper incisors forming a continuous row between the canines ....
....Order Carnivora, p. 233

4. Upper incisors absent 5
Upper incisors present 6

5. Orbits forming a bony ring; teeth sharp and complicated ....White-tailed Deer
(*Odocoileus virginianus*), p. 281
Orbits not forming a bony ring, teeth mere pegs................
....Nine-banded Armadillo
(*Dasypus novemcinctus*), p. 129

6. Large prominent chisel-shaped upper incisors separated from molariform teeth by wide diastema; never more than 8 teeth on each side of upper jaw................................7
Incisors not as above; no diastema; 9–11 teeth on each side of upper jaw....................... Order Soricomorpha, p. 63

7. Two pairs of upper incisors, a small pair directly behind the larger pair; lateral rostral area with perforations.........
....................Order Lagomorpha: Hares and Rabbits, p. 133
One pair of upper incisors; lateral portions of rostrum solid bone ....Order Rodentia: Rodents, p. 143

KEY TO SKULLS OF SPECIES OF ORDER SORICOMORPHA

1. Teeth white; zygomatic arch complete (but often broken) . . . Moles 2
Teeth with chestnut-colored tips; zygomatic arches absent . . . Shrews..3

2. Third upper tooth resembling a canine; premaxillaries extending well forward of the narial aperture (Fig. 5); 11 teeth above on each side..........................Star-nosed Mole
(*Condylura cristata*), p. 86
Third upper tooth not resembling a canine; premaxillaries not extending well forward of the narial aperture (Fig. 5); 10 teeth above on each side............... Eastern Mole
(*Scalopus aquaticus*), p. 82

3. Three or 4 unicuspids visible in lateral view (Figs. 6, 7) 4
Five unicuspids visible in lateral view 6

4. Four unicuspids visible in lateral view, fifth hidden (Fig. 7), posterior edge of braincase with ridge ....

5. Four unicuspids actually present, fourth hidden in lateral view (Fig. 6) .... Least Shrew (*Cryptotis parva*), p. 80
   Five unicuspids present, third and fifth tiny and hidden (Fig. 8) .... Pygmy Shrew (*Sorex hoyi*), p. 70

6. Total length of skull over 17 mm .... Smoky Shrew
   (*Sorex fumeus*), p. 68
   Total length of skull under 17 mm 6

7. Rostrum long and narrow (Fig. 9); third unicuspid not smaller than fourth (Fig. 9); inner ridge of upper unicuspids with pigment .... Masked Shrew
   (*Sorex cinereus*), p. 64
   Rostrum short, wider (Fig. 10); third unicuspid often smaller than fourth (Fig. 10); inner ridge of upper unicuspids lacking pigment .... Southeastern Shrew
   (*Sorex longirostris*), p. 73

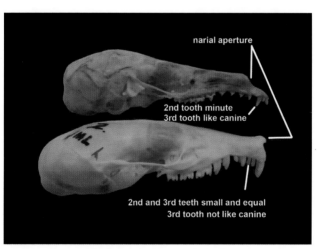

Figure 5. Star-nosed upper and eastern mole skulls

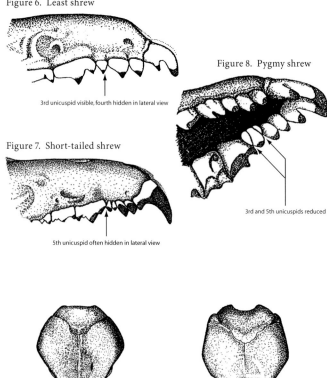

Figure 6. Least shrew

3rd unicuspid visible, fourth hidden in lateral view

Figure 8. Pygmy shrew

3rd and 5th unicuspids reduced

Figure 7. Short-tailed shrew

5th unicuspid often hidden in lateral view

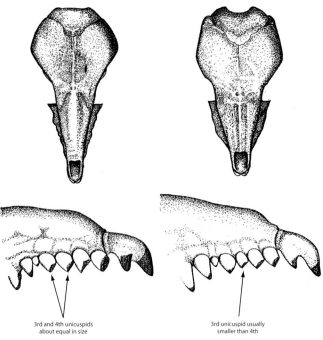

3rd and 4th unicuspids
about equal in size

3rd unicuspid usually
smaller than 4th

Figure 9. Masked shrew skull in dorsal view, *above;* note more elongate rostrum

Figure 10. Southeastern shrew skull in dorsal view, *above;* note shorter, wider rostrum

KEY TO SKULLS OF ORDER CHIROPTERA

1. One incisor on each side of upper jaw 2
   Two incisors on each side of upper jaw.............................4

2. Five upper molariform teeth, the first reduced in size and
   behind the canine in lateral view (Fig. 11); skull short and
   squarish 3
   Four upper molariform teeth, none reduced......................
   .... Evening Bat (*Nycticeius humeralis*), p. 118

3. Skull short, less than 15 mm total length .... Red Bat
                                    (*Lasiurus borealis*), p. 120
   Skull longer, more than 15 mm total length........................
   .... Hoary Bat (*Lasiurus cinereus*), p. 123

4. Four upper molariform teeth on each side, all about the
   same size (Fig. 12).. Big Brown Bat
                                    (*Eptesicus fuscus*), p. 115
   Five or 6 upper molariform teeth on each side, the first
   1 or 2 reduced in size (Figs. 13, 15), thus appearing as a
   gap in the toothrow, between the canines and the larger
   posterior molariform teeth...5

5. Five upper molariform teeth, the first 1 reduced in size
   (Fig. 13)...6
   Six upper molariform teeth, the first 2 reduced (Fig. 15)
   . . . *Myotis* (it is very difficult to separate skulls of this
   genus) 8

6. Skull about 15 mm in length; dorsal aspect of skull very
   convex or "bumped"; auditory bullae very large; an accessory cusp on first molar ...... Rafinesque's Big-eared Bat
                                    (*Corynorhinus rafinesquii*), p. 126
   Skull not humped, or else less than 14 mm long; no
   accessory cusp 7

7. Skull very flat or concave dorsally as viewed from side ....
   .... Silver-haired Bat (*Lasionycteris noctivagans*), p. 110
   Skull very small, less than 14 mm in length and convex
   in lateral view..Eastern Pipistrelle
                                    (*Perimyotis subflavus*), p. 112

8. Least width of interorbital constriction 4 mm or more ...9
   Least width of interorbital constriction less than
   4 mm 11

9. Total length of skull usually 15.7 mm or more ....
......................................Gray Myotis (*Myotis grisescens*), p. 98
Total length of skull less than 15.7 mm............................. 10

10. Skull with low median crest ....
............Southeastern Myotis (*Myotis austroriparius*), p. 96
Skull lacking median crest .... Little Brown Myotis
(*Myotis lucifugus*), p. 92

11. Skull lacking median crest; length from front of canine
to back of last molar greater than width across molars in
upper jaw ....Northern Myotis
(*Myotis septentrionalis*), p. 104
Skull with median crest; length from front of canine to
back of last molar less than width across molars................
.... Indiana Myotis (*Myotis sodalis*), p. 106

Figure 11. Red bat—first tooth reduced in size and wedged between canine and second molariform tooth

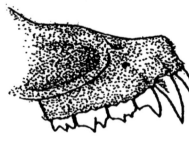

Figure 12. Big brown bat—premolar

Figure 13. Eastern pipistrelle—premolar

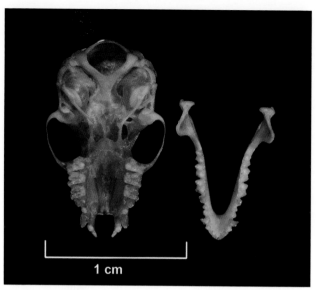

Figure 14. Ventral view of skull and lower jaw of *Myotis lucifugus*

Figure 15. Little brown myotis—2 small premolars immediately behind canine

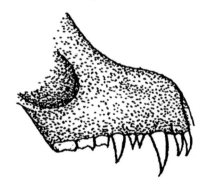

KEY TO SKULLS OF SPECIES OF LAGOMORPHA

1. Posterior extension of postorbital process connected
   to braincase for most of its length (Fig. 16), leaving no
   opening (or if opening present, tiny and not much more
   than 1 mm in length); anterior palatine foramina extending posteriorly not quite to the level of the first pair of
   molariform teeth.. Swamp Rabbit
   (*Sylvilagus aquaticus*), p. 138
   Posterior extension of postorbital process not connected
   to braincase (Fig. 17), or separated by a larger fenestra;
   anterior palatine foramina extending posteriorly to just
   beyond the level of the anterior edge of the first molariform teeth... Eastern Cottontail
   (*Sylvilagus floridanus*), p. 134

Figure 16. Swamp rabbit

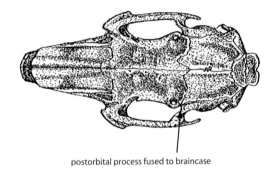

postorbital process fused to braincase

Figure 17. Eastern cottontail

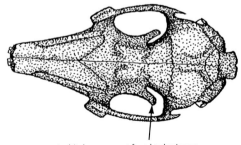

postorbital process not fused to braincase

KEY TO SKULLS OF SPECIES OF
ORDER RODENTIA

1. More than 3 upper molariform teeth per side 2
   Three upper molariform teeth per side 12

2. Skull with prominent postorbital processes (Fig. 18) ....
   Sciuridae 3
   Skull lacking prominent postorbital processes 10

3. Incisors white; top of skull flat; postorbital processes at
   right angles to skull (Fig. 18) .... Woodchuck
   (*Marmota monax*), p. 149
   Incisors orange or yellow; top of skull rounded;
   postorbital process not at right angle to skull 4

4. Infraorbital opening a foramen (opening through a thin
   plate) rather than a canal; 4 upper molariform teeth ....
   .... Eastern Chipmunk (*Tamias striatus*), p. 145
   Infraorbital opening a canal (opening through a thick
   plate) 5

5. Skull large, about 60 mm 6
   Skull smaller, no larger than about 54 mm 7

6. Four upper molariform teeth, none small ....
   .... Fox Squirrel (*Sciurus niger*), p. 164
   Five upper molariform teeth, the first small (less than
   one-half width of second) .... Gray Squirrel
   (*Sciurus carolinensis*), p. 160

7. Five upper molariform teeth, 3 posterior ones largest, the
   first small (but not minute, more than half the width of
   second); anterior portion of zygomatic arch bent out and
   downward, forming a relatively flat plate; distance from
   tip of rostrum to posterior edge of this plate is about
   48–52 percent of total length of the skull 8
   Four or 5 upper molariform teeth; if 5, the first small to
   minute; anterior portion of zygomatic arch more vertically positioned; distance from tip of snout to posterior
   edge of zygomatic plate is less than one-half total length
   of skull, usually less than 45 percent 9

8. Length of skull about 50–60 mm .... Franklin's Ground
   Squirrel (*Spermophilus franklinii*), p. 157

Length of skull about 40–45 mm ....
....Thirteen-lined Ground Squirrel
(*Spermophilus tridecemlineatus*), p. 153

9. Total length of skull about 43–49 mm; 4 large molariform teeth, but a tiny premolar is sometimes present anterior to these; notch over orbit absent or not well developed .....
...................Red Squirrel (*Tamiasciurus hudsonicus*), p. 168
Total length of skull less than 38 mm; 4 large molariform teeth preceded by a small premolar; smoothly rounded notch over orbit ....Southern Flying Squirrel
(*Glaucomys volans*), p. 172

10. Skull very large, more than 70 mm long; incisors not grooved ....Beaver (*Castor canadensis*), p. 179
Skull smaller, less than 70 mm; incisors grooved
(Figs. 20, 21)..11

11. Infraorbital opening large; skull less than 35 mm long .....
.... Meadow Jumping Mouse (*Zapus hudsonius*), p. 229
Infraorbital opening tiny; skull more than 35 mm long....
Plains Pocket Gopher (*Geomys bursarius*) (Fig. 22), p. 175

12. Molariform teeth with three longitudinal rows of cusps
(Fig. 22) . . . Muridae.. 13
Molariform teeth with two longitudinal rows of cusps
(Fig. 23), or with loops and triangles (Figs. 25, 26) rather than cusps . . . Cricetidae.. 14

13. Skull rounded and less than 25 mm long............................
.... House Mouse (*Mus musculus*), p. 225
Skull flat above and more than 25 mm long......................
.................................Norway Rat (*Rattus norvegicus*), p. 221

14. Cheek teeth usually with cusps, teeth rooted . . .
Neotominae.. 15
Cheek teeth with loops and triangles (Figs. 24, 25), teeth usually rootless . . . Arvicolinae... 18

15. Upper incisors grooved (Fig. 20) .... Western Harvest Mouse (*Reithrodontomys megalotis*), p. 186
Upper incisors not grooved... 16

16. Skull large, more than 35 mm; molars with prismatic pattern resembling rootless teeth .... Allegheny Woodrat
(*Neotoma magister*), p. 198

Skull smaller, less than 35 mm; molars with cusps.........17

17. Skulls of these two species are very similar; we have found no good characters that work for Indiana material..White-footed Mouse (*Peromyscus leucopus*), p. 194, and Prairie Deer Mouse (*Peromyscus maniculatus bairdii*), p. 190

18. Basal length of skull more than 50 mm.................Muskrat (*Ondatra zibethicus*), p. 213
Basal length of skull less than 40 mm 19

19. Incisors with faint longitudinal groove (Fig. 26), outer and inner angles of molariform teeth acute ....
........Southern Bog Lemming (*Synaptomys cooperi*), p. 218
Incisors lacking grooves, angles of molariform teeth rounded 20

20. Third upper molariform teeth usually with four triangles between the anterior and posterior loops (Fig. 24).............
..................Meadow Vole (*Microtus pennsylvanicus*), p. 203
Third upper molariform teeth with two (sometimes one in *Microtus ochrogaster*) triangles between the anterior and posterior loops (Fig. 25)..21

21. Squamosal width divided by total length usually less than 0.49; foramen above ear opening more than 3 mm long...................Prairie Vole (*Microtus ochrogaster*), p. 207
Squamosal width divided by total length usually more than 0.49; foramen above ear opening less than 3 mm long.............. Woodland Vole (*Microtus pinetorum*), p. 210

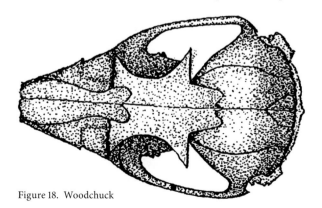

Figure 18. Woodchuck

Figure 19. Prairie deer mouse

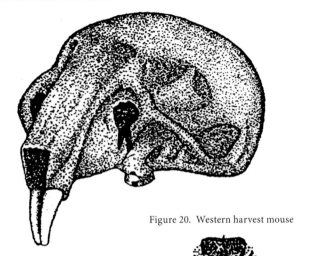

Figure 20. Western harvest mouse

Figure 21. Plains pocket gopher

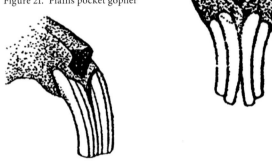

Figure 22. House mouse

Figure 23. Deer mouse

Figure 24. Meadow vole

Figure 25. Prairie vole

Figure 26. Southern
bog lemming

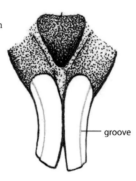

groove

KEY TO SKULLS OF SPECIES OF
ORDER CARNIVORA

1. Six upper and 6 or 7 lower molariform teeth 2
   Fewer than 6 upper and fewer than 6 lower molariform teeth..5

2. Posterior end of hard palate ending far beyond posterior molariform teeth; 6 lower molariform teeth (Fig. 27) ....Raccoon (*Procyon lotor*), p. 247
   Posterior end of hard palate ending at about level of posterior molariform teeth; 7 lower molariform teeth . . . Canidae..3

3. Postorbital processes thickened, convex dorsally; basal length of skull more than 147 mm.............................
   .... Coyote (*Canis latrans*), p. 235
   Postorbital process thin, concave dorsally; skull smaller..4

4. Sagittal ridges U-shaped (Fig. 28); posterior end of lower jaw with distinct notch...Gray Fox
   (*Urocyon cinereoargenteus*), p. 244
   Sagittal ridges V-shaped (Fig. 29); posterior end of lower jaw without notch...............Red Fox (*Vulpes vulpes*), p. 239

5. Five upper and 5 (occasionally 6) lower molariform teeth..........................River Otter (*Lontra candensis*), p. 253
   Usually 4 upper (3 in bobcat) and fewer than 6 lower molariform teeth..6

6. Skull short with smoothly rounded braincase; no sagittal crest; 3 or 4 upper molariform teeth....................................7
   Skull elongate, differently shaped and with a sagittal crest in adults; 4 upper molariform teeth 8

7. Three upper molariform teeth ....
   ....Bobcat (*Lynx rufus*), p. 276
   Four upper molariform teeth.........................Domestic Cat
   (*Felis catus*)

8. Palate not extending appreciably beyond last upper mo-lariform teeth (Fig. 30); top of skull as viewed from side forming an angle of about 60°........................Striped Skunk
   (*Mephitis mephitis*), p. 272

Palate extends appreciably beyond posterior edge of last molariform teeth (Fig. 31) 9

9. Braincase triangular (Fig. 32); skull more than 90 mm long; last molar with triangular grinding surface ....Badger (*Taxidea taxus*), p. 269

Braincase elongate; skull less than 90 mm long; last molar with dumbbell-shaped grinding surface 10

10. Total length of skull more than 55 mm .... Mink (*Mustela vison*), p. 266

Total length of skull less than 55 mm 11

11. Total length of skull less than 33 mm .... Least Weasel (*Mustela nivalis*), p. 259

Total length of skull more than 33 mm ....Long-tailed Weasel (*Mustela frenata*), p. 262

Figure 27. Raccoon, skull and lower jaw

Figure 28. Gray fox, skull and lower jaw

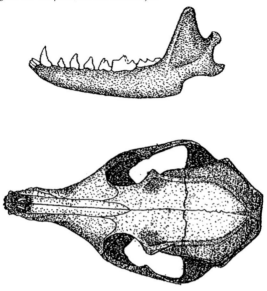

Figure 29. Red fox, skull and lower jaw

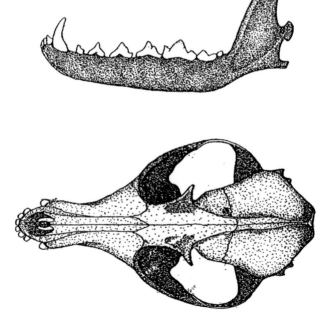

Figure 30. Striped skunk, ventral view of skull

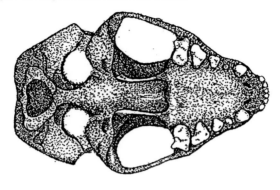

Figure 31. Mink, ventral view of skull

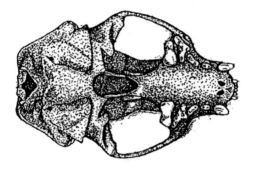

Figure 32. Badger, dorsal view of skull

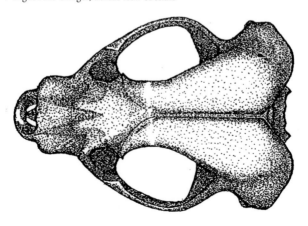

102|17

**SPECIES ACCOUNTS
LISTED BY FAMILY**

Order DIDELPHIMORPHIA—Opossums

FAMILY DIDELPHIDAE
Didelphis virginiana / Virginia Opossum

Order Didelphimorphia

Originally the opossums were established as one of the 10 families constituting a single order, the pouched mammals or Marsupialia. The pouched mammals have now been divided into seven orders. Marsupials occur primarily in the Australian region and in South America, with only one species, the American opossum, in Indiana. Didelphimorphia is presently the name of the order that includes our one marsupial, or pouched mammal, the opossum. The American opossum remains in the family Didelphidae.

FAMILY DIDELPHIDAE

The family Didelphidae, the American opossums, is a diverse group comprising about 63 species in 12 genera, all in the New World and most in South America. Of the 63 species, about 11 reach into Central America, and 1, the Virginia opossum, *Didelphis virginiana,* is distributed widely in North America. Didelphids vary greatly in size, habits, and habitat, but many have long, prehensile tails. Some of the species in the family have secondarily lost the marsupium (pouch), the mother in these cases presumably caring for her young in the traditional way—in a nest. The Virginia opossum is often referred to as a "living fossil" because of its primitive characteristics. The name "opossum" derives from a term for "white animal" in an Algonquian language of Virginia.

Virginia Opossum
Didelphis virginiana Kerr

Distinguishing Features and Measurements: The opossum is pale-colored (usually gray), medium-sized (about the size of a domestic cat), and has a long, nearly naked, scaly, prehensile tail. The large, dark eyes are conspicuous in the white to pale-grayish face. The prominent, naked, leathery-looking ears are black with pale tips (the tips sometimes are missing due to frostbite). The snout is long and pointed. The five toes on the front feet bear claws; the hind feet have four claw-bearing toes and an opposable toe without a claw. Females have a fur-lined pouch for carrying the young. Inside the pouch are usually 13 teats (in a circle or a U), but the number may vary from 9 to 17.

TL 559–964, T 206–394, HF 52–79, Wt. 1,820–5,556 (4–12.2 lbs)

Skull: Length: 105–141 (4.2–5.6').

An opossum skull can be immediately distinguished from that of all other Indiana mammals by its greater number of incisors (5 on each side above and 4 below), its small braincase, and its high, thin sagittal crest.

Dental Formula:

$$I \; \frac{5}{4} \quad C \; \frac{1}{1} \quad P \; \frac{3}{3} \quad M \; \frac{4}{4} \quad = \quad 50$$

Habitat: The opossum may occur in numerous habitats from wooded to open.

Food: The opossum is omnivorous and feeds on a great variety of vegetable foods such as persimmons, berries, apples, and hickory nuts, as well as cultivated items (corn, wheat, sorghum). It will also feed on animal matter of all kinds, including mammals, birds, amphibians, and reptiles. It is likely that much of the vertebrate food is carrion. Insects and other invertebrates, especially earthworms, are also eaten.

Reproduction: The gestation period of the opossum is only about 12–13 days, and the young are poorly developed at birth. The young climb hand over hand to find their way into the female's pouch, where they remain for several weeks. Up to 13 young may be found in the mother's pouch from March to October. Females probably produce two litters per year.

Range: Today, the opossum is common throughout Indiana but is more abundant in the southern half.

Habits and Comments: Mostly nocturnal, but the opossum is often abroad by day. It does not hibernate but in fall becomes fat. This allows it to remain inactive during inclement weather, although it may emerge even in bad weather. The tips of the ears or tails may be lost to frostbite.

Opossums are solitary wanderers, moving from den to den, staying 1 or more days depending on conditions there. They den or nest under brush piles or other debris, in burrows, hollow logs, trees and stumps, or drainage tiles. They also take shelter in buildings, caves, and even in garbage cans. Nests are of dry leaves, grasses, corn husks, or similar materials. Nest building is particularly interesting. Nesting materials are grasped in the mouth and then passed under the body to the tail, which is turned forward between the hind legs. The materials are then transported by the tail. The opossum does considerable climbing to obtain food or to reach dens. It can hang by its tail, and the tail also provides a useful "fifth hand." The usual walking gait is a slow waddle, but when sufficiently frightened the opossum can cover the ground in leaping bounds. Animals found on the ground can often be captured by hand; a frightened individual may expose the teeth, hiss, and exude saliva. Feigning death by lying immobile on its side and letting its tongue hang out (playing possum) is rather common when cornered. Even when handled, the animal may retain this posture. After the disturbance has passed, the opossum resumes its normal activities. The opossum can swim under water even for considerable distances.

SELECTED REFERENCES. Fitch and Sandidge 1953; Hamilton 1958; Hartman 1928; McManus 1974; Whitaker et al. 1977.

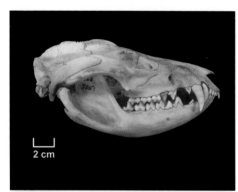

Side view of skull

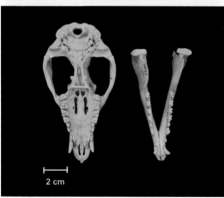

Ventral view of skull and lower jaw

Opossum.
Photo by J. Hill Hamon

Playing possum.
Photo by Kim Terry

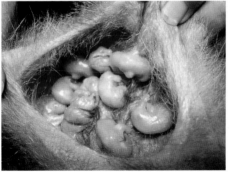

Pouch with young.
Photo by Norm Griggs

Order SORICOMORPHA—Shrews and Moles

FAMILY SORICIDAE
Sorex cinereus / Masked Shrew
Sorex fumeus / Smoky Shrew
Sorex hoyi / Pygmy Shrew
Sorex longirostris / Southeastern Shrew
Blarina brevicauda / Northern Short-tailed Shrew
Cryptotis parva / Least Shrew

FAMILY TALPIDAE
Scalopus aquaticus / Eastern Mole
Condylura cristata / Star-nosed Mole

Order Soricomorpha

The moles and shrews were previously classed as order Insectivora but are now in the order Soricomorpha. Only two families occur in North America: the shrews, Soricidae, and the moles, Talpidae. North American soricomorphs have five toes on front and rear feet, small eyes and ears, a long, tapering snout extending considerably beyond the jaw, and a wedge-shaped skull. The zygomatic arch is complete but reduced in size in moles and is lacking in shrews. Moles have white teeth, and North American shrews have chestnut-colored enamel on their teeth. There are six species of shrews and two species of moles in Indiana.

FAMILY SORICIDAE

Shrews include about 312 species of small mammals with soft fur that will lie either forward or backward. The first upper incisors, which protrude forward, are efficient in gathering the tiny prey on which shrews feed. They are enlarged and pincer- or sicklelike but have a posterior cusp as well. Behind these enlarged teeth are a series of 4 or 5 small teeth called the "unicuspids." The number and size of the unicuspids have been much used in shrew identification. We have not included standard tooth formulas for shrews, since it is not clear, in this case, how "unicuspids" might relate to the incisors, canines, and premolars of the standard formula. In North American shrews, all of which belong to the subfamily Soricinae, the "red-toothed shrews," the teeth have chestnut-colored tips.

Shrews are seldom seen but are exceedingly active, constantly running about, squeaking, wriggling their noses, and sniffing this way and that. They also have exceedingly high metabolic rates. The heart rate may reach 1,200 beats per minute, and respiration rates run from 168 breaths per minute when at rest to 750 per minute when undergoing "average" activity. Few individuals live much over a year. Shrews are among the smallest of mammals, and our pygmy shrew is the smallest of the shrews.

Shrews are often numerous. They consume great quantities of worms, insects and other invertebrates, and some vegetation. Shrews, *Blarina,* often feed on the minute subterranean fungus *Endogone* and related genera. Shrews have a number of glands that may impart an odor to the shrew, and many of them probably function to bring the sexes together. One might think these glands would deter predators, but predators often eat shrews. At least some shrews are known to use echolocation for navigational purposes.

Shrews have an interesting distribution in the state. As is often the case, shrews in the same area generally are of different sizes, eat different foods, and divide up the habitat in some way, thus avoiding competition. The six shrews of Indiana have evolved in this way. *Blarina brevicauda* and *Cryptotis parva* occur throughout the state, although *Cryptotis* is increasingly uncommon to the north. *Sorex cinereus* occurs throughout the state except in the south central hill country. *Sorex longirostris* occurs in the southern part of the state. In the southwest it occurs in the uplands, *S. cinereus* in the bottoms. In the southeast it occurs in uplands and bottoms. In the south central unglaciated hill country, *S. cinereus* is absent, *S. longirostris* occurs in the bottoms, and *S. hoyi* and *S. fumeus* inhabit the uplands.

Masked Shrew
Sorex cinereus Kerr

Distinguishing Features and Measurements: The masked shrew, the pygmy shrew (*Sorex hoyi*), and the southeastern shrew (*Sorex longirostris*) are the smallest Indiana mammals. All are long-tailed, brownish in color, and have pointed snouts and tiny beady eyes. The smoky shrew, *Sorex fumeus,* also occurs in Indiana, but it is somewhat larger and is usually gray or grayish. The ears in these species are small and nearly concealed in the fur, which is fine, soft, and dense. The pygmy shrew is the smallest of these species (averaging 2.2 grams) and is somewhat more grayish. However, the best character for identifying it is by the third and fifth unicuspid teeth, which are reduced in size and hidden, making it appear as though they number only 3. The masked and southeastern shrews have 4 large, followed by 1 smaller unicuspid tooth. Coloration and measurements of the masked shrew and the southeastern shrew are similar. Both have pale, silvery colored undersides. The masked shrew tends to have a longer, more haired tail.

TL 70–109, T 25–45, HF 9–13, Wt. 2.4–7.8

Skull: Length: 16.0–17.5 (0.64–>0.7').
Sorex skulls are tiny, somewhat flattened, rounded behind, with a pointed snout and with chestnut-tipped teeth.

As indicated above, the two species are best separated by skull characteristics. Both have 5 unicuspids with the posteriormost (fifth) being reduced in size. However, in the southeastern shrew, the third unicuspid is usually smaller than the fourth. The rostrum of the southeastern shrew is shorter and broader than that of the masked shrew.

Dental Formula:

$$I \ \frac{3}{1} \ C \ \frac{1}{1} \ P \ \frac{3}{1} \ M \ \frac{3}{4} \ = \ 32$$

Habitat: Masked shrews favor moist habitats with fairly dense ground cover. We have trapped masked shrews in swampy deciduous woods; marshy areas covered with grasses and brush; tamarack bogs; weedy and grassy fencerows bordering bluegrass pastures; rank weedy growths along the floodplain of small creek and ditch banks; young pine plantations in old field; fairly dense grasses on sandy prairies; and around the border of a bald cypress pond.

Food: Masked shrews eat caterpillars, beetle larvae, and slugs and snails, followed by spiders, crickets, and hemipterans. Earthworms, important to larger shrews, are seldom eaten by this species, while a variety of other invertebrates, especially insects, are also eaten.

Reproduction: The gestation period is thought to be about 18 days. Litters of 2–10 have been produced, but 5–7 is more common. Litters may be produced through the spring and summer and into the fall, with up to three litters per female.

Range: The masked shrew is common in Indiana, especially in the northern part of the state, although its distribution is spotty, reflecting the distribution of suitable habitat. It is much less common in southern Indiana and is entirely lacking in the south central unglaciated hill country.

Habits and Comments: The masked shrew is mostly nocturnal but is often observed in the daytime. It is active all year and may be out in extremely cold (−10°F) weather. Its movements are quick, as it darts back and forth, constantly starting, stopping, and shifting about, presumably navigating and hunting food using its echolocation. Masked shrews sometimes hide under rotten logs, stumps, boards, fallen fence posts, or other debris on the ground. They also make runs in leaf mold. In grassy areas, runs utilized by this shrew are not evident, and the animals are frequently trapped in runways made by voles or other species. Nests are constructed of grasses under logs, stumps, and other objects. As in other small shrews, the metabolic rate is high and the animals have to eat throughout the day to stay alive. People seldom see masked shrews, but some are caught by house cats.

SELECTED REFERENCES. French 1980; Whitaker 2004; Whitaker and Mumford 1972a.

Front part of skull of masked shrew

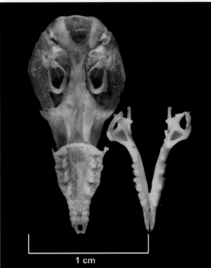

Ventral view of skull and lower jaw

Newborn masked shrew. *Photo by W. J. Hamilton, Jr.*

Southeastern shrew (*at left with shorter tail*) and masked shrew.
Photo by Tom French

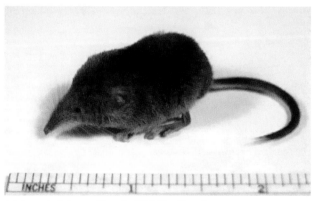

Adult masked shrew. *Photo by W. J. Hamilton, Jr.*

Smoky Shrew
Sorex fumeus Miller

Distinguishing Features and Measurements: The smoky shrew is gray and is the largest long-tailed shrew of Indiana. Its total length ranges from 110 to 125 mm, its tail from 37 to 47. As in other Indiana shrews, the snout is long and pointed and projects beyond the mouth, the eyes are small, and the ears are concealed in the fur. See under skull.

TL 103–122, T 39–46, HF 12–14, Wt. 5.4–10

Skull: Length: 18–19.2 (0.7–0.8').

The teeth are tipped with chestnut enamel. There are 5 unicuspids, with the fourth the smallest.

Dental Formula:

I $\frac{3}{1}$ C $\frac{1}{1}$ P $\frac{3}{1}$ M $\frac{3}{3}$ = 32

Habitat: Mature woodlands, especially the more moist parts of the oak and hickory woodlands of south central Indiana. Occupies runways in the leaf mold, and occurs under logs and rocks and in and under the lips of banks.

Food: Earthworms, centipedes, spiders, coleopteran larvae, and un-identified insect larvae. These items, cumulatively, comprised 56.8% of the food. Insect larvae collectively made up 24.1% of the food, coleopterans 10.7%.

Reproduction: They make nests of shredded vegetation in a rotted log, under a stump or rock, or in some other protected place. The first litter is generally in early April, and there is often a second litter in July, rarely in August. Two litters are usual, but sometimes there is a third litter in the fall. Lactating individuals may be found as late as October. There are 2–8 young per litter, averaging about 5.5. At 1 month, the young weigh about 4 grams, or half the weight of the adults. The young do not breed in the year of their birth but produce young, then usually die in their second summer or fall. Most of the smoky shrews present in winter are young of the year.

Range: Fairly common throughout the unglaciated hill country of south central Indiana.

Habits and Comments: The first smoky shrews ever taken in Indiana were taken in May 1981. Associated with the smoky shrew in southern Indiana are the short-tailed shrew, *Blarina brevicauda;* pygmy shrew, *Sorex hoyi;* white-footed mouse, *Peromyscus leu-*

copus; and woodland vole, *Microtus pinetorum.* The pygmy shrew and smoky shrew occur on the upper levels and the slopes of ravines; the southeastern shrew occurs in the lower portions of the ravines. They run about, poking their noses here and there in their nearly continuous quest for food. When disturbed, they may utter high-pitched notes, and if further riled they may throw themselves on their back and continue to utter this note. These shrews constantly utter soft twittering sounds when foraging, undoubtedly part of their echolocation repertoire. Smoky shrews have odor-producing glands, presumably helpful in bringing the sexes together.

SELECTED REFERENCES. Caldwell et al. 1982; Cudmore and Whitaker 1984; Hamilton 1940; Owen 1984; Whitaker and Cudmore 1987.

Side view of skull

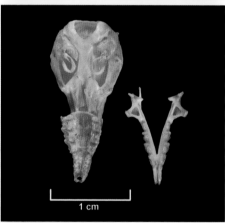

Ventral view of skull and lower jaw

Smoky shrew. *Photo by Roger Barbour*

Pygmy Shrew
Sorex hoyi (Baird)

Distinguishing Features and Measurements: The pygmy shrew is the smallest North American long-tailed shrew. As in other shrews, the snout is long and pointed and projects beyond the mouth, eyes small, ears concealed in the fur, and teeth tipped with chestnut enamel.

TL 68–82, T 21–28, HF 6–9, Wt. 1.3–2.9

Skull: Length: 15.0–16.5 (0.6–0.7').

Five unicuspids are present, but the third and fifth are tiny and hidden, thus it appears that there are just 3. You can best see the 2 hidden unicuspids by looking through the open mouth to the toothrow on the far side, or by turning the cleaned skull upside down. Unicuspids of all small long-tailed shrews should be checked for this species.

Dental Formula:

$$I \quad \frac{3}{1} \quad C \quad \frac{1}{1} \quad P \quad \frac{3}{1} \quad M \quad \frac{3}{3} \quad = \quad 32$$

Habitat: Pygmy shrews over their range have been taken in a variety of habitats, but all from Indiana were in moist oak and hickory woodlands of the unglaciated portion of south central Indiana.

Food: Spiders, unidentified beetles, unidentified insect larvae, lepidopteran larvae, and coleopteran larvae.

Reproduction: Data for Indiana are scant but suggest spring breeding from at least late March through April and at least some fall breeding.

Range: The pygmy shrew is fairly common throughout the unglaciated hill country of south central Indiana.

Habits and Comments: Ronald Caldwell set sunken can traps in Crawford County in southern Indiana and caught the first pygmy shrew, *Sorex hoyi,* ever taken in the state (Caldwell, Smith, and Whitaker 1982). The pygmy shrew is one of the smallest species of mammals of the world, and the individuals of this species from Indiana are the smallest known of their species, averaging only about 2.2 grams. Species associated with the pygmy shrew in southern Indiana are the short-tailed shrew, smoky shrew, southeastern shrew, white-footed mouse, and woodland vole. The pygmy and smoky shrews occur mostly on the upper levels and the slopes of ravines, and the southeastern shrew occurs in the lower portions of the ravines. Here they run about, poking their noses here and there in their nearly continuous quest for food. They may utter high-pitched notes as they forage, undoubtedly part of their echolocation repertoire. Pygmy shrews may be active at any time during the 24 hours and throughout the year.

SELECTED REFERENCES. Caldwell et al. 1982; Cudmore and Whitaker 1984; Whitaker and Cudmore 1987.

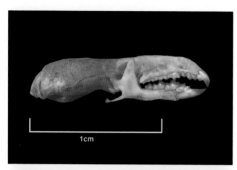

Side view of skull

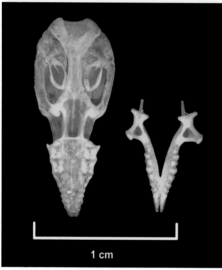

Ventral view of skull and lower jaw

Pygmy shrew. *Photo by Rob Simpson*

Least, short-tailed, and pygmy unicuspids (*top to bottom*)

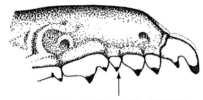

3rd unicuspid visible, fourth hidden in lateral view

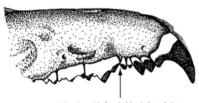

5th unicuspid often hidden in lateral view

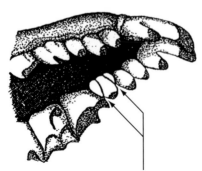

3rd and 5th unicuspids reduced

Southeastern Shrew
Sorex longirostris Bachman

Distinguishing Features and Measurements: Small brown or reddish-brown long-tailed shrew similar to masked shrew. See also *S. cinereus* account. Southeastern shrew differs from masked shrew in having a proportionately shorter tail, the skull is smaller and much shorter, and the rostrum is broader. Also, the pigmentation of the teeth is usually lighter and the inner ridges of the upper unicuspids lack pigment. See under skull.

TL 73–87, T 26–33, HF 9.5–11.0, Wt. 2.0–4.0

Skull: Length: 14.1–15.9 (0.5–0.6').

Probably the easiest character to use is the short, wide rostrum of *S. longirostris* as compared to the long, narrow rostrum of *S. cinereus.* This can be expressed as a ratio by dividing the distance across the outside of the first large molariform teeth into the distance from the posterior end of the palate to the anterior end of the first incisors. This value is usually more than 2 in *Sorex longirostris,* which has the rostrum short and wide, and less than 2 in *Sorex cinereus,* which has a long, thin rostrum.

Dental Formula:

I $\frac{3}{1}$ C $\frac{1}{1}$ P $\frac{3}{1}$ M $\frac{3}{3}$ = 32

Habitat: Moist often in moist to dry fields with rather heavy ground cover. Often found in dense grasses and sedges along wet areas but also often taken in woods.

Food: Main foods in Indiana are spiders, caterpillars, slugs and snails, centipedes, harvestmen, and roaches.

Reproduction: May produce young April through September. Embryos range in number from 4 to 6 (average 4.6). As with most shrews, two distinct age groups are readily discernible, first-year animals that have not yet overwintered and second-year animals—the breeding population of the year. Few shrews survive the second winter, so third-year animals are very rare.

Range: Occurs in the southwestern half of the state, southwest of a line from Benton to Jefferson counties. We currently have records of this species from 25 counties.

Habits and Comments: We formerly assumed that the southeastern shrew was rare in Indiana, but more recent data indicate that it is actually relatively abundant. The use of sunken cans for trapping has greatly increased our knowledge of all of the small shrews. In one field near Terre Haute, the southeastern shrew, masked shrew, meadow vole, and prairie vole were all taken. In other areas in the same county, masked shrews, short-tailed shrews, least shrews, meadow voles, woodland voles, meadow jumping mice, and white-footed mice were trapped in the same habitats with the southeastern shrew. Its habits are assumed to be similar to those of the masked shrew. The foods are clearly similar, and in Indiana, the two pretty much replace each other geographically or ecologically.

SELECTED REFERENCES. French 1980, 1984; Mumford and Rippy 1963; Whitaker and Mumford 1972a.

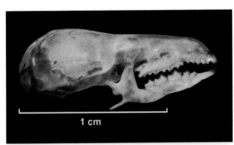

Side view of skull

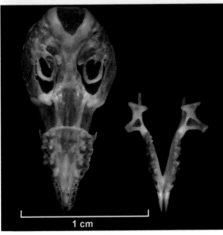

Ventral view of skull and lower jaw

Southeastern shrew. *Photo by Tom French*

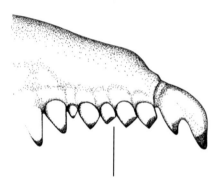

Southeastern shrew—third unicuspid
usually smaller than fourth

Northern Short-tailed Shrew
Blarina brevicauda (Say)

Distinguishing Features and Measurements: This is the largest Indiana shrew, silvery-gray to black, with tail much shorter than the body. Underparts slightly paler than dorsal areas. Snout long, pointed, and projects beyond the mouth. Eyes tiny and black, external ear opening is large but concealed in the fur. Five clawed toes on each foot, with hind feet somewhat larger than the front. Fur velvety, with no differentiation into guard hairs and underfur. See under skull.

TL 95–126, T 17–28, HF 9–20, Wt. 11–26.3

Skull: Length: 20.8–23.4 (0.8–0.9").

As in all North American shrews, *Blarina* has teeth with chestnut-colored enamel. Five unicuspids, with the fifth behind a lobe of the fourth, therefore hidden from the side. Third and fourth unicuspids smaller than the first and second; the fifth is still smaller. The anterior most incisors are enlarged, protrude forward, and have a posterior lobe.

Dental Formula:

$$I \ \frac{3}{1} \ C \ \frac{1}{1} \ P \ \frac{3}{1} \ M \ \frac{3}{3} \ = \ 32$$

Habitat: Occurs in most Indiana habitats, woodlands, open fields, wetlands, fencerows. Mature woodlands with a thick ground litter and partially rotted logs and stumps on the forest floor frequently harbor large populations.

Food: Earthworms, slugs and snails, caterpillars, crickets, and centipedes are the most important foods. A northern short-tailed shrew sometimes splits open the outer covering of larger insects to extract the internal organs. The fungus *Endogone* is also eaten. *Blarina* often stores food in small caches and sometimes uses plant material. One living under a large piece of plywood in a hedgerow along a cornfield made a series of tunnels with several caches of corn in blind passages. It takes several days for the shrews to consume a cache.

Reproduction: Reproductive activity may occur through most of the year. Breeding peaks from March through May, with a smaller peak in fall. No females with embryos were taken between October and February. Gestation is about 17–21 days.

Range: This species is common or even locally abundant over much of

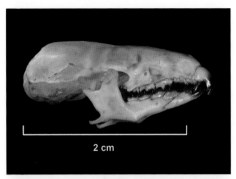

Side view of skull

2 cm

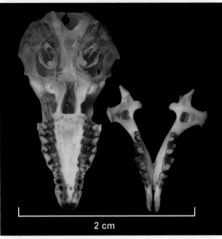

Ventral view
of skull and
lower jaw

2 cm

Northern short-
tailed shrew.
*Photo by Terry L.
Castor*

Corn stored by *Blarina brevicauda*

the state. It and the white-footed mouse are two of the most common native Indiana mammals. It is more common in the north; may be scarce in some parts of south central Indiana.

Habits and Comments: The species most commonly associated with *Blarina* in wooded areas is the white-footed mouse. In mature forest, both may be quite abundant and may constitute most of the small mammal population. In moist woods with soft soil, *Blarina* and the woodland vole (*Microtus pinetorum*) often occur together, even using the same burrows. Burrows of the short-tailed shrew can often be distinguished from those of the woodland vole because the latter tend to be round in cross section instead of somewhat flattened from top to bottom. Since the short-tailed shrew is found in a wide variety of habitats, most species of mammals found in Indiana are at some place associated with it. In the wooded hills of south central Indiana, *Blarina* occurs with *Sorex longirostris, S. fumeus,* and *S. hoyi,* but these species tend to partition the environment and habitat, thus reduce competition. *Blarina* occurs in all habitats, whereas the largest and the smallest of the long-tailed shrews occur mostly on the upper slopes and the southeastern shrew occurs in the bottoms. *Blarina* feeds on larger items, especially earthworms. The smoky shrew feeds on medium-sized prey, including smaller earthworms. The southeastern and pygmy shrews feed heavily on tiny insect larvae and spiders. The short-tailed shrew spends considerable time running (and sniffing) from place to place, apparently searching for food and quite oblivious of its surroundings. It is active both day and night but is primarily nocturnal and is active throughout the year. Nocturnal activity is reflected in the number of short-tailed shrew skulls one finds in owl pellets. Cats and dogs often kill this shrew but usually discard kills rather than eat them. Short-tailed shrews are often found along paths, roads, and trails where they are probably discarded by foxes and other predatory mammals. Vocalizations include squeaks, chipping or clicking sounds, and chattering.

This shrew has small flank glands that produce a strong, musky secretion. It is produced in males all year and in females during the nonbreeding season. Secretions from the glands scent the burrows, and individuals avoid burrows scented by other individuals, although males enter unscented (female) tunnels during the breeding season. The submaxillary glands of *Blarina* produce a strong poison, which functions to immobilize prey. These glands open into the mouth between the large lower incisors.

SELECTED REFERENCES. Dapson 1968; George et al. 1986; Martin 1981; Pearson 1944; Whitaker and Cudmore 1987; Whitaker and Mumford 1972a.

Least Shrew
Cryptotis parva (Say)

Distinguishing Features and Measurements: This is the smaller of the two species of short-tailed shrews in Indiana. Total length less than 90 mm. Least shrews are usually brown or grayish-brown (rarely grayish), slightly paler below than above. The snout is long, extending well beyond the mouth. Eyes black, external ears are small, with the large ear openings hidden in the fur. Hind feet 9–12 mm. Fur soft, with no differentiation into underhair and guard hairs. See under skull.

TL 61–88, T 9–21, HF 9–12, Wt. 2.0–6.5

Skull: Length: 16–17.2 (0.64–0.69").

Usually 30 teeth, but 2 are sometimes missing. Skull can be immediately separated from that of other Indiana shrews because it has only 4 unicuspids, the fourth hidden behind the third in lateral view (see key, Fig. 6). Other Indiana shrews have 5 unicuspids. As usual in North American shrews, the teeth have chestnut-colored tips and the zygomatic arch is absent.

Dental Formula:

$$\text{I } \frac{3}{1} \text{ C } \frac{1}{1} \text{ P } \frac{2}{1} \text{ M } \frac{3}{3} = 30$$

Habitat: The least shrew in Indiana is primarily a mammal of old fields, particularly drier ones.

Food: The most important foods are caterpillars, earthworms, spiders, internal organs of orthopterans, and beetle larvae. Nearly 10% of the food appears to be internal organs of larger insects, probably mostly grasshoppers, crickets, and beetles.

Reproduction: Least shrews produce young at least in spring and fall but likely all through the summer. Young range from two to seven. Gestation about 21–23 days.

Range: Species seems by trapping records to be rare to uncommon. However, it is sometimes locally abundant and may actually be relatively common throughout much of the state, since it may be fairly common in owl pellets. We have examined least shrews from 45 Indiana counties.

Habits and Comments: Least shrews are quite secretive and mostly nocturnal. They are active throughout the year and form some small runways. We have noted no burrows, but they are undoubtedly small and easily overlooked. Nests are usually constructed in hidden sites, and numerous individuals sometimes occupy the same nest. The least shrew often utters chirping sounds. Cats regularly kill least shrews, and there is circumstantial evidence that foxes also kill (and discard) this species. As indicated earlier, various birds of prey feed on least shrews.

SELECTED REFERENCES. Choate 1970; Davis and Joeris 1945; Hamilton 1944; Whitaker 1974; Whitaker and Mumford 1972a.

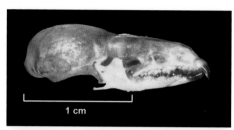

Side view of skull

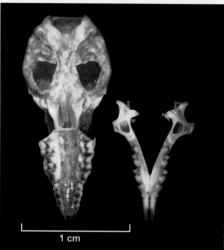

Ventral view of skull and lower jaw

Least shrew with earthworm. *Photo by Roger Barbour*

Moles are highly modified for burrowing existence. Their eyes are reduced and barely functional. Their forelimbs are enlarged, turned outward, and tipped with very large claws. They are formidable digging tools. Moles are almost completely fossorial and their soft and velvety fur can lie in either direction, thus permitting movement either backward or forward in their burrows. Their teeth are sharp, like those of shrews, but unlike those of New World shrews, they are white. The zygomatic arch is complete. In moles, the testes and the rest of the male reproductive tract become extremely large during the breeding season, forming as much as 14% of total body weight. There is but one litter per year, but this is sufficient to maintain population size, because predation on animals that remain below ground most of the time is low. Growth is rapid and the young are nearly full grown when they leave the nest. Moles are good swimmers.

Worldwide, there are 17 genera and 42 species of moles. They occur from southern Canada to northern Mexico. Three species occur in the eastern United States.

Eastern Mole
Scalopus aquaticus (Linnaeus)

Distinguishing Features and Measurements: The eastern mole is grayish and has greatly enlarged front feet, short legs, a short and nearly naked tail, and small eyes concealed in the fur. Some individuals appear silvery or gray, others brownish to blackish. The fur is dense and soft. The front feet are rotated outward so that the palms are almost vertical. They are broad, naked below, lightly furred above, and have large flattened claws on the toes. The elongate hind feet are considerably smaller than the forefeet and have smaller claws. The palms of all feet are surrounded by a fringe of hairs, which aid in digging. The front feet are rotated outward. The separation between head and body is indistinct. The snout is conical, naked, and flexible and projects beyond the mouth. No external ears or eyes are visible.

TL 164–223, T 22–35, HF 19–29, Wt. 80–140

Skull: Length: 35–40 (1.4–1.6").

There are 36 teeth, none with a typical canine form, but the anterior incisors are enlarged. The zygomatic arches are complete (but thin).

Dental Formula:

$$I \quad \frac{3}{2} \quad C \quad \frac{1}{0} \quad P \quad \frac{3}{3} \quad M \quad \frac{3}{3} \quad = \quad 36$$

Habitat: The eastern mole is found in most Indiana habitats, even in some areas that are periodically flooded. Open fields, especially with sandy or other loose soils, lawns, roadsides, open woods, gardens, and cultivated fields are all habitats likely to contain moles. Loose soil is apparently necessary for this species to thrive, while excessive soil moisture inhibits it.

Food: The most important foods of this species are earthworms, scarabaeid larvae (grubworms), vegetation, ants, and ground beetles (Carabidae), although numerous other foods are eaten in lesser amounts. The vegetation often includes seeds, especially of the grass *Digitaria.*

Reproduction: The eastern mole produces a single litter per year, in early spring, after a gestation period of about 30–42 days. Harmon P. Weeks, Jr., found a nest in the edge of his lawn. It was a ball of leaf fragments less than an inch square. It was 12" below the surface in a nongrassy area. When found on 28 April, it contained four young, about 3" long. Nearly all moles found are of near-adult size, because the young remain in the nest until nearly full grown.

Range: This mole is found throughout the state and is common in most sections. The number of moles in an area is probably often less than one might think from the amount of activity, for a single mole constructs many feet of burrows.

Habits and Comments: Moles are seldom seen because they spend most of their time below the ground, but their presence is easily detected by the characteristic molehills and by the elevated ridges that mark their shallow forage tunnels. Burrowing is so important to moles that most of their characteristics are adaptations to fossorial life. These include large front feet for digging, a movable snout, a naked tail that serves as a sensory organ (especially when the mole moves backward), and eyes and ears that are covered with fur. The eyes are fused shut and serve only to distinguish between light and dark.

When digging, moles use the front feet to loosen the soil and brace themselves with the hind feet. Soil is pushed backward beneath the animal, then the mole turns around and pushes the soil farther to the rear with its front feet. Excess soil is pushed into an unused burrow or to the ground surface, where it forms the "molehills." Foraging tunnels are near the surface, and when a mole is actively extending one, an observer can see the soil being pushed up. During this time, the mole can often be captured by hand by inserting the blade of a shovel or spade behind it so that it cannot retreat back into the completed burrow, then digging the mole up. Burrowing speed varies with the texture of the soil, but may occur at a rate of 15' per hour. Moles are active day and night and throughout the year. When the ground surface becomes frozen, they use deeper burrows. Mounds may be pushed up through the snow when soil conditions permit. Numerous new mounds may be observed after a heavy rain, particularly when the rain follows a dry period. During spring thaw, a flurry of activity takes place and many forage tunnels and mounds are constructed. A live mole placed on the ground usually begins to dig into the soil. Eastern moles can swim, but, unlike the star-nosed mole, probably do so only under stress. Owls and domestic dogs and cats often capture eastern moles, dogs and cats usually by digging them from their foraging burrows. Cats sometimes watch the tunnels being formed and may pounce and dig the moles out; they often abandon the moles then, apparently because of their bad odor. How owls catch moles is unknown; perhaps they take some as carrion or find the moles aboveground.

SELECTED REFERENCES. Arlton 1936; Whitaker and Schmeltz 1974; Yates and Schmidley 1978.

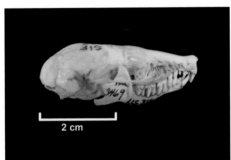

Side view of skull

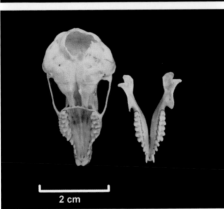

Ventral view of skull and lower jaw

Eastern mole

Mole hill. *Photo by Linda K. Castor*

Raised area along mole burrow. *Photo by Linda K. Castor*

Star-nosed Mole

Condylura cristata (Linnaeus)

Distinguishing Features and Measurements: The star-nosed mole is blackish above and below, with soft, shiny dense fur. The eyes and ears are small, and the "star" on the end of the long, pointed snout consists of 22 fleshy tentacles around its tip. The tail is long and black, constricted at the base, and becomes much enlarged with stored fat in winter. The hind feet are elongate, the front feet shorter and broad with their palms turned outward.

TL 152–198, T 57–71, HF 21–29, Wt. 30–58.6

Skull: Length 33–35 (1.3–1.4").

The skull is narrow, with incomplete auditory bullae, and the third incisor is caniform in shape.

Dental Formula:

$$\text{I } \frac{3}{3} \text{ C } \frac{1}{1} \text{ P } \frac{4}{4} \text{ M } \frac{3}{3} = 44$$

Habitat: Marshes, bogs, ditch and stream banks, and swampy areas are the favored habitats of the star-nosed mole. *Condylura* is semiaquatic and spends considerable time in the water. On the Pigeon River Fish and Wildlife Area, we captured star-nosed moles in burrows in a grass-covered bank along a pond, a brushy willow thicket along a lake, a tamarack swamp, brush and brushy river bank, and a shallow, leaf-filled gully draining into a lake. Some of the trap sites were saturated, others were relatively dry, but the soil in most cases was mucky.

Food: In 18 star-nosed moles from Indiana, the only major food was earthworms, comprising 100% of the food in nine stomachs and 10, 66, and 90% in three others. Other items were insects, slugs, vegetation, and aquatic foods.

Reproduction: One litter per year is produced, in spring. The gestation period is about 45 days. The nest is a flattened sphere of grasses or leaves, about 5–7" in diameter, placed above high water. It is usually in a little hillock or knoll, often beneath a stump or log.

Range: Occurs only in about nine counties in the northeast part of the state.

Habits and Comments: Star-nosed moles form forage tunnels and mole-hills but do not push up as many ridges as eastern moles. We noted rather extensive areas where the muck had been disturbed on the Pigeon River Fish and Wildlife Area. We have observed burrows in banks along lakes and ponds, in saturated soil along lake shores, and under a thick layer of leaves in partially dried-up swamps. This species also enters wet portions of lawns, where it may push up mounds. It is active day and night and throughout the year, and mounds sometimes appear on top of snow. It is an excellent swimmer and diver, well adapted for its semiaquatic habitats. Entrances to its burrows often are below water.

SELECTED REFERENCES. Eadie and Hamilton 1956; Gould et al. 1993; Hamilton 1931; Peterson and Yates 1980; Van Vleck 1965.

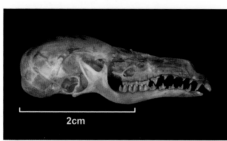

Side view of skull

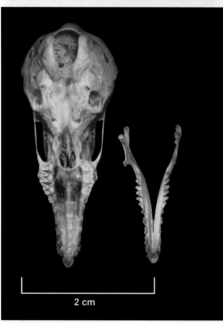

Ventral view of skull and lower jaw

Star-nosed mole. *Photo by Clarence Owens*

Pigeon River star-nosed mole habitat, *above and below.*
Photos by Terry L. Castor

Order CHIROPTERA—Bats

FAMILY VESPERTILIONIDAE

Myotis lucifugus / Little Brown Myotis
Myotis austroriparius / Southeastern Myotis
Myotis grisescens / Gray Myotis
Myotis leibii/ Eastern Small-footed Myotis
Myotis septentrionalis / Northern Myotis
Myotis sodalis / Indiana Myotis
Lasionycteris noctivagans / Silver-haired Bat
Perimyotis subflavus / Eastern Pipistrelle
Eptesicus fuscus / Big Brown Bat
Nycticeius humeralis / Evening Bat
Lasiurus borealis / Red Bat
Lasiurus cinereus / Hoary Bat
Corynorhinus rafinesquii / Rafinesque's Big-eared Bat

Order Chiroptera

Bats are the only truly flying (winged) mammals. Their wings are of skin stretched over the finger and arm bones, and they usually connect and include the tail. Many bats exhibit echolocation and hibernation. All bats of Indiana exhibit delayed fertilization; that is, they mate in fall, the sperm are stored in the uterus, and fertilization occurs in spring. There may also be winter or spring matings in some species. All of the bats of Indiana feed on flying insects. Bats are the second largest order after rodents and make up nearly a fourth of the species of mammals of the world. The "mouse-eared" bats (the big genus *Myotis*) are best called myotis, e.g., little brown myotis, but the names are often used interchangeably. The other bats of Indiana are called bats.

The most common bats in Indiana are the big brown and red bats and little brown myotis. The big brown bat and little brown myotis both form most of their maternity colonies in buildings in summer, while most northern myotis have their maternity colonies in trees, and pipistrelles have theirs in very small numbers in leaf clusters. Evening bats used to form maternity colonies in buildings but now do so in tree hollows. Indiana myotis usually form maternity colonies under sloughing bark in the sun. Northern myotis usually form theirs in cracks of trees or under sloughing bark. Silver-haired bats migrate through Indiana twice a year, forming maternity colonies in hollow limbs in summer to the north of Indiana and hibernating mostly south of Indiana. Most big brown bats hibernate in buildings, and this is the only species that does so in Indiana. However, some big brown bats hibernate in caves. The main species that hibernate in caves are the Indiana myotis, the little brown myotis, the pipistrelle, and the northern myotis. The Indi-

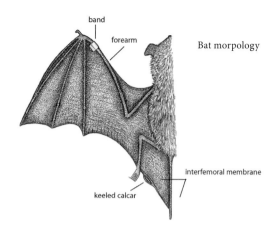

band
forearm
Bat morpology
interfemoral membrane
keeled calcar

ana myotis hibernates in huge clusters in a few caves. The little brown myotis hibernates in smaller clusters; the pipistrelle does not cluster. The northern myotis is seldom seen in hibernation because it usually hibernates deep in cracks, powderholes, or stalactites. The only true cave bat (forming summer colonies and hibernating in caves) in Indiana is the gray myotis. However, there is only one colony of gray myotis in the state (Clark County), and it hibernates to the south of the state. Exactly where is unknown, but it could be in Tennessee or Alabama. The red bat and hoary bat are solitary bats, hang in the foliage, and generally migrate south for the winter. The eastern small-footed bat, *Myotis leibii,* had been expected in Indiana for many years, and indeed the first three ever found there were captured in bat traps just as this book was going to press.

The last verified record of the southeastern myotis, *Myotis austrorparius,* in the state was one banded on 4 February 1977 by J. B. Cope in Donnehue's Cave, Lawrence County. The big-eared bat, *Corynorhinus rafinesquii,* is of accidental occurrence in the state. The last verified *Corynorhinus rafinesquii* was seen in 1962 in a cave near Smedley, Washington County. A big-eared bat was reported from Squire Boone Cave several times over a period of about a month in the summer of 1992. This appears to be a valid record. In addition, two individuals of *Lasiurus seminolus,* the Seminole bat, were captured by a cat just west of Evansville in a driveway in Posey County on 15–16 August 1994. They were submitted by the cat's owner to the rabies laboratory. The Seminole bat's nearest native range is in southern Tennessee, about 150 miles away from Posey County. It was a mystery as to how the bats got in the driveway, but this species has been previously captured far from its natural range in Wisconsin, New York, and Pennsylvania. Another Seminole bat was taken in 2001 in western Evansville. There were shreds of Spanish moss tangled in its foot. The bat was caught in a flower shop that commonly purchases bundles of Spanish moss (as do other flower shops in the area). We believe all three bats originated from this source.

FAMILY VESPERTILIONIDAE

The vespertilionids are the largest family of bats. "Evening bats" is a poor name for the family, however, since most bats fly in the evening, and one species, *Nycticeius humeralis,* is formally known as the evening bat. The family includes about 35 genera and 318 species occurring essentially in temperate and tropical areas throughout the world. Only on small, remote islands are there no vespertilionid bats. *Myotis* is the biggest genus, with about 84 species, many of which are difficult to distinguish. Most North American bats and all but four species of eastern U.S. bats belong to this family. All are insectivorous, and all have well-developed echolocation. They have plain noses, the earlobe forms a tragus, and the tail extends slightly beyond the hind edge of the interfemoral membrane. The front of the skull is flattened, and there is a space between the two front incisors. A few make long migrations to their wintering grounds, and most make at least short migrations. Many exhibit delayed fertilization, mating usually in the fall but sometimes in the spring or even in winter, and with fertilization occurring in the spring. Delayed fertilization may serve as an energy-saving mechanism, and as a mechanism for ensuring that all females are bred. Many of the species hibernate, and they may readily enter torpor on cool days even during the nonhibernating season, as a means of conserving energy.

There are six main events in the life history of many of our northern insectivorous bats. In the spring, which is relatively short, bats gradually begin emerging from hibernation, and there is much activity or "swarming" at the cave entrance. Spring feeding begins and some copulations may occur during the nightly swarming. The bats reenter hibernation each day. For females at least, this is followed by spring migration to the summer or maternity roosts, where birthing takes place. The males are often solitary or aggregated into small groups, sometimes near the maternity roosts, sometimes elsewhere. Fall migration back to the hibernacula proceeds gradually, beginning in late summer, the males tending to precede the females. In the fall, there is a great deal of swarming activity at cave entrances, and most copulations apparently occur at this time. In northern areas, feeding ceases toward the end of this period, and hibernation begins.

Little Brown Myotis
Myotis lucifugus (Le Conte)

Distinguishing Features and Measurements: The little brown myotis (*Myotis lucifugus*) is a small, brownish bat with relatively short ears and a short, rounded tragus. It is easily confused with other *Myotis*. Examination of teeth will verify whether you are dealing with a *Myotis,* for in this genus there are two tiny teeth between the canine and the large, posterior teeth. The little brown myotis differs from the Indiana myotis in having larger feet and longer and much more conspicuous hairs on toes (extending to or beyond the tips of the claws). Also, there is usually a distinct keel on the calcar of the Indiana myotis but little or none on the little brown myotis. The northern myotis has longer ears and a longer tragus than other *Myotis* of Indiana.

TL 75–94, T 24–48, HF 9–11, FA 35–38, Tragus 7–9, Wt. 5–14

Skull: Length: 14.1–15.4 (0.56–0.62").

The skulls of *Myotis* characteristically have 2 upper incisors in each jaw and 2 tiny teeth behind the upper canines, but otherwise the skulls of *Myotis* are difficult to tell apart, other than that of the gray myotis is larger.

Dental formula:

$$\text{I } \frac{2}{3} \text{ C } \frac{1}{1} \text{ P } \frac{3}{3} \text{ M } \frac{3}{3} = 38$$

Habitat: Female little brown myotis in summer normally form large maternity colonies in human structures: mostly houses, churches, and barns. Males are solitary and spend the day in secluded places: in trees, buildings, caves, or mines, but a few in the same buildings with females. In winter, little brown myotis hibernate in caves and mines.

Food: Little brown myotis eat various flies, moths, caddisflies, and beetles. True flies include many unidentified flies, about 31% of the total, but also some midges and a few mosquitoes.

Reproduction: Most mating is in autumn but some occurs in winter and early spring. In April, females begin gathering in maternity colonies, where the young are produced. Up to several thousand females may occupy a single maternity colony. Daytime temperatures in maternity roosts may be in excess of 100°F. This heat promotes rapid growth of young. Females usually produce a single offspring per year, between late May and early July. Growth of young is rapid; the young can fly at about 4 weeks.

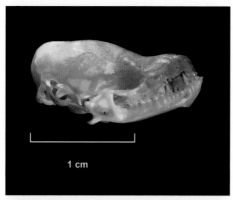

Side view of skull

Ventral view of skull and lower jaw

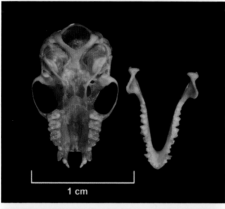

Little brown myotis. *Photo by Linda K. Castor*

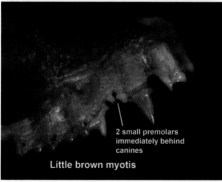

2 small premolars immediately behind canines

Little brown myotis

Range: The little brown myotis is common and found throughout Indiana. It is one of our most abundant bats but apparently is declining, partly because of loss of habitat and possibly because it is being slowly outcompeted by the big brown bat for roosts in buildings.

Habits and Comments: The little brown myotis is probably the third most abundant bat in Indiana, after big brown and red bats. It forms the second greatest number of colonies in buildings, after the big brown bat. Regular trapping of the entrance to Copperhead Cave throughout the year has shown that these bats start swarming in August and do so until well into the fall. Some bats may fly outside at any time in winter, but they do not feed then. However, there are particles of chitin in their intestine, which are digested during the winter, aided by the enzyme chitinase, which is produced by bacteria in the digestive tract. Many individuals return to the same colony each year, but some may occupy different colonies in different years. The longevity record for a little brown myotis is 34 years, as indicated by banding research.

SELECTED REFERENCES. Anthony and Kunz 1977; Barbour and Davis 1969; Cope et al. 1958; Fenton 1970, 1977; Fenton and Barclay 1980; Humphrey and Cope 1976; Thomas et al. 1990; Whitaker et al. 2004; Whitaker and Rissler 1992a,b, 1993.

Little brown myotis
ear and tragus

Little brown myotis colony

Little brown myotis

Little brown myotis. *Photo by Adam Mann*

Southeastern Myotis
Myotis austroriparius (Rhoads)

Distinguishing Features and Measurements: This species is probably extirpated in Indiana as of the early 1980s. Like the gray-pelaged gray myotis, most of the southeastern myotis that lived in Indiana had a gray dorsum and a whitish venter. However, the gray myotis has a longer forearm, dorsal fur the same color from base to tip, and less white (more grayish) on the venter. Brown-pelaged individuals are best separated from other *Myotis* in Indiana by forearm length and (in life) by pink noses. Winter individuals have white underparts.

TL 70–95, T 27–41, HF 9–11, Tragus 5.5–9, Forearm 34–39, Wt. 4.1–9.1

Skull: Length: 14–15.2 (0.56–0.6").
See under little brown myotis.
Dental Formula:

$$I \ \frac{2}{3} \ C \ \frac{1}{1} \ P \ \frac{3}{3} \ M \ \frac{3}{3} = \ 38$$

Habitat: In earlier years (through the 1970s), this species hibernated in small numbers in a few caves in south central Indiana.

Food: There is little information on food of this species, but it apparently feeds heavily on flies (Diptera) and on some beetles as well.

Reproduction: Females produce two young in May. We have no evidence that the southeastern myotis ever had young in Indiana.

Range: The southeastern myotis has always been rare in Indiana and was known only from Crawford, Greene, Lawrence, and Washington counties. Most records are from Lawrence County, either from Donaldson's Cave in Spring Mill State Park or from Donnehue's Cave, but there are records of single individuals from other caves. A fair number of records occurred through the 1950s, and then the numbers decreased. The last individuals were seen in hibernation in Bronson's Cave (1970), Donnehue's Cave (1973), and Donaldson's Cave in 1974. The last southeastern myotis seen hibernating in the state was in Ray's Cave in 1977.

Habits and Comments: Maternity colonies are in caves, buildings, or other protected sites such as hollow trees, but no breeding individuals were ever found in Indiana. Nursery colonies would probably form in late April or May in Indiana. During late April to mid-May, about 90% of the bats of this species in Florida produce two young. All other *Myotis* in Indiana regularly produce only one young. Southeastern myotis hibernate in caves in Indiana from about October/November to April. All of the southeastern bats found in Indiana were in caves in the southern part of the state.

SELECTED REFERENCES. Barbour and Davis 1969; Jones and Manning 1989; LaVal 1970.

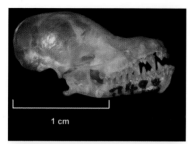

Side view of skull

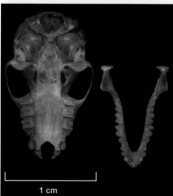

Ventral view of skull and lower jaw

Southeastern myotis.
Photo by Roger Barbour

Gray Myotis
Myotis grisescens Howell

Distinguishing Features and Measurements: The gray myotis is the largest member of the genus *Myotis* in the United States. It can be separated from other *Myotis* in Indiana by its forearm length (42–45 mm), dorsal hair the same color from base to tip, and the attachment of the wing membrane to the tarsus instead of to the side of the foot.

TL 92–107, T 35–46, HF 9–12, Tragus 7–10, FA 42–45, Wt. 10.7–12

Skull: Length: 16 mm (0.7").
Dental Formula:

$$I \ \frac{2}{3} \ C \ \frac{1}{1} \ P \ \frac{3}{3} \ M \ \frac{3}{3} \ = \ 38$$

Habitat: This species is a true cave bat. It forms large maternity colonies in caves in summer, then migrates south to other caves for hibernation in winter. There is one maternity colony in Indiana in a quarry at Sellersburg with individuals also using caves at nearby Charlestown.

Food: The major foods of the gray myotis at Sellersburg appear to be midges and other true flies (Diptera) in spring and fall, and various kinds of beetles in summer. Bats have even eaten pupal midges, presumably skimming them from the surface of the water. Beetles include May beetles, ground beetles, and spotted cucumber beetles, *Diabrotica undecimpunctata.* The latter item is a favored food of big brown and evening bats and an important agricultural pest of melons and other vine plants. Also, moths are often eaten, and caddisflies form a significant part of the diet in April, June, and September, and brown lacewings (Hemerobiidae) are of some importance throughout the year. A few spiders and crickets are also eaten.

Reproduction: Gray myotis give birth to one young in late May or early June, and the young are weaned in about 2 months.

Range: The gray myotis is a southeastern species but there is one colony in Clark County, southern Indiana. The distribution of this species has always been patchy, but fragmentation and isolation of populations has increased in recent decades. Prior to 1975 only 32 individuals had been seen in the state. In 1982, Brack, Mumford, and Holmes (1984) located the colony in an old quarry. There is a lake associated with the quarry, extending throughout the entire area where the bats live.

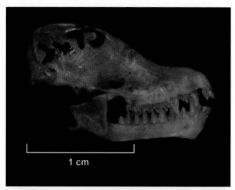

Side view of skull

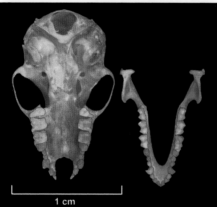

Ventral view
of skull and
lower jaw

Gray myotis. *Photo by James Kiser*

Habits and Comments: It is not known when the gray myotis maternity colony became established in Indiana. Occasional gray myotis at various localities in Indiana could indicate that the colony existed for some time, perhaps as far back as 1958 or even farther. However, the most likely scenario to us is that gray myotis became established in Clark County in the 1970s, with earlier records representing accidental occurrence from Kentucky. Gray myotis form maternity colonies in caves, then migrate and hibernate in other caves to the south. The species is on the U.S. Fish and Wildlife Service endangered species list because it lives in a small number of large colonies, and those colonies are extremely intolerant of human disturbance. About 95% of the entire population hibernates in only nine caves in Alabama, Arkansas, Kentucky, Tennessee, and Virginia.

The gray myotis population at Sellersburg was estimated at about 400 individuals in 1982, but it has increased since then. Our estimate in 2006 was over 6,400.

Selected References. Barbour and Davis 1969; Brack et al. 1984; Decher and Choate 1995; Tuttle 1975, 1976a,b 1979; Tuttle and Stevenson 1977; Whitaker, Pruitt, and Pruitt 2001.

Eastern Small-footed Myotis
Myotis leibii (Audubon and Bachman)

Distinguishing Features and Measurements: This is the smallest bat species in the eastern United States, with only the eastern pipistrelle approaching it in size. The most diagnostic characteristics are that the face, ears, and muzzle are black and form a "mask" that contrasts sharply with the fur. The calcar has a definite keel and the feet are tiny, measuring 6–7.5 mm. Forearm length is 31–34 mm. Eastern small-footed bats have thick glossy dorsal fur with a yellowish-brown to golden-brown appearance. The ventral fur varies from gray to whitish in color.

This species is similar to other species of *Myotis* in Indiana but can be identified by its small size, small foot, shorter forearm, and the black facial mask. The eastern pipistrelle is similar in size, but that species has pink ears and face as opposed to the black ears and facial mask of the eastern small-footed bat.

TL 73–82, T 30–35, HF 6–7.5, FA 31–34, Wt. 3–7

Skull: Length: 12.1–13.4 (0.47–0.52").

Dental Formula:

$$I \ \frac{2}{3} \ C \ \frac{1}{1} \ P \ \frac{3}{3} \ M \ \frac{3}{3} \ = \ 38$$

Habitat: This is one of the rarest bats in North America and relatively little is known about its ecology and life history. It hibernates in caves or mines. It appears to be more tolerant of low temperatures than other bat species. It is often thought to be our hardiest cave bat, with the possible exception of the big brown bat. Eastern small-footed bats arrive at hibernacula in October or November and depart in early March, long before other hibernating bats. They may hibernate, either solitary or in small clusters, near the cave entrance, where temperatures may drop below freezing and humidity is relatively low. Often overlooked by cave biologists, these bats wedge themselves into cracks and crevices of the hibernacula ceiling or wall, and they have also been found hibernating horizontally under rock slabs and talus on the cave floor.

Food: Moths are heavily eaten by this species and beetles are also important. Moth remains were found in all but one sample. Coleopterans, especially June beetles and leaf beetles, are also important, and other insect groups may be eaten such as leafhoppers. Spiders are commonly eaten also, suggesting these bats often glean directly from vegetation.

Reproduction: Males and females occupy different roosts during the summer, with females forming small maternity colonies and males roosting alone or in small groups. Maternity roosts are usually underneath rocks on exposed slopes and ridges, and in the fissures and cracks of cliff faces and rocky outcrops, although one colony was found in a barn in Ontario. Like other species of *Myotis,* eastern small-footed bats exhibit swarming behavior and breed in the fall. Sperm are stored in the female's uterus, throughout hibernation, until spring ovulation occurs. Females give birth to a single pup in May or June.

Range: This species was first recorded in Indiana in the spring of 2009 when three individuals were taken in a bat trap at Wyandotte Cave, Crawford County, on three different dates. The first, a female, was caught on 25 February and weighed 4.0 grams. The second was a male and was caught 16 March and weighed 4.3 grams. It is not known whether the species has hibernated there in low numbers for an extended period, or if some individuals from elsewhere, probably northern Kentucky, have rather recently started hibernating there. There is no information on this species producing young in Indiana to date.

Habits and Comments: As indicated, relatively little is known about this species. Eastern small-footed bats in Canada were found to move less than 12.5 miles (20 kilometers) between winter and summer habitat, while in Maryland, distances of 0.6–3 miles (1–5 kilometers) have been reported. It will be interesting to determine if this species now produces young in Indiana, probably in the vicinity of Wyandotte Cave.

Shortly after sunset, these bats emerge from their roosts to feed. Their flight pattern is weak and erratic, and they often forage 3–10' above ponds, streams, and along forested corridors. Common food items include moths, flies, and beetles, although the presence of spiders in fecal samples suggests this species may glean prey as well.

Selected References. Best and Jennings 1997; Gikas et al. submitted.

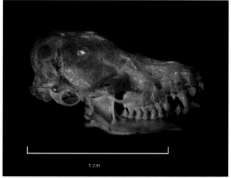

Side view of skull

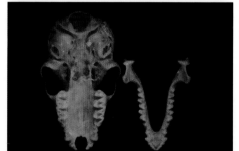

Ventral view of skull and lower jaw

Eastern small-footed myotis. *Photo by Roger Barbour*

Northern Myotis
Myotis septentrionalis (Trouessart)

Distinguishing Features and Measurements: Among Indiana species, the northern myotis (*Myotis septentrionalis*) is most similar in appearance to the little brown myotis (*Myotis lucifugus*). The best distinguishing characters of northern myotis are the long ears (average 17 mm) and the long, thin, pointed tragus (average 9 mm). The tragus is often somewhat curved.

TL 75–95, T 27–42, HF 8–11, FA 35–41, Tragus 8–11, Wt. 4.7–9.2

Skull: Length: 14.5–15.5 (0.58–0.62").
See under little brown myotis.
Dental Formula:

$$I \frac{2}{3} \quad C \frac{1}{1} \quad P \frac{3}{3} \quad M \frac{3}{3} = 38$$

Habitat: This species forms maternity colonies in cracks, crevices, and cavities or under loose bark of trees, although occasionally in buildings. Also they often use bat houses, even in shade. They hibernate in caves and mines. Although they are common, it is very difficult to find hibernating individuals in any numbers in caves and mines because most crawl far back out of sight into cracks and crevices. An interesting but common roosting site is the hollow core of a broken stalactite, often just large enough for a single bat.

Food: The major foods of this species are flies, beetles, and moths, but they do often glean spiders from surfaces.

Reproduction: Birth occurs during June, over a span of perhaps 2–3 weeks. Litter size is one.

Range: The northern myotis probably occurs throughout Indiana, but it seems to be quite rare in the northern part of the state.

Habits and Comments: Myotis septentrionalis is generally a solitary species, except during the breeding season, when aggregations of females and young form. In August and September northern myotis swarm in some numbers at the entrances of a number of caves and mines.

SELECTED REFERENCES. Barbour and Davis 1969; Fitch and Shump 1979 (much of the material included is on the eastern species, *M. septentrionalis*).

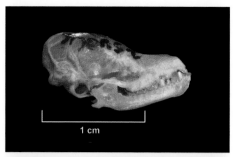

Side view of skull

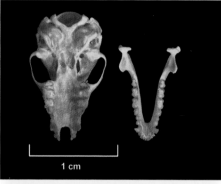

Ventral view of skull and lower jaw

Northern myotis. *Photo by Adam Mann*

Northern myotis, ear and tragus

Indiana Myotis
Myotis sodalis Miller and G. M. Allen

Distinguishing Features and Measurements: The Indiana myotis is dark pinkish-brown above and paler (more pinkish) below. It is most apt to be confused with the little brown myotis, which is much more variable in color. The best characters for separating the Indiana myotis from the little brown myotis are in the feet and calcar. The Indiana myotis has smaller feet than the little brown myotis, and the hairs on the toes are fewer and shorter, not extending beyond the knuckles, and much less obvious. Most Indiana myotis also have a more or less distinct keel on the calcar. The keel is usually easy to see in whole specimens but is much more difficult to see in dry skins.

TL 73–100, T 26–40, HF 7–10, FA 34–41, TR 6–8, Wt. 6–11

Skull: Length: 14–15 (0.56–0.6").
See under little brown myotis.
Dental Formula:

$$I \ \frac{2}{3} \ C \ \frac{1}{1} \ P \ \frac{3}{3} \ M \ \frac{3}{3} \ = \ 38$$

Habitat: During the nonhibernating period, females and young form maternity colonies under loose bark of a variety of tree species in riparian or upland woodlands, in patches of trees, or even in relatively open areas. The trees are usually fairly large (over 20" diameter) and have areas with sloughing bark toward the sun, as the developing young need much heat. Most roost trees are dead or dying, thus they serve for only 2–8 years. At any time, a colony may be using one to three primary roost trees, and there may be much movement between roost trees. This is beneficial to the bats, providing them other roosts should one or more of their primary roost trees be lost. In winter Indiana myotis hibernate in large numbers in relatively few caves.

Food: Indiana myotis primarily feed on dipterans (including a few mosquitoes), coleopterans, and lepidopterans.

Reproduction: Females mate and then enter hibernation in fall soon after arriving at the hibernacula. One young is born usually in the first 3 weeks of June. Gestation is about 40 days. Maternity colonies consist of up to or even more than 100 adult females.

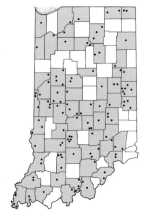

Range: The overall range for the Indiana myotis is given as the entire state. However, few reproductive adults or juveniles are found in the southern part of the state during summer. In winter they hibernate in the cave region of south central Indiana. Although there has been a rangewide decline, Indiana populations have remained stable.

Habits and Comments: Myotis sodalis was not described as a separate species from the little brown myotis until 1928, when Miller and Allen described it as a new species with the type locality as Wyandotte Cave, Crawford County, Indiana. This is an indication of the Indiana myotis's similarity to the little brown myotis. The Indiana myotis was listed as federally endangered by the U.S. Fish and Wildlife Service on 11 March 1967, and gained legal protection by the United States when the Endangered Species Act was passed in 1973 (Public Law 93-205, amended 1982). The main reason this species is so vulnerable is because it forms huge masses in a very few caves. Numbers up to 125,000 have been seen in single hibernacula in Indiana. Vandalism or natural disasters (such as flooding) can easily destroy large numbers. Indiana is now the state with the most hibernating Indiana myotis, currently over 200,000. Hibernation occurs from mid-November to mid-April. Hibernating groups containing both sexes form dense clusters on cave ceilings, but singles and small groups are commonly found as well. Indiana myotis form huge blankets such as the estimated 36,000 in a single cluster in Twin Domes Cave. Migrating Indiana myotis arrive at the hibernacula starting in late July and extending through mid-October. Males may

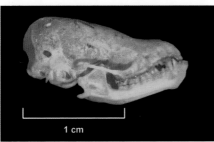

Side view of skull

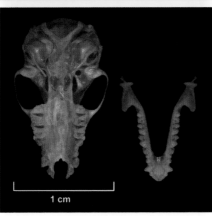

Ventral view of skull and lower jaw

remain active into late fall, presumably to mate with late arrivals. In fall, Indiana myotis "swarm" at hibernacula entrances; that is, they fly in and out of the entrances at night, whereas there are very few individuals in the caves during the day. Swarming period is from late August into early November but peaks in September. The bats leave the hibernacula in April and May.

SELECTED REFERENCES. Cope et al. 1974; Humphrey and Cope 1977; Humphrey et al. 1977; Kurta and Kennedy 2002; Mumford and Calvert 1960; Mumford and Cope 1958; Richter et al. 1978; Thomson 1982.

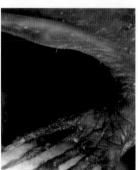

Indiana myotis, *above.*
Photo by Adam Mann

Foot and calcar of
Indiana myotis

Maternity roost.
Photo by Al Kurta

Twin Domes Cave showing 36,000 Indiana myotis

Silver-haired Bat
Lasionycteris noctivagans (Le Conte)

Distinguishing Features and Measurements: The silver-haired bat is a medium-sized, chocolate-colored or blackish bat with whitish hair tips (frosting) both above and below. The amount of silver tipping varies considerably among individuals. It is not likely to be confused with any other species of bat occurring in Indiana.

TL 84–113, T 27–47, HF 7–11, FA 39–44, Tr. 4–8, Wt. 7–16

Skull: Length: 16.1–17 (0.64–0.68").

The skull has 2 upper canines in each jaw, has 1 tiny tooth in space behind the upper jaw, and is rather flat as viewed from the side.

Dental Formula:

$$\text{I} \ \frac{2}{3} \ \ \text{C} \ \frac{1}{1} \ \ \text{P} \ \frac{2}{3} \ \ \text{M} \ \frac{3}{3} \ = \ \ 36$$

Habitat: These bats are usually found in trees in cracks or under bark in summer, and in caves (usually solitary) in winter.

Food: Silver-haired bats feed on moths, brown lacewings, ants, some beetles, and various flies.

Reproduction: These bats have their young in small colonies in hollow limbs to the north of Indiana.

Range: The silver-haired bat is a spring and fall migrant and a rare winter resident in Indiana. Spring migrants are found mostly from 18 April to 28 May, although we have netted a few individuals into early June. Fall migrants occur from 29 August to 6 November. Some hibernate in central and southern Indiana, but most hibernate to the south of Indiana.

Habits and Comments: Silver-haired bats usually begin foraging early in the evening. They usually fly fairly low, hawking insects from 15 to 30' above the ground, along woods borders.

Selected References. Barbour and Davis 1969; Kunz 1982.

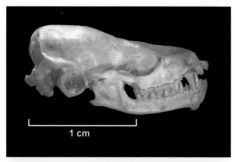

Side view of skull

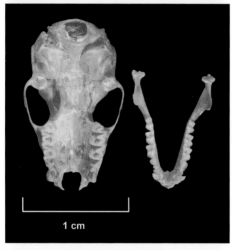

Ventral view of skull and lower jaw

Silver-haired bat. *Photo by Tony Brentlinger*

Eastern Pipistrelle
Perimyotis subflavus (F. Cuvier)

The eastern pipistrelle was known until 2003 as *Pipistrellus subflavus*.

Distinguishing Features and Measurements: The eastern pipistrelle is the smallest bat of Indiana. In color, it varies from pale yellowish-brown or grayish-brown to dark reddish-brown above. It is distinguished by having tricolor fur, with each strand having a broad, blackish basal band, then a narrower, yellowish band, and dusky tips. Immature individuals are gray. The belly is less grayish because hairs there are not dark-tipped. The forearm is usually reddish and contrasts sharply with the blackish wing membranes, especially in live animals. The first upper molariform tooth is reduced, creating a space that contains 1 tiny tooth immediately behind the canine.

TL 74–91, T 31–42, HF 7–10, FA 32–35, TR 4–6.5, Wt. 4–8,

Skull: Length: 12.5[–13.3 (0.5–0.53").

The skull has 2 incisors on each side of the upper jaw and 1 tiny tooth in the space behind the upper canines, is less than 14 mm long, and is somewhat "humped" behind as viewed from the side.

Dental Formula:

$$I \frac{2}{3} \quad C \frac{1}{1} \quad P \frac{2}{2} \quad M \frac{3}{3} = 34$$

Habitat: Perimyotis subflavus appears to be most abundant in well-wooded regions of southern Indiana that contain streams and ponds. In winter, they hibernate in caves and mines usually within 35 or 40 miles of their summer roosts.

Food: Leafhoppers and other "hoppers" are one of the most commonly eaten foods, followed by ground beetles, flies, other beetles, and moths.

Reproduction: Most mating occurs in fall in conjunction with swarming, but some also occurs in winter. Two young are usually produced, and most are born in June.

Range: The pipistrelle is common in southern Indiana north to Tippecanoe County in western Indiana, to Wells County in the west.

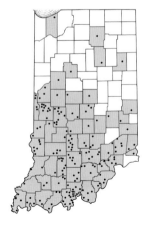

Habits and Comments: Colonies start to form in mid-April. Most pipistrelles in Indiana in summer live in clusters of leaves (mostly dead leaves) in trees in woods, but a few form small colonies (up to about 30 individuals) in buildings in summer. We had thought that pipistrelles in woods were using hollow trees since they would live in buildings, but we were surprised to

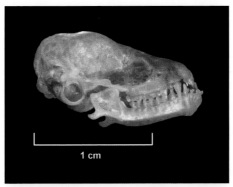

Side view of skull

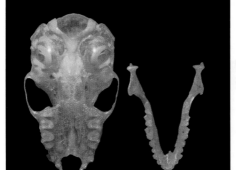

Ventral view
of skull and
lower jaw

Eastern pipistrelle. *Photo by Charles Oberst*

learn, via radio-tracking, that they lived in the leaf clusters. In winter they hibernate in caves and mines not far from their summer quarters. Consequently they are pretty much restricted to southern Indiana where most of the caves and mines occur. They hibernate alone, so there are usually few in any one cave or mine. A few pipistrelles, mostly males, may be found in caves throughout the summer.

SELECTED REFERENCES. Brack and Mumford 1984; Cope et al. 1961; Davis and Mumford 1962; Fujita and Kunz 1984; Hoofer et al. 2006; Kurta et al. 1996; Veilleux et al. 2003; Whitaker 1998; Winchell and Kunz 1996.

Pipistrelles in leaf cluster. *Photo by Brianne Walters*

Big Brown Bat
Eptesicus fuscus (Beauvois)

Distinguishing Features and Measurements: This is the second-largest bat of Indiana. It is brownish with blackish membranes and ears. The tragus is broad and blunt at the tip, and the ears are relatively short. The wingspan is 310–355 mm, and the forearm varies from 42 to 54 mm (average 46 mm). The only other brownish bat in Indiana with a forearm reaching 42 mm is the rare gray myotis, which has a forearm ranging from 42 to 45 mm and a relatively long, narrow, pointed tragus.

TL 94–129, T 29–50, HF 9–13, FA 42–54, TR 5–8, Wt. 12.4–26.5

Skull: Length: 18.5–20.7 (0.74–0.83").

The skull is large and has 2 incisors on each side. There are no tiny teeth, thus no space behind the upper canines.

Dental Formula:

$$I \frac{2}{3} \quad C \frac{1}{1} \quad P \frac{1}{2} \quad M \frac{3}{3} = 32$$

Habitat: Summer roost sites of *Eptesicus fuscus* include buildings, bridges, silos, rocky escarpments, and caves, but the species is most common in buildings. Of 306 big brown summer colonies in buildings, 102 were in barns, 69 in houses, 64 in churches, 7 in schools, 5 in sheds and garages, 51 in an assortment of other buildings (stores, factories), 6 in "other" (silos, mausoleum, parking garage, press box), and 2 were under bridges. Almost all colonies were in buildings that were occupied. We have seen buildings that harbor up to about 600 individuals, including volant (flying) young. In winter, a few hibernate in caves and mines, but the great majority hibernate in heated buildings.

Food: Beetles and true bugs are the most important foods of big brown bats in Indiana. Beetles include June bugs, spotted cucumber beetles,

and stinkbugs (mostly bright green ones). Flying ants are often eaten. This species also eats crickets (a few flying forms, as well as nonflying forms). Leafhoppers and ichneumonid wasps are also eaten.

Reproduction: Copulation has been observed in big brown bats in Indiana from spring through fall. Since relatively few big brown bats hibernate in caves, and since there is relatively little swarming there, we think much of the big brown bats' mating occurs in buildings or elsewhere. Two young are born in late May or June. Pregnancies

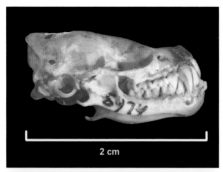
Side view of skull

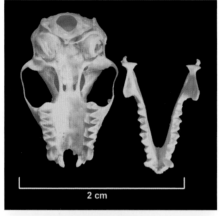
Ventral view
of skull and
lower jaw

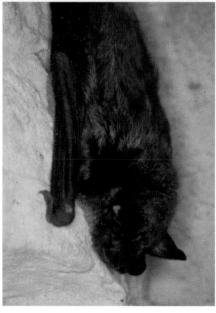
Big brown bat

have been recorded from 18 May through 11 July, lactating bats between 9 June and 30 July, and postlactating bats starting 10 July.

Range: This is the most abundant bat throughout the state, summer and winter.

Habits and Comments: Big brown bats have adapted to the human environment in summer and in winter. They start arriving at the maternity roosts in mid-March, even though it still may get quite cold. Twenty-six big brown bats were found in torpor on 26 March in a barn north of Terre Haute, but undoubtedly they came there from some other area after initial arousal from hibernation, as the barn was too cold (below freezing at times) to harbor them through the winter. Several times bats have left buildings lacking enough heat to maintain the temperature above freezing. Maternity colonies begin to disband in late August, and by mid-November essentially all individuals have gone to their hibernacula. This species, like other hibernators, wakens and becomes active periodically during the winter. On unusually warm winter evenings (temperature around 55–60), they may occasionally be seen in flight.

We do not think that very many big brown bats winter and summer in the same roost. Most big brown bats summer in places that become too cold to winter, so all those bats have to move to different winter roosts. Also, when big brown bats do winter in the same building in which there is a maternity colony, the numbers are much reduced. There seems to be a time in April when nearly all of the bats have left the winter quarters—even when the winter quarters also house a maternity colony.

Selected References. Beer 1955; Beer and Richards 1956; Christian 1956; Hamilton 1933; Kurta and Baker 1990; Rysgaard 1942; Whitaker 1995; Whitaker and Gummer 1992, 2000.

Evening Bat
Nycticeius humeralis (Rafinesque)

Distinguishing Features and Measurements: The evening bat is a small brown bat with black membranes, short ears, and a short tragus. It resembles certain *Myotis,* or a small big brown bat. Big brown bats are much larger than evening bats, having forearms usually much over 40 mm, whereas the forearm of the evening bat is 40 or under. The evening bat can be separated from *Myotis* by its short, rounded tragus and lack of a space behind the upper canines. *Myotis* has a much longer tragus, as well as longer ears and a "space" behind the canine produced by the first 2 molariform teeth being tiny.

TL 80–106, T 25–42, HF 8–11, FA 28–40, TR 3.0–7, Wt. 6–14.8

Skull: Length: 14.4–15.1 (0.57–0.6").

Skull with 1 upper incisor on each side, with 4 molariform teeth, none reduced in size.

Dental Formula:

$$I \ \frac{1}{3} \ C \ \frac{1}{1} \ P \ \frac{1}{2} \ M \ \frac{3}{3} \ = \ 30$$

Habitat: All of the earlier known maternity colonies in Indiana were in buildings. However, all the known evening bat colonies currently in Indiana are in hollows in trees; we suspect this was their original primary habitat. This is the only species of bat in the state we have not found in a cave.

Food: Beetles, moths, and leafhoppers are the major foods eaten by these bats.

Reproduction: Two young per litter are usually produced in early to mid-June.

Range: The evening bat is most abundant in the southern part of the state. However, it is uncommon in Indiana. All 11 earlier known colonies (in the 1950s) were in buildings and all were roughly along tributaries of major rivers. All 11 sites were revisited in 1989 and 1990, and netting was conducted in the vicinity of each. At this time all of the original colonies were inactive. A colony was found in a church near Clay City, Clay County, in 1987, but the bats were evicted in 1993. In July 1994, a large population of evening bats was found along Prairie Creek in southern Vigo County. There were also scattered populations along the Wabash all the way to Evansville, and there are a few other colonies in woods in the state.

Habits and Comments: Where evening bats from Indiana spend the winter is unknown, but we suspect that they move southward and hibernate in hollow trees. Essentially all adult evening bats at Prairie Creek are female, whereas in Posey County, at the southern tip of Indiana, both males and females occur. Since males of some species tend to remain near the hibernacula, this suggests that Posey County is on the northern edge of the wintering range.

Selected References. Humphrey and Cope 1968, 1970; Jones 1967; Mumford 1953; Watkins 1972; Whitaker and Gummer 1994, 2003.

Side view of skull

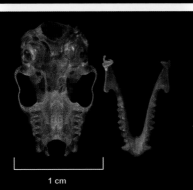

Ventral view of skull and lower jaw

Evening bat. *Photo by Adam Mann*

Red Bat
Lasiurus borealis (Müller)

Distinguishing Features and Measurements: The red bat can be distinguished from all other bats of Indiana by its reddish coloration. Males are a clear, brick red and females are a duller red. This is a unique example of sexual dimorphism in color among mammals. There is a small whitish-yellow patch forming an epaulet in front of each shoulder. Red bats have short, rounded ears and a short, rounded tragus. The dorsal and ventral surfaces of the wing are furred close to the body and along the forearm. The top of the interfemoral membrane is densely furred over its entire surface.

TL 90–123, T 32–59, HF 7–11, FA 36–47, TR 4–7.5, Wt. 9–22

Skull: Length: 13.1–14.6 (0.52–0.58").

Skulls of *Lasiurus* can be separated from those of other bats of Indiana by their short, squarish shape and by the presence of a tiny "peg" tooth behind and between the first incisor and canine tooth. Those of red bats can be separated from those of hoary bats by size; the skulls those of red bats are about 13–14 mm long, while those of hoary bats are about 17–20 mm long.

Dental Formula:

$$I \ \frac{1}{3} \ C \ \frac{1}{1} \ P \ \frac{2}{2} \ M \ \frac{3}{3} \ = \ 32$$

Habitat: Red bats seem to favor areas of scattered deciduous trees, and thus are often seen about orchards, parks, cemeteries, grazed woodlots, and residential areas, but they also occur in larger forested areas.

Food: Red bats feed on moths, June bugs, tree and leaf hoppers, flying ants, and many other insects.

Reproduction: Mating occurs in August and September and is apparently initiated in flight. Several copulating pairs have been seen as they fall to the ground. Red bats usually produce three or four young, which is a large number for bats. This is probably an indication that more predation occurs on this species than on most bats. Most young are born in June.

Range: Occuring throughout Indiana, it is abundant in many sections, but is least numerous in the prairie region of northwestern Indiana. A few red bats winter in Indiana, but there is an extensive migration in spring and fall. In summer, it is one of the most abundant bats in Indiana, ranking second only to the big brown bat.

Habits and Comments: The red bat spends the day hanging among vegetation and flying out to feed, usually just before dark. Its flight can be exceptionally rapid, especially on windy evenings. The bat may make sudden side forays to pursue an insect, or it may dive at high speed to chase prey close to the ground. At times red bats flying at altitudes of more than 100' may dive suddenly, almost vertically, to the surface of a pool, level off, and gracefully drink by skimming the surface. The few red bats that winter in Indiana probably hibernate in leaf litter. They waken by passive warming and, on warm nights, in contrast to most other species in Indiana, will feed in winter (Boyles et al. 2003; Dunbar et al. 2007).

SELECTED REFERENCES. Barbour and Davis 1969; Boyles et al. 2003; Davis and Lidicker 1956; Dunbar et al. 2007; Mumford 1973; Shump and Shump 1982a; Whitaker 1972b.

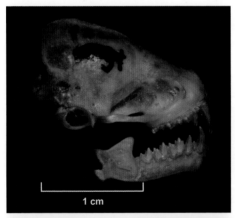

Side view of skull

1 cm

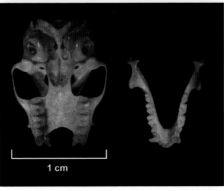

Ventral view of skull and lower jaw

1 cm

Red bat. *Photo by Adam Mann*

Juvenile female red bat. *Photo by Adam Mann*

Hoary Bat
Lasiurus cinereus (Palisot de Beauvois)

Distinguishing Features and Measurements: The hoary bat is a large, grayish bat with short, broad, rounded ears bearing black borders. It is the largest bat in Indiana. Its forearm is 47–59 mm. The whitish tips of the body hairs give the bat the appearance of being covered with hoarfrost, hence its common name. The dorsal surface of the interfemoral membrane is completely furred. The throat is yellowish, and there is a small, irregular yellowish spot at the base of each thumb.

TL 120–152, T 44–65, HF 10–14, FA 47–59, TR 5–11, Wt. 20–38

Skull: Length: 17–18.5 (0.68–0.74").
The skull of *L. cinereus* is roughly square and similar to that of *L. borealis,* but larger.
Dental Formula:

$$I \ \frac{1}{3} \ C \ \frac{1}{1} \ P \ \frac{2}{2} \ M \ \frac{3}{3} \ = \ 32$$

Habitat: The hoary bat is a tree-inhabiting species, roosting by day among the foliage. It often roosts in areas where trees are scattered and have openings below their crowns, such as pastures, residential areas, lake shores, campuses, and even brush or old field areas.

Food: Hoary bats feed heavily on moths when available but will eat a variety of other insects.

Reproduction: As in other bats in temperate zones, mating takes places mostly in fall, and fertilization takes place in spring, a process called delayed fertilization. Hoary bats give birth to two young, usually in late May and early June. Lactating females have been observed between 28 May and 14 July.

Range: The hoary bat no doubt occurs throughout Indiana but appears to be uncommon.

Habits and Comments: The hoary bat is primarily solitary, except at favored feeding and drinking areas, where three or more may be seen together. Family groups consisting of a female and her two young are also encountered. The flight of the hoary bat is usually strong, fast, and direct. The wing beats seem regular, rather deliberate, and somewhat birdlike. Amazingly erratic flight may be exhibited by foraging individuals, especially on windy evenings.

The species is highly migratory, being found in Indiana in summer (mostly females). Most individuals migrate southward and spend the winter in southern California, Baja, or Central America. A few migrate to the southeast (Louisiana to South Carolina).

Selected References. Barbour and Davis 1969; Mumford 1969b; Provost and Kirkpatrick 1952; Shump and Shump 1982b; Whitaker 1967b.

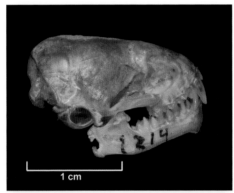

Side view of skull

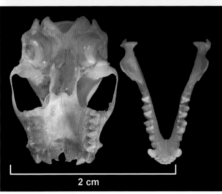

Ventral view of skull and lower jaw

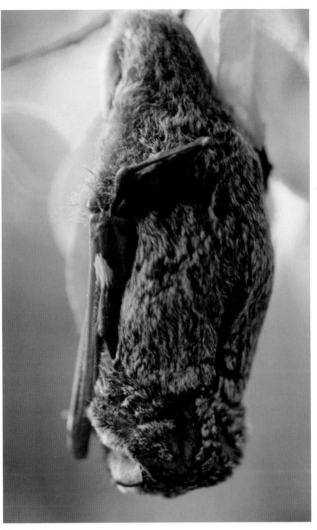

Hoary bat

Rafinesque's Big-eared Bat
Corynorhinus rafinesquii (Lesson)

Distinguishing Features and Measurements: This medium-sized bat is brownish above and whitish below. It has much longer ears than those of any other bat in Indiana. The ears of this species are 27–35 mm, more than 1" long.

TL 84–104, T 43–50, HF 9–11, FA 43–45, TR 13–15, Wt. 10–11

Skull: Length: 15.5–16.5 (0.62–0.66").

The skull of this species has 1 upper incisor on each side, is humped behind, and has 1 reduced tooth in the space behind the canine.

Dental Formula:

$$\text{I} \ \frac{2}{3} \ \text{C} \ \frac{1}{1} \ \text{P} \ \frac{2}{3} \ \text{M} \ \frac{3}{3} \ = \ 36$$

Habitat: There are only 17 records of this species from Indiana, hence it is classed as an accidental. All but one individual were from caves in areas of deciduous woodlands; a single individual was taken from a long, concrete culvert.

Food: We have no data on the food of this species from Indiana, but we assume that it feeds heavily on moths, its normal food elsewhere.

Reproduction: The species has not been known to reproduce in Indiana. Delayed fertilization occurs, and one young is produced in May or June.

Range: The earliest record of Rafinesque's big-eared bat in Indiana was from Putnam County, where two individuals were taken in a cave near Greencastle. Including those, only 17 records of this species have occurred in over a century. Most records are from Lawrence (8 individuals) and Washington (5 individuals) counties.

Habits and Comments: Most big-eared bats observed in Indiana were single animals, but two were found in one cave on three occasions. The big-eared bat usually roosts, even in winter, in the twilight zone near cave entrances. Here, the temperature is often quite cool and air movement is sometimes considerable. The only other bat occurring in Indiana that chooses similar winter roosting sites is the big brown bat.

Selected References. Barbour and Davis 1969; Hall 1963; Hoffmeister and Goodpaster 1963; Jones and Suttkus 1975; Wilson 1960.

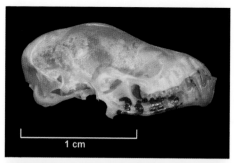
Side view of skull

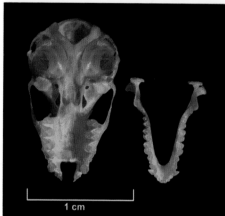
Ventral view
of skull and
lower jaw

Rafinesque's big-eared bat. *Photo by Edward Pivorun*

Order CINGULATA—Armadillos

Dasypus novemcinctus / Nine-banded Armadillo

Order Cingulata

The armadillos were previously classed with the sloths and anteaters but more recently have been placed in their own order, the Cingulata. There is only one family, the Dasypodidae, and its characteristics are those of the order.

FAMILY DASYPODIDAE

Armadillos are unique among living mammals in having ossified dermal plates covered by leathery epidermis. These plates form a shell with 7–11 transverse, usually movable bands, the shell completely covering the dorsal surface of the animal. The forefeet, furnished with strong claws, are powerful digging tools. Only one species of armadillo (*Dasypus novemcinctus,* family Dasypodidae) occurs in the United States, but there are 21 species of armadillos ranging widely through much of Central and South America.

Nine-banded Armadillo
Dasypus novemcinctus Linnaeus

Distinguishing Features and Measurements: The armadillo is opossum-sized and can be confused with no other species. It has a shell-like, scaly skin with 7–11 (usually 9) transversely joined bands over the back. Bony scutes cover the tail and the top of the head as well as the carapace. The simple, peglike teeth (usually 8 above, 8 below), the long, apparently segmented tail (it carries 12–15 rings of scutes), and the prominent claws further distinguish this peculiar animal. There are four claws on the forefeet, five on the hind. Soft, sparsely haired skin covers the belly and limbs. The prominent, erect ears are nearly half the length of the head. The eyes are small and weak, and the animal has a piglike snout. There are four mammary glands, two pectoral, two inguinal. Males are larger than females; females weigh 3.6–6.0 kg (8–13 lbs), males 5.5–7.7 kg (12–17 lbs). The generic name means hairy-footed, and the specific name means nine-banded.

TL 615–800, T 245–370, HF 75–107, Wt. 3.6–7.7 kg (8–17 lbs)

Skull: Length: 92–102 (3.6–3.9").
Dental Formula:
$$\frac{7 \text{ to } 9}{7 \text{ to } 9} \quad \text{(usually 8)} \quad = \quad 14\text{-}18$$

Habitat: The nine-banded armadillo is found in many habitats—such as brushy or waste lands, moist forests, pastures, and scrub—where the soil permits easy digging and supports enough food for its needs.

Food: The food of the armadillo is primarily insects and their larvae and other invertebrates, particularly ants, beetles, caterpillars, centipedes, millipedes, earthworms, and snails and slugs, although some plant food (up to 10% or so of the diet) is eaten. Vertebrates, particularly lizards and their eggs, may constitute up to 25% of the diet, especially in winter, but small birds or mammals and birds' eggs may be eaten when available. The armadillo exposes insects with its sharp claws, then flicks them into its mouth with its long, sticky tongue. The scats of this beast are round mudballs, in which are found numerous insect remains. Mortality on the highway probably accounts for more deaths than does predation, although the dog can be an important predator. Armadillos are short-lived. In the wild, few live more than 2 years. The subterranean fungus *Endogone* is commonly eaten.

In spite of persecution and unwitting destruction, armadillos seem to thrive, as the amazing extension of their range within recent decades so dramatically demonstrates.

Reproduction: This species almost always produces four young per litter, the four always of the same sex. The early embryo divides by fission to form twin embryos, and immediately these divide to give rise to two pairs of duplicate twins, or quadruplets. Thus the young are all derived from one fertilized egg and all inherit the same assortment of genes. Mating occurs in summer, but implantation is delayed into November, following which 4 months will elapse before the birth of the young. The young are born in an advanced condition;,and although the armor is soft and pliable at birth, it soon hardens. One litter a year is the rule, and armadillos apparently remain paired for the season. Because of the shell, copulation requires that the female lie on her back.

Range: Only four armadillos have been taken in Indiana, two in Gibson County, one in Vanderburgh County, and one in Pike County.

Habits and Comments: John J. Audubon and John Bachman first reported the armadillo in the United States. It was from southern Texas, and it has continually increased its range since then. By 1925 it had entered Louisiana; by 1936 it occurred throughout Louisiana west of the Mississippi; and by 1943 it had moved east of the Mississippi River and now occupies western and southern Mississippi (Humphrey 1974). It became established in Alabama by 1952 and is now widespread in the southern part of that state. The armadillo was introduced in Florida in the 1920s, and by 1952 could be found throughout much of the state. From this center it has also spread and now occurs in southern Georgia, western Tennessee, and South Carolina. Most recently it has moved into Kentucky and Southern Illinois, and of course now apparently into Indiana.

The armadillo is primarily crepuscular and nocturnal, usually becoming active near dusk, but during cold weather the animal often is active during the day. It forages by rooting here and there in the manner of a pig. While foraging, the armadillo will sometimes stand up on its hind legs, braced by the tail, and sniff the air. Its sight and hearing are poor, and the armored skin gives it a stiff-legged gait and immobile body.

The small head and short neck give it the appearance of a small pig. Because its eyesight is poor, it may be approached within about 30 yards, often much closer. The animal is an accomplished digger and makes prominent burrows, from which trails radiate in several directions. Each armadillo maintains several burrows. Cottontail rabbits, opossums, skunks, and other animals may use the burrows of armadillos. Burrows in Texas averaged about 4 feet in length. About half of 26 burrows studied there ended in an enlarged chamber housing a nest. Burrows are about 7 inches diameter, and the enlarged nest chamber averages about 14 inches in diameter. The nest is usually in a burrow but is sometimes in a small cave or crevice. When alarmed an armadillo will run rapidly away, traveling with considerable speed for such a clumsy-appearing beast. However, it may be overtaken by a man on foot. If overtaken, it does not roll into a tight ball, as often claimed, although it may partially curl up, protecting the soft belly from attack. Often when alarmed an armadillo will jump straight into the air and arch its back, a behavior responsible for many highway deaths. When cornered in a burrow, the animal arches its back, making it extremely difficult to extract.

In loose soil an armadillo can burrow out of sight in a few minutes. The nose and front feet dig into the soil, which is then pushed under the abdomen. The animal then balances tripodlike on the forefeet and tail and swings the hind feet forward over the dirt. The back is then arched, and a sudden straightening of the body, coupled with a thrusting back and up with the hind limbs, throws the dirt behind. The armadillo swims in the manner of a dog. Occasionally, if the distance is short, it will walk across on the bottom—underwater. That its specific gravity exceeds one allows this behavior but also means that the animal must ingest air by repeated gasping if it is to swim (or walk) any distance.

Because of the hard plates, it appears much less subject to ectoparasites than many other mammals of comparable size. Armadillos may carry ticks and chiggers, but fleas are rare. However, a number of internal parasites have been found. The armadillo may harbor *Trypanosoma cruzi,* the causal agent of Chagas disease. Many armadillos are killed and their armored skins prepared as baskets for the tourist and curio trade. Armadillos are used for food, roasted "in the shell." Natural cases of leprosy have been found in armadillos, and the species is an important laboratory animal in leprosy research.

SELECTED REFERENCES. Breece and Dusi 1985; Clark 1951; Fitch et al. 1952; Hofmann 2005; McBee and Baker 1982.

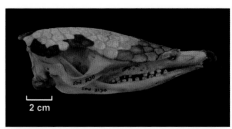

Side view of skull

Ventral view of skull and lower jaw

Nine-banded armadillo

Order LAGOMORPHA—Hares, Rabbits, and Allies

Order Lagomorpha

Lagomorphs resemble rodents, with which they have much in common. Apparently lagomorphs and rodents have common ancestry. Lagomorphs possess 2 pairs of upper incisors. The first pair is large and rodentlike, with a broad groove on the front surface. The second pair, emerging directly behind the first, is small, lacks the cutting edge, and is nearly circular in outline. Another feature of lagomorph dentition is that the lateral distance between the cheek teeth of the left and right sides of the lower jaw is considerably less than that between the 2 molar-tooth rows of the upper jaw. Consequently, only 1 molar row of the upper jaw and 1 of the lower jaw meet at one time, resulting in a sidewise chewing movement. Lagomorphs also have numerous fenestrae—small openings in the rostral area that serve to lighten the skull.

FAMILY LEPORIDAE

The order Lagomorpha includes two families: the Leporidae, or rabbits (including cottontails) and hares (including jackrabbits), and the Ochotonidae, the much smaller pikas, or coneys. There are two species of lagomorphs in Indiana, the common and ubiquitous cottontail and the swamp rabbit, a rare species of the river "bottoms" of southwestern Indiana.

The terms "hare" and "rabbit" are much misused. Hares are generally larger and have longer ears and longer legs. Most species of hares, the snowshoe being an exception, live in more open habitat than rabbits and tend to outleap and outrun predators. Rabbits, by contrast, tend to run for cover when threatened. Hares do not make nests for their young; rather, the young are well developed (precocial) when born—fully furred and open-eyed. They are able to move about within hours after birth but remain in the vicinity of their birth. Rabbits, for their part, are altricial, that is, born in a relatively immature state, as are most mammals; at birth, they are pink and usually hairless, and their eyes are closed. Rabbits and hares often lie on the ground in a "form," which may be under cover or out in the open. The form is simply a shallow, temporarily cleared depression. When in the form they remain completely still, ears back, and are thus almost invisible. If discovered, they burst forth, depending on their great speed and acceleration to outrun a predator. Lagomorphs are exceedingly prolific, their high reproductive rates offsetting the great numbers killed by predators, people, and the automobile. Ovulation is induced by copulation—which helps ensure that ovulation occurs at the optimum time for fertilization. The scrotal sac, entirely covered with hair, is visible only during the breeding season, when the testes are scrotal.

Rabbits and hares form the familiar hard, brown fecal pellets seen in the field. But in an alternative—faster and minimally digestive—process often practiced by rabbits and hares, soft, greenish pellets are formed and re-eaten. The soft pellets still contain much nutritive material and large amounts of vitamin B. This process is called *coprophagy* or *reingestion* and allows the animals to feed on a large amount of food in a short time, then return quickly to the safety of the form, thicket, or brush pile, where the soft pellets are eaten directly from the anus and digested more slowly.

Lagomorphs are generally silent except for foot thumps, alarm or aggressive signals, and the distress screams of captured animals. These animals appear to rely heavily on scent signals for communication.

Eastern Cottontail
Sylvilagus floridanus (J. A. Allen)

Distinguishing Features and Measurements: This is the only rabbit common throughout Indiana, and among native mammals can be confused only with the larger swamp rabbit, currently found in a few localities in Knox, Gibson, and Posey counties of southwestern Indiana. Released or escaped domestic ("San Juan") rabbits (*Oryctolagus cuniculus*) may be encountered occasionally. The eastern cottontail is grayish to brownish above and sprinkled with black. The upper surfaces of the hind feet are whitish; the upper surface of the tail is grayish. The swamp rabbit is more reddish-brown and has more black on the back; the upper surface of its tail is brownish and the upper surfaces of the hind feet are tan or pale brown. Both species have a reddish nape patch, which is somewhat variable in color. Young and subadult cottontails have a white spot on the forehead that is absent in the swamp rabbit.

TL 355–537, T 30–67, HF 80–110, Wt. 900–1,800

Skull: Length: 69–81 (2.7–3.2").

The skull of the cottontail is smaller and differs in other ways from that of the swamp rabbit (see figures and the species account for the swamp rabbit). Rabbits are the only Indiana mammals in which the 2 pairs of upper incisors are situated 1 pair directly behind the other.

Dental Formula:

$$\text{I } \frac{2}{1} \quad \text{C } \frac{0}{0} \quad \text{P } \frac{3}{2} \quad \text{M } \frac{3}{3} \quad = \quad 28$$

Habitat: Cottontails are encountered in many habitats but are most numerous in overgrown fields of weeds, briers, and brush near croplands. They occur in extensive woodlands sparingly, usually near openings, but may be found in ungrazed woodlots, smaller wooded tracts, and in young pine tree plantations. Many thrive in cities where they can be found in vacant lots, gardens, shrub plantings, golf courses, parks, and other areas that afford enough shelter and food. Heavy ground cover is one prerequisite for optimum cottontail habitat, and thickets of blackberries or wild roses are especially good.

Food: Cottontails feed on many species of plants, such as hydrangea, hepatica, ironwood, shellbark hickory, black walnut, clover, Christmas fern, wahoo, sugar maple, dogwood, sassafras, alfalfa, corn, cabbage, peas, beets, and apples. They may feed on fruit trees in winter and may completely girdle trees in obtaining bark. Such damage usually occurs when snow cover hides more desirable food items. During heavy snows cottontails may strip the bark from sumac, black cherry, and tree-of-heaven. We have observations of their feeding on multiflora rose, red osier dogwood, sycamore, persimmon, and cultivated beans and apples. Blackberry briers as large as ⅜" in diameter are sometimes clipped off by cottontails in deep snow. Sprouts have been noticed that had their bark removed to a height of 2.5' above the ground. Cottontails sometimes completely consume individual plants of dry lamb's-quarters during winter.

Reproduction: Courtship activities commence in late winter and early spring. Pairs or small groups may be seen actively chasing each other about. At times one or more individuals may jump straight up into the air to a considerable height. Mating occurs after this activity, and the members of the pairs then go their separate ways. Gestation is about 28–32 days. Several litters are produced each year. The number of young in cottontail litters usually ranges from three to seven. At birth, the young are blind and without hair, so a warm nest is important to their survival. The young are born in nests usually in open sites with sparse vegetation. Nests appear as shallow, cuplike depressions in the ground. The nests are constructed of grasses and other soft plant materials, to which is added considerable hair from the female's body. They are so well hidden and covered that even on a well-kept lawn they may be difficult to detect. The young are fed near dawn and dusk. The behavior of an adult female at her nest containing young was witnessed by R. E. Mumford on a 5 April. At 6:30 PM (sunset was at 7:15), the female came slowly hopping and walking across a lawn to the nest near the foundation of a house. She stopped at the nest site and scratched briefly with her feet, undoubtedly uncovering the young in the hidden nest. She then sat perfectly motionless for 10 minutes nursing the young. The next 4 minutes she sat in the same position, but preened her feet and chest. The last minute she was at the nest she scratched at the leaves and grass briefly, turned 90 degrees and scratched again, then turned another 90 degrees and repeated the process before hopping away. Thus, she spent 15 minutes at the nest. When the young leave the nest, they are still relatively small (4–5" long). Because of their size and the fact that they are mainly on their own after leaving the nest, they are vulnerable to many predators and accidents.

Range: The cottontail occurs throughout the state where suitable habitat is present and may be locally abundant.

Habits and Comments: Cottontails spend most of the daylight hours in a "form" or bed on the ground. Forms are usually in good cover, especially in winter, so that the animal is sheltered from sight from all directions except the one it faces and escapes to when disturbed. Sometimes old rolls of fence wire, old farm machinery discards, stacks of lumber, brush piles, pipes, tiles, small culverts, or other objects serve as resting sites. Forms may be used more than once, but a new form may also be used each day. A cottontail occupied a form in a small clump of grass on Whitaker's closely mowed lawn for several days. If one looked closely, the rabbit could easily be seen from several feet away. Cottontails frequently construct a form at the base of a stump or tree, so that they are more protected from the rear. Ground burrows made by larger mammals, particularly woodchucks, also serve as daytime resting places for cottontails, especially in winter or inclement weather. Most cottontail activity is in early morning, late evening, or at night, although it is not unusual in early spring to see rabbits out in the daytime.

An individual probably spends most of its life within a fairly small area. When a cottontail is chased by dogs, it will soon circle back near the site where it was originally flushed; rabbit hunters take advantage of this behavior by staying near where the animal was flushed. Cottontails swim well, using convulsive kicks of the hind feet. They are not normally gregarious, and even where rabbits are plentiful they are not usually seen in large groups. Two or more may be seen together during the courtship and mating season, but one most often sees a single animal. Cottontails sometimes squeal loudly when handled by humans or captured by predators.

The cottontail eats a great amount of food in a relatively short time, thus reducing its exposure to predators while it is feeding in the open. The food is partially chewed and gulped down but not immediately digested. It moves into the small intestine, where it forms soft, green fecal pellets. When the rabbit reaches a protected spot, it defecates these green pellets and reingests them, a process called coprophagy. These pellets are about the same size and shape as completely digested pellets but are merely masses of green vegetation. The cottontail has a number of enemies. It makes up a large percentage of the diets of foxes and coyotes. Many fall prey to domestic cats and dogs; many other carnivores, bird predators, and large snakes prey on them.

SELECTED REFERENCES. Chapman et al. 1980; Demaree 1978.

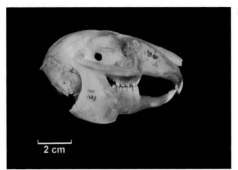

Side view of skull

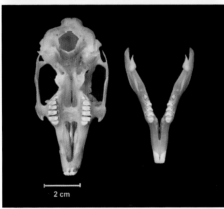

Ventral view of skull and lower jaw

Eastern cottontail. *Photo by Terry L. Castor*

Swamp Rabbit
Sylvilagus aquaticus (Bachman)

Distinguishing Features and Measurements: The swamp rabbit resembles a large cottontail and is difficult to distinguish except by size. The swamp rabbit is darker brown and has a more liberal sprinkling of blackish on the back. The rump tends to be brownish, rather than grayish as in the cottontail. The tail is narrower and browner above than that of the cottontail. The dorsal surface of the hind feet is tan in the swamp rabbit, whitish in the eastern cottontail. There is a distinct reddish or rusty-colored nape patch in both species, but that of the swamp rabbit is duller. Habitat and range help a great deal, as swamp rabbits presently occur only in floodplain woods of Knox, Gibson, and Posey counties. The skulls of the two species are similar, but that of the swamp rabbit is larger (greatest length about 90 mm, compared to about 70 mm in the eastern cottontail).

TL 462–545, T 40–60, HF 101–113, Wt. 1,780–2,800

Skull: Length: 83.7–94.6 (2⅜–3⅝").
   Dental Formula:

$$I \quad \frac{2}{1} \quad C \quad \frac{0}{0} \quad P \quad \frac{3}{2} \quad M \quad \frac{3}{3} \quad = \quad 28$$

Habitat: Swamp rabbits occur in bottomland woods with good ground cover, and particularly with cane, *Arundinaria gigantea,* or elderberry, *Sambucus canadensis.* Major tree species found at swamp rabbit localities are shellbark hickory, sugarberry, sugar maple, bitternut hickory, pecan, elm, sweet gum, ash, pin oak, cottonwood, sycamore, Shumard's oak, box elder, and black walnut. The forest floor vegetation includes heath aster, poison ivy, stinging nettle, grasses, sedges, trumpetvine, cane, lizard's-tail, greenbrier, and spotted touch-me-not. Apparently the most important factor as to whether swamp rabbits are present or not in otherwise good habitat is whether raised areas or "refugia" are present where they can avoid flooding. The refugia are most often in the form of levees or raised ridges. In areas where swamp rabbits were present earlier but are now gone, one can often see that the refugia have now been cleared and cultivated.

Food: Winter foods eaten by swamp rabbits, as revealed by tracking rabbits in the snow, are crossvine leaves; poison ivy and sedge; greenbrier; willow bark and shoots; blackberry and silver maple seedlings; and trumpetvine, cane, box elder, aster, and ragweed. Swamp rabbits have been recorded feeding on cane and spotted touch-me-not during the first week of August. The rabbits also eat honey locust, blackberry, shellbark hickory, and wahoo.

Reproduction: The gestation of the swamp rabbit is about 38 days. Young are born in a nest much like that of the eastern cottontail but larger. Nests of both rabbits in Indiana are difficult to locate, for

they are well hidden and are covered when the female is away. Young are produced throughout the growing season, but peak birth times occur in April and July.

Range: The swamp rabbit presently occurs only in floodplain woods of Knox, Gibson, and Posey counties. It is listed as endangered by the state of Indiana.

Habits and Comments: Home ranges vary from 10 to 50 or more acres. During the day, swamp rabbits usually rest in forms, often in brush piles, grapevine tangles, cane thickets, grassy open areas, standing hollow trees, at bases of trees, buttonbush sloughs, or blackberry thickets.

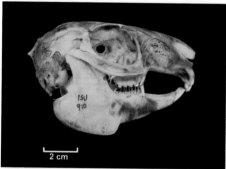

Side view of skull

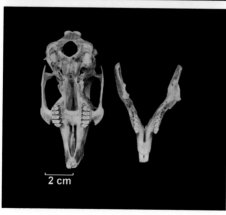

Ventral view of skull and lower jaw

Swamp rabbits frequently deposit fecal pellets on top of stumps and logs in winter (from October through May), but this information is not reliable for determining distribution of swamp rabbits in summer or early fall, as log usage is virtually nonexistent from early June to mid-September. Eastern cottontails rarely deposit pellets on logs. We believe the fecal deposition on logs is because the rabbits spend much time sitting on logs as observation posts during winter when ground cover is sparse and the rabbits can see for some distance.

SELECTED REFERENCES. Chapman and Feldhamer 1981; Hunt 1959; Terrel 1972; Whitaker and Abrell 1986.

Swamp rabbit. *Photo by NealyBob@Pbase.com*

Swamp rabbit pellets on log, *above and opposite, top*

Swamp rabbit habitat at Long Pond, in Gibson County

Order RODENTIA—Rodents or Gnawing Mammals

FAMILY SCIURIDAE

Tamias striatus / Eastern Chipmunk
Marmota monax / Woodchuck
Spermophilus tridecemlineatus / Thirteen-lined Ground Squirrel
Spermophilus franklinii / Franklin's Ground Squirrel
Sciurus carolinensis / Gray Squirrel
Sciurus niger / Fox Squirrel
Tamiasciurus hudsonicus / Red Squirrel
Glaucomys volans / Southern Flying Squirrel

FAMILY GEOMYIDAE

Geomys bursarius / Plains Pocket Gopher

FAMILY CASTORIDAE

Castor canadensis / Beaver

FAMILY CRICETIDAE

SUBFAMILY NEOTOMINAE—New World Rats and Mice

Reithrodontomys megalotis / Western Harvest Mouse
Peromyscus maniculatus bairdii / Deer Mouse
Peromyscus leucopus / White-footed Mouse
Neotoma magister / Allegheny Woodrat

SUBFAMILY ARVICOLINAE—Voles, Muskrats, and Bog Lemmings

Microtus pennsylvanicus / Meadow Vole
Microtus ochrogaster / Prairie Vole
Microtus pinetorum / Woodland Vole
Ondatra zibethicus / Muskrat
Synaptomys cooperi / Southern Bog Lemming

FAMILY MURIDAE

Rattus norvegicus / Norway Rat
Mus musculus / House Mouse

FAMILY DIPODIDAE

SUBFAMILY ZAPODINAE—Jumping Mice

Zapus hudsonius / Meadow Jumping Mouse

Order Rodentia

Rodents are found throughout the world, far surpassing all other mammalian orders in numbers of individuals and in numbers of genera and species. There are about 443 genera and 2,021 species. There are 22 species of rodents living in Indiana at present, 20 native. Among them are terrestrial, fossorial, arboreal, and semiaquatic species, and even a glider. As a group, they are best characterized by their large, chisellike incisors, a single pair of them in each jaw, and the absence of canines. There is thus a wide space, the diastema, between the incisive and molariform or cheek teeth. Some rodents, such as rats and mice, and field "mice" or voles (*Microtus*), often cause great loss to agriculture, and some are notorious disease carriers. Conversely, rodents are exceedingly important as prey species. Also, many of them eat weed seeds and insects. The muskrat and beaver are or at least have been valuable furbearers, and squirrels are heavily hunted for food. Also, squirrels and chipmunks provide us with much entertainment.

Recently, there has been considerable discussion regarding the classification of rodents. Rodents currently are placed in five suborders, four occurring in North America: the Sciuromorpha (squirrel-like rodents); the Myomorpha (mouse- and ratlike rodents); the Castorimorpha (beavers, pocket gophers, and kangaroo rats and relatives); and the Hystricomorpha, or porcupines and allies. One member of the Hystricomorpha, the native American porcupine (Erethizontidae, *Erethizon dorsatum*) did occur in Indiana but is now extirpated. Only one sciuromorph family occurs in Indiana, the squirrels (Sciuridae). The Sciuromorpha have a small infraorbital canal (not enclosing muscle tissue), a well-developed postorbital process, and 4 or 5 upper and lower molariform teeth. The Myomorpha have a small to large infraorbital canal through which part of the main jaw muscle passes before inserting on the side of the rostrum, and there is no postorbital process. The Myomorpha includes three North American families. Myomorph rodents of Indiana, as now classified, include the mice and rats proper (New World mice, Cricetidae, and the introduced Old World mice, Muridae) and jumping mice (family Dipodidae, subfamily Zapodinae). Muroids have 3 molariform teeth above and below; the zapodines have a large, oval infraorbital foramen, 3 molariform teeth below and 3 or 4 above; and castorids have a small infraorbital foramen and 4 molariforms above and below.

The muroid mice and rats currently include two families with representatives in North America. One is the Muridae (Old World rats and mice) with two genera, *Mus* and *Rattus,* occurring in North America through introduction. The other family is the Cricetidae (New World rats and mice and the voles).

FAMILY SCIURIDAE

Squirrels are conspicuous over much of the world, except for Australia, southern South America, Malagasy (Madagascar), and many islands. There are eight species of squirrels in Indiana. Squirrels generally have large eyes; tree squirrels have long, bushy tails. Ground squirrels have smaller tails with less fur (Indiana has two species of ground squirrels). Squirrels often sit on their haunches and feed using their front feet. The thumb is reduced on the front foot, and there are five toes on the hind. There are 4 molariform teeth in each half of the lower jaw and 4 or 5 in each half of the upper jaw. Squirrels are of various sizes and differ greatly in habits and habitats, which tends to reduce competition among them. Most squirrels are diurnal, the flying squirrels being an exception. Some are primarily arboreal (red, fox, gray, and flying squirrels), some are burrowers (ground squirrels and the woodchuck), and one in Indiana (chipmunk) is both. There is a general increase in tail bushiness with increased time spent in trees. The tail aids in balance and helps act as a parachute in case of a fall.

Squirrels have a great awareness of their environment. Their feeding strategy is one of moving about, sampling various items, and thus locating a variety of foods as they become available. All species that live primarily on the ground hibernate (chipmunks, woodchucks, and ground squirrels). The chipmunks, however, awake periodically and eat from the food they have stored, whereas other hibernating squirrels use stored fat for maintenance energy during hibernation. Tree squirrels are active all year. Most squirrels are primarily vegetarian, but some are highly insectivorous (flying and thirteen-lined ground squirrels), and some will take eggs, young birds, or other young vertebrates when opportunity arises. Indiana squirrels range in size from the southern flying squirrel, averaging about 52 grams, to the woodchuck, which weighs up to 6 kg (13 lbs). The family name is taken from the generic name *Sciurus* (*sci* = shade; *urus* = tail), from the tree squirrels' habit of positioning the broad tail over the back like an umbrella when at rest.

Eastern Chipmunk
Tamias striatus (Linnaeus)

Distinguishing Features and Measurements: The chipmunk is a small, brownish squirrel with two pale and five blackish longitudinal stripes on the back, and two pale and two brownish stripes on each side of the face. The underparts are white and the rump is rusty-colored. The tail is dorsoventrally flattened and has long, reddish hairs, tipped with black. Chipmunks have well-developed internal cheek pouches.

TL 83–275, T 8–111, HF 8–44, Wt. 90–149

Skull: Length: 38–42 (1.5–1.7").

The skull is about the same size as that of the thirteen-lined ground squirrel, and the two types of skulls are sometimes confused. However, the eastern chipmunk has 4 upper molariform teeth, whereas the ground squirrel has 5. Also, the infraorbital foramen goes through a thin plate in the chipmunk but forms a canal through a thick plate in the ground squirrel.

Dental Formula:

$$I \ \frac{1}{1} \quad C \ \frac{0}{0} \quad P \ \frac{1}{1} \quad M \ \frac{3}{3} \ = \ 20$$

Habitat: The eastern chipmunk is essentially a woodland-dwelling animal that also inhabits woodland border habitats such as cemeteries, parks, residential tracts, roadsides, lake borders, and brushy localities.

Food: Chipmunks eat a wide variety of food items but mainly seeds, nuts, acorns, blackberries, and strawberries. They also consume significant amounts of animal material, including many kinds of insects and other arthropods. They store nuts and acorns in autumn, and these form the staple article of food for several months.

Reproduction: The gestation period is about 31 days. There are two breeding seasons for chipmunks in Indiana, one in early spring and one in mid-July to mid-August. It appears that young chipmunks do not emerge from their nesting burrows until they have attained considerable size.

Range: We have records of chipmunks from 88 counties, and they may be present in every county. They are locally abundant in northeastern and west central Indiana, but they appear to be uncommon along the Ohio River.

Habits and Comments: Chipmunks are diurnal, largely terrestrial mammals that spend much of the winter in hibernation. In late fall or early winter, they prepare to enter hibernation by storing large amounts of food, but they put on little fat, unlike other hibernators, which use stored fat as energy. The chipmunk wakes occasionally to feed on its stored food. The hibernation period ends about late February or early March, but chipmunks may be aboveground during every month of the year, especially in warmer weather. On 20 February 1977, during one of the coldest winters on record in Indiana, a chipmunk was observed in a Clay County woodlot. The temperature reached about 30°F that day.

Chipmunks are good climbers but are usually seen on the ground. They are most apt to climb trees for food or to escape a disturbance. We have often seen them collecting acorns from white oaks. A frightened chipmunk will often scamper away and climb a few feet up the trunk of a tree, where it may watch or scold the intruder. Chipmunks hold the tail straight up when running. Vocalizations are variable and play an important role in the daily life of the species. The low, clucking sounds so often heard are often mistaken for those of birds, such as yellow-billed cuckoos. When calling, chipmunks often twitch their tails. There is an apparent cessation of chipmunk activity in July, and few vocalizations are heard, not even the titter as they enter their burrows.

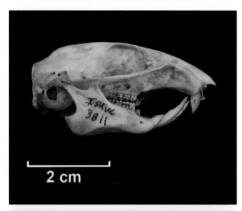

Side view of skull

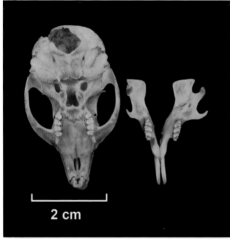

Ventral view
of skull and
lower jaw

Eastern chipmunk with pouches full. *Photo by Linda K. Castor*

The chipmunk spends a considerable amount of its active period foraging, transporting, and storing food. Nuts, acorns, seeds, and other foods are gathered and cached in underground burrow systems. Food is carried in the large internal cheek pouches, which accommodate items up to the size of a red oak acorn. The chipmunk pushes the food into its cheek pouches with the front feet. To remove the food from the pouches, the chipmunk pushes its front feet forward along the cheeks, squeezing items from the pouches. One can find small piles of food refuse such as acorn and nut parts dropped by the animals on top of stumps, logs, rocks, or other objects where chipmunks have fed.

Burrows are usually excavated under rocks, tree stumps, logs, buildings, bridges, walls, standing trees, or other objects, but some may be in the open. The entrance to the burrow usually slants downward steeply or may even be vertical for nearly a foot or more. Burrows may be 20–30' long. Enlarged chambers (up to 12" long and 8" high) may be constructed along them for nesting and food storage.

On bright, sunny days, chipmunks may spend considerable time sunning or preening while perched on rocks, logs, or stumps, about buildings, or even in trees. Many chipmunks may be heard in good chipmunk habitat in late summer or early fall, and they can often be seen on a lookout perch, unmoving, totally silent, and aware of the observer.

Selected References. Allen 1938; Snyder 1982; Yerger 1953.

Woodchuck

Marmota monax (Linnaeus)

Distinguishing Features and Measurements: The woodchuck is the largest member of the squirrel family in Indiana. It is grizzled, grayish-brown above, sometimes with decided blackish or reddish tones. The underparts are pale reddish-brown. The hair is coarse, and that of the belly is so sparse that the skin shows through it. The ears and eyes are small, and the tail is relatively short and slightly bushy. There are four claws on the toes of each front foot and five on the hind foot.

TL 475–700, T 107–182, HF 75–100, Wt. 2–5.8 kg

Skull: Length: 73–95 (2.9–3.8").

The enamel of the incisors, unlike other Indiana squirrels, is white. The skull is flat above, with prominent transverse postorbital processes projecting outward from the upper rim of the orbit (see Fig. 18 in key).

Dental Formula:

$$I \ \frac{1}{1} \quad C \ \frac{0}{0} \quad P \ \frac{2}{1} \quad M \ \frac{3}{3} \ = \ 22$$

Habitat: Woodchucks occur most often in grassy or weedy areas in rolling country. However, they may be seen in cultivated and fallow fields, in abandoned gravel pits, in fencerows, along levees, about stone piles in a field, in wooded areas, and often in the dirt floor of barns or other outbuildings. Brushy, uneven land interspersed with cultivated fields appears to be chosen when available. Large numbers of woodchucks sometimes occur along railroad grades and ditch banks far from forested areas.

Food: The woodchuck is practically 100% vegetarian. They eat ferns, shrubs, grasses, the tender shoots of young trees, and ripe apples, but also corn, dandelion blossoms, sassafras, persimmon pulp, blooming spring beauties, and the leaves of small red elm trees. Woodchucks may do extensive damage in gardens. Red clover, wheat, sorghum, and alfalfa are locally important food plants. Larry L. Schmeltz and Whitaker observed a woodchuck that appeared to remain active all winter (Vigo County), which fed on standing corn near its burrow.

Reproduction: The woodchuck presumably mates soon after emerging from hibernation in February and March. Gestation is about 28 days. Litters of three to eight are produced from late March to late April, with most born the first 3 weeks of April. Females apparently bear one litter per year, but two are possible.

Range: The woodchuck was common throughout the state, although it may be locally rare to abundant. However, it appears to be decreasing with increased coyote populations.

Habits and Comments: The woodchuck is primarily diurnal and terrestrial but is occasionally out at night. Tree climbing appears to be relatively common and is often associated with feeding.

The most obvious signs of woodchucks are the burrow entrances, usually one major and two or three subsidiary ones that lead into an extensive underground system, which may reach depths of 3–4'. The main entrance usually has a pile of soil at its mouth; the other openings often lack mounds and may be more hidden by vegetation. Woodchuck mounds often interfere with farm operations. The burrows may extend from 15 to 50' horizontally, may have several side passages leading to the nest, and may contain a latrine area or a hibernating chamber. Nests of leaves are built in the burrows. Burrows are most likely to be constructed on a hillside or the side of a bank, embankment, or levee, but some are dug into level ground. Considerable time seems to be spent sunning, and an animal will often lie flat on the mound of soil at the burrow entrance to sun. Woodchucks are slow, clumsy runners, but the presence of well-used trails probably enables them to return to the safety of their underground dens more easily.

The woodchuck feeds mostly in morning and evening but may be seen aboveground at nearly any time. There is a minor feeding period around noon. Feeding forays may take the animals 75' or more from their dens, to which the woodchucks return quickly if disturbed. Rarely does a woodchuck stray more than a few hundred feet from its den. While foraging, they stand up about every 30 seconds or so and scan their surroundings. When alarmed, the animals scurry back to the burrow, usually by the shortest and most direct route. The woodchuck becomes fat in late summer in preparation for hibernation. In southern Indiana the animals usually retire about mid-October, although there are numerous sightings for October and November, a few records for December, and at least one for January. Emergence from hibernation, contrary to folklore, does not occur on Groundhog Day (2 February). We do not know whether the single January observation (date not available) indicated an animal late to enter hibernation, one early to emerge, or one that simply came aboveground for some reason. Schmeltz and Whitaker recorded the earliest emergence on 5 February 1971 and 8 February 1972, but in 1978, a year of record cold temperature, Whitaker observed a freshly opened burrow on Groundhog Day, with the excavated soil deposited directly on the snow. Woodchucks are good swimmers. Their usual call is a shrill, somewhat quavering whistle (giving rise to the name "whistle-pig"). This call can often be heard when the animal has been frightened into its burrow. Automobiles (and to a lesser extent, trains) take a considerable toll on woodchucks.

Woodchucks share their habitats with many other species. Trapping woodchuck burrow openings along a levee along the Wabash River at

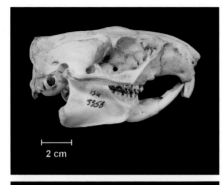

Side view of skull

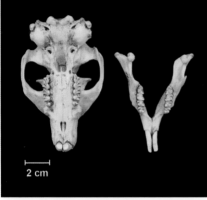

Ventral view of skull and lower jaw

Burrow of wood-chuck in bank at Willow Slough

Terre Haute yielded 22 eastern cottontails, 20 opossums, 8 raccoons, and 1 gray and 1 red fox besides woodchucks. Also captured in entrances to dens were 104 white-footed mice, 2 meadow voles, 32 house mice, 29 prairie deer mice, 10 short-tailed shrews, 2 meadow jumping mice, and 2 masked shrews.

SELECTED REFERENCES. Grizzell 1955; Hamilton 1934; Kwiecinski 1998; Schmeltz and Whitaker 1977.

Woodchuck. *Photo by Mark Romesser*

Thirteen-lined Ground Squirrel
Spermophilus tridecemlineatus (Mitchill)

Distinguishing Features and Measurements: This is a chipmunk-sized, short-legged ground squirrel with a tail of medium length. Its unique dorsal color pattern consists of alternating brownish and buff longitudinal bands from the ears to the tail. Inside the dark bands are rows of pale spots. The sides are buff and the underparts are buff to yellowish-white. The hair is relatively sparse and individual hairs are rather stiff. The ears are short and protrude little beyond the hair of the head.

TL 232–291, T 75–97, HF 32–40, Wt. 95–234

Skull: Length: 37–41 (1.5–1.6").

The skull is most similar to that of the eastern chipmunk, from which it can be separated by the presence of 5 upper molariform teeth (the chipmunk has 4). The skull of the thirteen-lined ground squirrel is considerably smaller than that of the Franklin's ground squirrel, except in immature specimens of the latter species.

Dental Formula:

$$\text{I } \frac{1}{1} \quad \text{C } \frac{0}{0} \quad \text{P } \frac{2}{1} \quad \text{M } \frac{3}{3} = 22$$

Habitat: Large populations often occur on closely cut lawns as in cemeteries, golf courses, pastures, airports, and in other open habitats of similar nature, such as grassy roadsides or school campuses. Sometimes colonies are established in abandoned gravel pits or in taller vegetation (usually weeds) with some brush. Weedy or cultivated fields, sand dunes, and fencerows are also inhabited, but the species shuns the woods. Draining of wetlands, increased cultivation, and removal of forest land all helped open the land to invasion by this species. Dispersal routes were furnished by ditch banks, railroads, and roadsides.

Food: The various parts of clover plants (leaves, seeds, flowers, and fruits) combined constituted the most food in 135 individuals from Indiana by volume, followed by caterpillars. Heads of clover and chickweed were eaten whole. Other common foods were seeds of finger grass, grasshoppers, ground beetles, and June bug adults and larvae (Scarabaeidae). Three kinds of vertebrates were found, birds in 4 of the 135 individuals, and a short-tailed shrew and a young prairie king snake in one each.

Reproduction: This species mates 2–4 weeks after emerging from hibernation, usually in April. Gestation is about 27–28 days. There is usually one litter per female per year, but sometimes two. The number of embryos per female ranges from 4 to 12, averaging over 8. Most Indiana litters are born in May in a nest of dry plant material. The first young are usually seen aboveground in late June.

Range: This ground squirrel moved southeastward across the state from 1909 to 1960. By 1960, its range extended over the northern two-thirds of the state north of a line connecting Vigo, Johnson, and Franklin counties. Since 1961, this movement continued as follows: north edge of Decatur County in 1965; along U.S. Route 31 a mile north of Edinburg (Johnson County) in May 1965; 2.5 miles north of Taylorsville, Bartholomew County, along U.S. 31, June 1966; Camp Atterbury, in the northwest corner of Bartholomew County, February 1970; 4 miles northeast of Columbus, Bartholomew County, July 1970; about a mile north of Greencastle, Putnam County, fall of 1970; along Route 59 about 2.5 miles north of Brazil, Clay County, 27 June 1976. R. E. Mumford sighted the Clay County specimen. Although he had driven this road often with his wife for the previous 30 years, this was the first individual they had seen in this area.

Habits and Comments: This is a diurnal species and thus is easily observed in open habitats. It spends the winter in hibernation. Ground squirrels are burrowers; they excavate numerous and sometimes complicated tunnel systems. Because of their burrowing, and the fact that they often live in cemeteries, golf courses, lawns, pastures, and other open locations, they frequently are in conflict with man. The animals seldom venture far from their burrows to feed, sun themselves, or play, and are always alert for danger. When disturbed, they may stand straight to view the disturbance, thus resembling a short stake driven into the ground. If sufficiently frightened, they return to the burrow, sometimes again standing at the entrance to look about before entering. The animals usually go just inside the burrow and may partially or completely emerge in a few minutes. They run with the body near the ground and the tail straight out behind.

Burrows are up to 2' deep and have one or two openings to the surface. The openings may have a mound or scattered loose soil at their entrances, or they may lack soil. Burrows may be 15–20' long and often have side passages. Burrows are 1.7–3" in diameter, and have enlargements for nests that are 5–7" in diameter. Runways in the grass form irregular patterns and often can be followed to a burrow system.

This species is active mostly during the warmest part of the day. On warm summer days they emerge about the time the dew dries up. Much of the time aboveground is spent foraging for food or engaging in chases, some of which appear associated with reproductive activity. They give a birdlike chattering call, which probably serves as a warning between members of the colony. The call is often heard as one approaches a burrow into which a squirrel has just disappeared. This

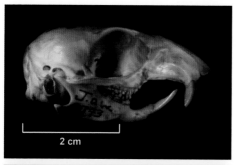

Side view of skull

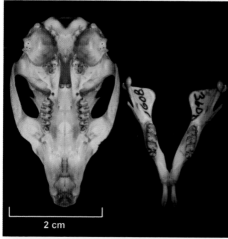

Ventral view
of skull and
lower jaw

Juvenile thirteen-lined ground squirrels.
Photo by Russell E. Mumford

rapid chatter or chirping call is similar to the prolonged chirping of a house cricket. Groups of immature ground squirrels foraging about the burrow entrance will scamper into the burrow when disturbed, and then, one by one, poke their heads and forequarters out of the burrow to look about. Mumford photographed seven such animals (evidently a litter), with their heads and forequarters out, their hindquarters and bodies entwined in the burrow entrance. In some habitats well-used runways radiate from the burrow openings into foraging sites, but these are not always readily visible.

Hibernation is from October or November to March or April, although there are some late dates for November through January. On the later dates, the daily temperature ranged from 59 to 72°F. In preparation for hibernation, the animals accumulate large quantities of fat. During hibernation, the animals curl into a ball in a nest of leaves or grasses below the frost line. In late September and October some individuals have as much as 11 grams of fat. Breathing rates of 187–213, 13–27, and 7–9 per minute were recorded when ground squirrels were awake, sleeping but not hibernating, and hibernating. Heart rates ranged from 350 beats per minute in excited animals, 100–113 in sleeping individuals, and 5–7 during hibernation. The animals lost up to 39% of their body weight during hibernation.

This ground squirrel is colonial and often locally abundant. In the early 1950s, this species was so abundant in pastures at the edge of the Purdue University campus (Tippecanoe County) that Mumford sometimes snared as many as eight animals per hour by hand. In August 1977, Whitaker's family collected 147 ground squirrels in a 10-day period from a cemetery. The capture area was about 28 acres of mowed lawn with scattered trees. It was felt that three or four times the number of squirrels taken were occupying this area.

Selected References. Streubel and Fitzgerald 1978; Whitaker 1972c.

Thirteen-lined ground squirrel

Franklin's Ground Squirrel
Spermophilus franklinii (Sabine)

Distinguishing Features and Measurements: Spermophilus franklinii is a relatively large ground squirrel, exceeded in size among the ground squirrels of Indiana only by the woodchuck. Franklin's ground squirrel is near the size of the gray squirrel, for which it is sometimes mistaken. The upperparts are a grizzled, brownish gray and may appear spotted. The underparts are dull yellowish-white. The tail is relatively long and bushy for a ground squirrel and is flattened dorsoventrally. The ears are rounded and short, and the legs are relatively short. Immatures are darker than adults.

TL 340–390, T1 20–152, HF 45–66, Wt. 280–520

Skull: Length: 52–57 (2.1–2.3").

The skull is similar to that of the thirteen-lined ground squirrel but is much larger.

Dental Formula:

$$I \ \frac{1}{1} \ C \ \frac{0}{0} \ P \ \frac{2}{1} \ M \ \frac{3}{3} \ = \ 22$$

Habitat: Most Franklin's ground squirrels today are seen along roadsides and railroad embankments, where mixed grasses and tall weeds are dominant. Scattered shrubs or small trees are sometimes present. Some individuals have been noted in weedy pastures, weedy/brushy old fields, along ditch banks, and in waste areas in shrub and mixed weeds. We have seen them along the sand dunes bordering Lake Michigan and in overgrown marsh borders with scattered trees around Wolf Lake (Lake County). This squirrel does not occur in woodlands and is usually in more dense, tall cover than thirteen-lined ground squirrels.

Food: Based on a small number of animals from Indiana, we found that green vegetation (including clover leaves) was the most important food, making up 43% of the volume, and plant material, collectively, made up 85% of the total volume. Caterpillars were the most prominent animal

food (8.5%), followed by ants (Formicidae, 3.5%). Flower heads of clover and dandelion were sometimes eaten.

Reproduction: Mating occurs soon after the animals emerge from hibernation, and the 4–11 young are born after a gestation of about 28 days. The young leave the maternal burrow in about 40 days.

Range: This species is relatively rare in Indiana and is decreasing. As of 1982, it was known or recently had occurred in 16 contiguous counties in northwestern Indiana. In 1992, DNR

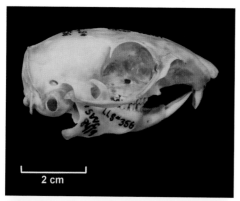

Side view of skull

2 cm

Ventral view
of skull and
lower jaw

2 cm

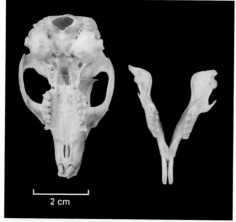

Franklin's ground squirrel. *Photo by Roger Barbour*

personnel trapped in all the counties where it had been taken previously. They captured 120 individuals at 36 (9.7%) of the study sites. It appears that the range of this species has receded to the west in recent years, as no Franklin's ground squirrels were captured in eight counties at the eastern periphery of the species' previously known range: St. Joseph, Marshall, Pulaski, Fulton, White, Cass, Carroll, and Montgomery. The DNR captured seven animals at three sites in Vermillion County, a new county for the species, and one individual was caught in northwestern Vigo County.

Habits and Comments: This species is diurnal. It hibernates for several months and may be seen aboveground from about 20 April to 21 October. Franklin's ground squirrels live in burrows and forage out in all directions, using well-defined trails into favored feeding areas. Unlike the thirteen-lined ground squirrel, this species usually does not leave a mound at the entrance to its burrow but scatters excavated soil. Burrows are a little more than 3" in diameter. Both species have been trapped in Indiana at the same burrow entrance, presumably at the larger Franklin's burrow. These animals are most often seen near the edge of highways or railroads, where they feed on vegetation and possibly insects. A chattering call is often given by startled individuals. This species is much less social and more secretive than the thirteen-lined ground squirrel.

SELECTED REFERENCES. Johnson and Choromanski-Norris 1992; Ostroff and Finck 2003.

Gray Squirrel
Sciurus carolinensis Gmelin

Distinguishing Features and Measurements: The gray squirrel is slightly smaller than the other large tree squirrel of Indiana, the fox squirrel. The underside and lateral portions of the tail are normally silvery in the gray squirrel, orangish in the fox squirrel. The tail is long, bushy, and dorsoventrally flattened. The upperparts of the gray squirrel are usually grizzled gray, with scattered buffy tones. Many color variations occur. Black gray squirrels occur in Goshen (Elkhart County); they were introduced from Michigan. Black squirrels also occur in Decatur, Adams County.

TL 400–530, Tl 77–285, HF 60–76, Wt. 400–610

Skull: Length: 59–64 (2.4–2.6").

The skull of the gray squirrel is about 59–64 mm long, rounded above, with orange-fronted, rootless incisors. The infraorbital foramen forms a canal through the zygomatic arch. The gray squirrel has a small premolar anterior to the molariform tooth row. It is lacking in the fox squirrel.

Dental Formula:

$$I \frac{1}{1} \quad C \frac{0}{0} \quad P \frac{2}{1} \quad M \frac{3}{3} = 22$$

Habitat: The best gray squirrel habitat in Indiana is probably extensive, mature, mixed deciduous woodlands with a well-developed understory on hilly terrain. In some of the most productive areas today, these woodlands are interspersed with brushy fields. Mature and overmature trees usually provide den sites, which are essential for high populations. Good habitat includes a wide variety of plants, especially trees, ensuring that some foods are available throughout the year. Gray squirrels have been introduced into several towns, where they often do quite well, probably because of the presence of old trees with natural cavities and protection from hunting.

Food: The gray squirrel consumes a wide variety and constantly changing array of vegetable foods. For example, they may feed on bark of basswood or maple twigs in February; red maple buds in March; and elm and maple seeds, oak, maple, cottonwood, elm buds, flowers of shagbark hickory and green ash in April and May. Late spring and early summer foods include tulip poplar flowers, maple leaves and stems, and mushrooms. Hickory nuts, tulip poplar fruits, acorns, black walnuts, butternuts, and the seeds and/or fruits of black cherry, black gum, hackberry, dogwood, sassafras, blackberry, huckleberry, flowering dogwood fruits, corn, beech, honey locust, and the like are often consumed in August and September. Gray squirrels will feed on buckeye fruits and even oak galls.

Reproduction: Pairing begins in January and February with mating chases. Gestation is about 45 days. Females produce one or two litters per year, depending on food conditions the previous season. After a good mast year most females have first litters in February and March and second litters about June. Following a season of poor mast, most litters are in July or August and few second litters occur. The number of young ranges from two to five. Young squirrels spend their first several weeks in the den, their eyes open at about 5 weeks, and they leave the den at about 90 days.

Range: Gray squirrels are found throughout the state. They are common in southern Indiana and are much more sporadic in the north, although they are increasing there. They are common at Turkey Run, Shades, and other parts of Parke County, and also in Lafayette and Muncie.

Habits and Comments: Gray squirrels are most active early in the morning, with a second activity period in the evening. More midday activity occurs on cool cloudy days. During late August to mid-September the squirrels spend most of their time in trees. Later they spend more time on the ground, where they forage for and bury acorns and nuts.

The usual calls of gray squirrels are short "barks," a rather drawn out nasal call, a squeal, and, occasionally, a chattering call. The first two appear to be scolding or alarm notes. They are often heard when humans, a dog, or some other intruder has been detected. Tail-jerking usually accompanies the barking call. Some calls of the gray squirrel resemble those of a domestic cat, hence this species is sometimes known as the cat squirrel.

The gray squirrel normally lives in tree cavities or in leaf and twig nests. The leaf nests are temporary shelters, occupied mainly in warmer weather. The coldest weather is spent in tree holes and cavities where there is more protection from the elements. Some leaf nests are small and cup-shaped and the animals lie on top of them, mainly in hot weather. A more substantial, roughly globular nest of leaves and twigs is most commonly constructed. The squirrels cut twigs with leaves attached, usually in spring or summer (thus the cut twigs retain their leaves for some time). Nests are usually placed in a limb or tree fork where they can be anchored more easily. The average nest is about 12" high and 14" wide, but size varies from smaller masses to nests as large as a bushel basket. Some nests have a definite entrance hole. Others do not, and the squirrels simply push their way into the nest through the loose leaves. Nests are lined with shredded bark (usually of grape or tulip poplar). Nest height ranges from 20 to 70' or more. A single squirrel appears to build each nest, sometimes completing the job in

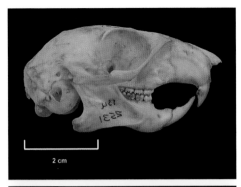

Side view of skull

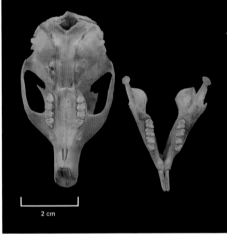

Ventral view of skull and lower jaw

Gray squirrel. *Photo by Linda K. Castor*

a day. Damaged nests are frequently rebuilt. Most leaf nests are used for less than a year, although a few are maintained for 3 years or more. Leaf-nest construction starts in late May and reaches a peak about 15 July. Den trees with cavities are of major importance, for they are required for escape, shelter in inclement weather, and sites to rear the young. Nests of leaves and other materials are constructed in the dens.

The gray squirrel does not hibernate but may remain relatively inactive during extremely cold weather. Squirrels store food for winter and normally enter winter at their greatest weight. Food caching begins in early September, and about 10 days later much of the activity of the squirrels is on the ground, where food is buried. The animals dig holes about 1.5–2″ deep with their front feet, place one or two acorns or nuts in each hole, pushing and tamping them with the head, jaws, and shoulders, then scrape soil and leaves over the site with the front feet. The animals usually tamp down the covering with their feet. Cached food may be unearthed and consumed until a new crop is available the next fall. During winter the squirrels progressively lose weight until spring foods are available, then quickly regain lost weight in spring. Food stored in the ground during fall is located and excavated in winter by returning to likely storage areas and using olfaction. The squirrels can even distinguish edible from nonedible items by olfaction. The home range of a gray squirrel in good habitat may be relatively small, perhaps the area within 100 yards of the den, larger in poorer habitat. Dispersal of gray squirrels occurs from about the first week of August through October, peaking with the ripening of the nut sources. Squirrels routinely cross busy city streets by walking or running along horizontal cables strung between utility poles.

SELECTED REFERENCES. Allen 1952; Koprowski 1994a.

Fox Squirrel
Sciurus niger Linnaeus

Distinguishing Features and Measurements: The fox squirrel is the largest tree squirrel in Indiana. Its upperparts are a tawny brown grizzled with gray; the underparts are usually yellowish-brown or rufous. The dorsoventrally flattened tail is mixed rufous and black, and underneath it appears yellow, in contrast to the gray squirrel, in which the tail looks silvery. The ears are medium-sized, rounded, and yellowish in the fox squirrel. Albinos, partial albinos, individuals with entirely black underparts, and individuals with white tails have been reported.

TL 500–627, T 190–342, HF 61–82, Wt. 700–1,210

Skull: Length: 62–70 (2.5–2.8").

The skull of the fox squirrel is rounded above and has a relatively small postorbital processes. The infraorbital opening forms a canal. The incisor enamel is orange. The skull is similar to that of the gray squirrel but has only 4 upper molariform teeth; the small anterior premolar present in the gray squirrel is absent in the fox squirrel.

Dental Formula:

$$I \ \frac{1}{1} \ \ C \ \frac{0}{0} \ \ P \ \frac{1}{1} \ \ M \ \frac{3}{3} \ = \ 20$$

Habitat: Fox squirrels generally occupy woodlands that have less understory or are more "parklike" than those occupied by gray squirrels. Fox squirrels readily adapt to pastured woodlots, windbreaks, residential areas, city parks, cemeteries, wooded fencerows, and even isolated clumps of non-mast-bearing trees in intensively farmed regions.

Food: Fox and gray squirrels eat similar foods, particularly corn, nuts, and acorns through much of the year, although the fox squirrel probably eats more corn. Hickory nuts are a major food of the species from late summer through fall, although acorns and beechnuts are also important, and walnuts are occasionally used. In spring and early summer a variety of buds, flowers, and seeds are eaten, along with nuts from the previous year. Maple seeds are often eaten when ripening, and the young fruit of the tulip tree is a staple food in July and early August. Bark is often eaten and twigs of maples or other trees are often stripped. Squirrels will lick highways, apparently for salt. Fox squirrels extract the seeds from the large globular fruits of Osage orange, and they will feed on blackberries and cockleburs. Fox and gray squirrels both readily come to bird feeders.

Reproduction: Males usually become sexually mature at about 11 months of age. Courtship begins at least by January and squirrels will undergo extensive courtship chases, on the ground or in the trees. The gestation period is about 45 days, and young may be produced throughout most of the year, at least from February to December, but most young are born from February to March and from June to August, with litters of one to five.

Range: Apparently most historical accounts of squirrel numbers and their damage to settlers' crops in Indiana involved the gray squirrel. When Indiana was being settled, the fox squirrel had a much more restricted range and occurred in lesser numbers than it does today. It is now common throughout much of the state.

Habits and Comments: Fox squirrels are evidently somewhat nocturnal. Several individuals have reported that on moonlit nights their dogs treed fox squirrels while they were hunting raccoons along cornfields. Gray and fox squirrels are excellent swimmers (gray squirrels have been known to swim the Ohio River) and fast runners. A fox squirrel running along the ground was clocked at 10 miles per hour for 50 yards. Squirrels depend upon short bursts of speed to elude predators, then they seek

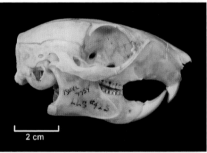

Side view of skull

2 cm

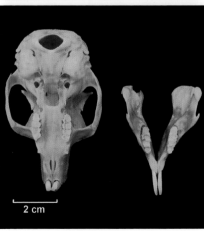

Ventral view of skull and lower jaw

2 cm

Fox squirrel.
Photo by
Terry L. Castor

Fox squirrel nest

Tulip tree blossoms
cut by fox squirrel.
Photo by Angela
Chamberlain

the shelter of a tree. When caught at a distance from a suitable retreat, they are often captured by dogs. If they are able to reach a safe perch in or on a tree, some will pause, watch the intruder, and scold with barking notes and jerking tails. The speed and agility with which both species can move from tree crown to tree crown are remarkable. They can leap gaps of several feet in moving from one tree to another. Occasionally one misses its footing and falls to the ground; unhurt, it runs rapidly away. Fox squirrels forage into cornfields and carry ears (or partial ears) of corn back to the trees. They usually climb a tree and feed from an elevated perch, dropping the cobs to the ground. Dens and nests of fox squirrels are similar to those of gray squirrels. Nests can be from 8 to 40' or more above the ground. The relative wariness of fox squirrels and gray squirrels (with respect to man) has been discussed under the latter species. Fox squirrels are more likely to stay in the tree where first observed. They hide in clumps of leaves, by flattening themselves out on top of horizontal branches and keeping the tree trunk or large branches between them and the observer. Sometimes fox squirrels will climb a tree and enter a leaf nest to escape humans, and they sometimes enter burrows in the ground to escape danger.

Fox squirrels produce mostly barking sounds. Tail-twitching accompanies the barking of both species. In hot weather, fox squirrels may come out of their nests and dens and lie in exposed sites. Feeding and sunning during midday are not unusual for the fox squirrel. Foxes, great horned owls, screech owls, and red-tailed hawks are predators, and large numbers of squirrels are killed by vehicles.

SELECTED REFERENCES. Allen 1952; Baumgartner 1939; Koprowski 1994b.

Red Squirrel
Tamiasciurus hudsonicus (Erxleben)

Distinguishing Features and Measurements: The red squirrel is the smallest diurnal tree squirrel in Indiana. It is rusty-reddish above and whitish below. In summer, the upperparts are uniformly reddish to reddish-brown, the belly is white or whitish, and a short black stripe separates the underparts from the upperparts. In winter, the middorsal region is reddish, bordered by grayish-olive, the upper surface of the tail is mostly reddish, the belly is whitish to grayish-white, and the black stripe on either side is faint or absent. The ears usually bear tufts of relatively long hairs in winter, which are absent in summer.

TL 262–390, T 100–190, HF 40–52, Wt. 150–252

Skull: Length: 44–47 (1.8–1.9").

The skull is intermediate in size (for Indiana squirrels, about 45 mm long). It is larger than that of the chipmunk, flying squirrel, or thirteen-lined ground squirrel, and smaller than that of the fox squirrel, gray squirrel, Franklin's ground squirrel, or woodchuck. The anterior upper premolar is usually absent, but when present is small and poorly formed.

Dental Formula:

$$I \ \frac{1}{1} \ C \ \frac{0}{0} \ P \ \frac{2 \text{ or } 1}{1} \ M \ \frac{3}{3} \ = \ 22 \text{ (or 20)}$$

Habitat: The red squirrel is found in conifers and mixed forest and in hardwoods. Wooded stream borders and adjoining swamps are favored habitats. It occurs in isolated woodlots surrounded by cultivated fields and in residential areas, parks, cemeteries, and on campuses, especially where some conifers are present.

Food: Red squirrels consume a great variety of seeds, fruits, nuts, and other plant materials, and they sometimes rob birds' nests of young or eggs. They will eat nuts and acorns and the cones of several conifers, including jack pine and Scotch pine, and store them for winter. They less often eat white pine. Red squirrels store much food (nuts and pine-cone mainly) in the ground for the winter and early spring. They also store food such as mushrooms by placing them on top of horizontal branches or in forked branches in trees. Pinecones are gathered in large stores, often called "middens." This behavior is sometimes used by foresters, who search out the middens to obtain pine seed rather than cutting cones from the trees. One red squirrel harvested black-berries by hanging upside down in the briers, suspended by its hind feet, and picking the berries with its front feet. Red squirrels eat ripe mulberries in late June; in late November they feed on fruits of Osage orange. Red squirrels have a characteristic method of extracting the meat from black walnuts and butternuts. They gnaw an irregular hole, measuring about ½–¾", on either side of the shell, and they remove the meat through these holes. The entire shell is not gnawed into fragments (a habit of gray squirrels and fox squirrels) but remains mostly intact.

Reproduction: Gestation is about 38 days. Pregnant females have been examined from 19 February to 1 September. There are two peaks of litter production, one in spring and another in late summer.

Range: The red squirrel, or "piney" as it is often called, is a northern species in Indiana, but it has been extending its range to the south. Widespread planting of pines may have been a factor in range extension. Although red squirrels do not require evergreen trees, practically all pine stands other than of white pine within their range are occupied by this squirrel. For example, Willow Slough Fish and Wildlife Area (Newton County) was established in the early 1950s. Red squirrels were first observed there in 1971, and by 1977, they were present at numerous sites throughout the area (mostly pine plantations).

Side view of skull

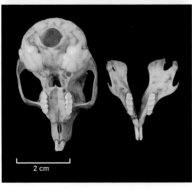

Ventral view of skull and lower jaw

Red squirrel,
above.
*Photo by Roger
Barbour*

White pine
cones eaten by
red squirrel

Red squirrel
habitat along
the Kankakee
River in Lake
County.
*Photo by
Terry L. Castor*

Habits and Comments: The red squirrel is often conspicuous as it is diurnal and has a variety of vocalizations. It is occasionally active at night. It spends much more time on the ground than do the other Indiana tree squirrels. It makes extensive use of burrows in the ground and it burrows in snow. Such burrows are most in evidence in pine plantations, where the squirrels store piles of cones for winter. The animals frequently make burrows in their cone and refuse piles. The red squirrel is active all year but may stay in its den in severe weather. Red squirrels are ever-active, nervous, and alert. They move about in trees and from tree to tree with astonishing speed and can run swiftly on the ground. They appear to be good swimmers, also. They seem inquisitive and can be called within view, sometimes quite near, by squeaking noises. The squirrel peers intently at the disturbance, apparently poised for instant movement, and may call. The usual call is a distinctive chatter, often heard before one sees its source. The tail can be twitched, curled over the back, hung loosely downward, or held in other positions, depending upon the occasion and the behavior of the individual animal.

Nests are constructed in tree holes and cavities or among the crowns of trees. Many treetop nests in Indiana were built in the crowns of conifers. Such nests are globular and are smaller (about 10" in diameter) and more compactly built than those of fox or gray squirrels. They contain more soft materials, including shredded bark, grasses, or other soft vegetation, and less leaves and twigs than those of the larger tree squirrels.

Red squirrels readily enter houses (occupied or unoccupied) and other buildings, building nests in convenient sites. Sometimes this creates quite a nuisance, for the animals carry in nesting material and food in some quantity. Food refuse is scattered about. Gnawing is also a problem; the squirrels may gnaw through house siding to gain access to an attic and may gnaw at insulation or electric wires. Mothballs have been used successfully to drive red squirrels from an attic.

In a hardwood forest with several large hollow beech and other large trees on the Willow Slough Fish and Wildlife Area, Whitaker watched red squirrel behavior patterns several hours on a day in April. Several squirrels were present and much chasing was evident. At dusk, other squirrels were still chasing and calling, and one squirrel, calling from inside a hollow beech tree, continued calling until 12–15 minutes after dark. The presence of a red squirrel is often first detected by hearing the characteristic chattering call. Some individuals are quite vocal and will call persistently when disturbed.

Selected References. Hatt 1929; Layne 1954; Steel 1998.

Southern Flying Squirrel
Glaucomys volans (Linnaeus)

Distinguishing Features and Measurements: This small brownish-gray squirrel is the only Indiana rodent with a well-developed gliding membrane (patagium). It extends from the wrist to the ankle on either side of the body. The tail is greatly flattened dorsoventrally. The upperparts are pale-brownish or pinkish-gray. The underparts are white. The fur is dense and soft. The eyes are large and black.

TL 220–256, T 82–133, HF 25–34, Wt. 42–85

Skull: Length: 33–36 (1.3–1.4").

The skull is most similar to that of the thirteen-lined ground squirrel and the eastern chipmunk. It is about 33–36 mm long and has 5 upper molariform teeth; the infraorbital foramen is formed as a canal through a thick plate. The eastern chipmunk has only 4 molariform teeth, and the infraorbital foramen opens through a thin plate. The ground squirrel has the zygoma turned outward in such a way that they are more horizontal, whereas they are more vertical in the flying squirrel.

Dental Formula:

$$I \ \frac{1}{1} \ C \ \frac{0}{0} \ P \ \frac{2}{1} \ M \ \frac{3}{3} \ = \ 22$$

Habitat: Most wooded areas that provide den sites may support populations of flying squirrels, but the species is most abundant in mature woods with numerous dead snags. The squirrels readily take over holes made by woodpeckers and will occupy such holes and natural cavities ranging from 5' above the ground upward. Individuals are present in towns and cities and often take up residence in buildings.

Food: Flying squirrels feed on nuts, seeds, fruits, and insects. Acorns and hickory nuts make up much of the diet, and remains of such foods are present in dens and roosts. Flying squirrels are said to eat young birds and eggs. They also have been known to eat seeds of bittersweet, English ivy, butternut, crickets, grasshoppers, and many other items.

Reproduction: The breeding season extends from March to October, and an individual female probably produces a single litter per year. Litter size ranges from two to five, averaging about three. Gestation is about 40 days. Young are born naked and blind, and the eyes open in about 28 days.

Range: The flying squirrel is found in suitable habitat throughout Indiana. It may be locally common but, statewide, should probably be considered uncommon. It has been collected in 39 counties and observed in 6 more. Flying squirrels are not easily seen because they are nocturnal, and their presence in an area may go undetected. No doubt the removal of the native forest from most of Indiana reduced the numbers of this interesting animal, although we believe it is considerably more abundant than available data indicate. They sometimes move into bird houses, and also they often come to bird feeders at night.

Habits and Comments: The southern flying squirrel is largely nocturnal and arboreal, although some time is spent foraging on the ground. The day is normally spent in a dark place, usually a tree hole. Nests are usually of grasses and shredded bark. Old woodpecker holes are excellent retreats and nesting sites. Flying squirrels are most easily found by searching wooded areas for dead stumps with woodpecker holes. Tapping on the stump with a stick will induce the squirrels to poke their heads out of the holes. If the disturbance is stopped, the animals will retreat back into the hole. But if one persists in tapping, the animals will come out of the holes, usually remaining on the trunk of the tree. Additional disturbance will usually cause the animals to climb to the top of the tree and glide to another. We have found flying squirrels most often in woodpecker holes from 5 to 15' from the ground in fairly small dead snags. The squirrels also use natural cavities in living trees, but it is very difficult to get them to emerge from a living tree by tapping.

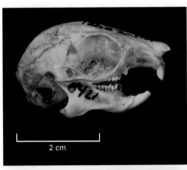

Side view of skull

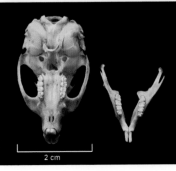

Ventral view of skull and lower jaw

Flying squirrels can glide from the top of one tree to another tree up to 90' away. Most glides are shorter, for the squirrels are usually found in wooded areas where trees are close together. The squirrel may start the glide at a considerable angle but just before alighting, it pulls up to a nearly vertical position and lands on the tree with all four feet. The tail is held straight out behind and is moved, probably as a rudder.

Flying squirrels often can be located by their high-pitched squeaking or birdlike calls. When disturbed, the mother readily moves her young, one by one, in her mouth. Aggregations of flying squirrels too large to represent family groups (up to at least 16) have repeatedly been observed together in tree holes or bird boxes. The largest groups have been discovered from late November to February. Young flying squirrels are easily tamed and make interesting pets.

SELECTED REFERENCES. Dolan and Carter 1977; Sollberger 1940, 1943.

Southern flying squirrel, *above. Photo by Jerry Gingerich*

Typical roost of southern flying squirrel

Pocket gophers are short-furred burrowing rodents, characterized by prominent, fur-lined, external cheek pouches, small eyes and ears, prominent claws on the forefeet, and a short to medium-length, nearly naked tail. They are confined to North and Central America and extreme northern South America, ranging from Saskatchewan to Colombia. In the eastern United States the Geomyidae are represented by two species of the genus *Geomys,* one restricted in its distribution to the southeastern states (Alabama, Florida, and Georgia) and the other to parts of Indiana, Illinois, and Wisconsin.

These animals are admirably modified for a subterranean existence. The skull is massive and angular, and the incisors are large and somewhat protruding. Each upper incisor often has one or two grooves on the anterior surface, a large one in the center and a smaller one toward the inner side. These grooves and the iron-oxide content of the outer enamel layer, which give the incisors their orange pigment, render them stronger and harder cutting and digging tools.

Plains Pocket Gopher
Geomys bursarius (Shaw)

Distinguishing Features and Measurements: This gopher is nearly the size of a gray squirrel and has a relatively short, hairless, tapered tail. Males average larger than females. The eyes and ears are small and the ears are naked and flattened against the head. The front feet are larger than the hind feet and are equipped with large, elongated claws for burrowing. *Geomys* has external, fur-lined cheek pouches that extend back to the shoulder region. Color varies geographically, usually similar to the prevailing soil color. The animals in Indiana, however, are uniformly slate gray above and below, the undersides often having a wash of beige or whitish. The feet and distal half of the tail are white or whitish.

TL 252–324, T 51–105, HF 28–38, Wt. 190–451

Skull: Length: 47–55 (1.9–2.2").

The skull of *Geomys* is relatively broad and flattened; at first glance it is similar in size and shape to that of the muskrat. Each upper incisor of the gopher has two distinct grooves on the anterior face (see Fig. 21 in key). The muskrat has no such grooves.

Dental Formula:

$$\text{I} \ \frac{1}{1} \ \text{C} \ \frac{0}{0} \ \text{P} \ \frac{1}{1} \ \text{M} \ \frac{3}{3} \ = \ 20$$

Habitat: The major habitat requirements of the species appear to be open areas with well-drained soil that permits easy burrowing. Pocket gophers occur in fine sand, sandy loam and gravel, silt loam, and silty clay loam. A colony near Battle Ground lived along a railroad grade that was composed mostly of cinders. *Geomys* lives mostly in grasslands, in grassy and weedy ditch banks, along roadsides and railroad grades, and in fallow fields. It also may be found in cultivated fields. Some colonies have been observed in open savannalike stands of trees. Where trees are too dense, burrowing is hampered and gophers do not persist. Drainage is of major importance; many colonies are located on moraines that are slightly higher and better drained than surrounding areas. Artificial drainage has rendered some habitats suitable, but intensive cultivation is often harmful. *Geomys* is found in greatest abundance in northern Jasper and Newton counties, perhaps because much of this region is relatively dry and sandy, thus less attractive to the farmer for growing crops.

Food: Pocket gophers in Indiana are known to eat alfalfa, red clover, wheat, oats, rye, soybeans, bluegrass, roots of ragweed, sunflower, and black-eyed Susan. In uncultivated sites, almost all plants are used as foods. Two food caches discovered in burrows consisted almost entirely of heavy rootstocks of alfalfa. Sometimes the roots are eaten away and the dead plant will still be standing in place aboveground. Succulent vegetation is gathered mostly at night; the animals probably come to the surface, remain near their burrow openings, and graze about the opening. Food is transported in the cheek pouches. A captive individual carried 54 grains of corn, and plant stems 3" long were also carried in the pouch. Material too large for the pouch was grasped by the incisors and dragged along the burrow, the gopher moving backward to do so. Food is routinely stored in the burrows.

Reproduction: Gestation is about a month. One litter is produced per year. The breeding season in Indiana extends from late February through early June. The number of embryos ranges from one to seven and averages four.

Range: The plains pocket gopher was known from six counties between the Kankakee and Wabash rivers and east to Pulaski County, all in northwestern Indiana. One mounted specimen represents the sole record for Pulaski County and was said to have been taken near Winamac. It may be extirpated in that county. Earlier, there were small, isolated colonies in Benton, Tippecanoe, and Warren counties, but most gophers occur in Jasper and Newton counties. Isolated mounds were found in Benton County and a single mound was found in White County in 1989, but no evidence of pocket gophers was found in Warren or Pulaski counties.

Side view of skull

Ventral view of skull and lower jaw

Plains pocket gopher. *Photo by Tony Brentlinger*

Habits and Comments. The pocket gopher is largely subterranean, rarely venturing aboveground except to feed. It is active day and night and throughout the year. Individuals are solitary other than occasionally for mating and raising young.

The most obvious behavior of *Geomys* is its burrowing. Underground tunnel systems are extensive. Foraging tunnels are usually 6–8" below the surface. Vertical or near-vertical short burrows connect the foraging burrows to other deeper tunnels. Excavated soil is pushed above the ground surface in the form of mounds. After a mound has been constructed, the opening used in its construction is plugged with soil. Mounds vary from several inches to 2' (or more) in diameter and may be nearly a foot high. In open areas, dozens of mounds may be visible from any one spot. The pocket gopher digs mostly with its front claws but may use the incisors to cut through roots. Gophers placed on top of the ground have usually tunneled out of sight within 5 minutes. They dig with their front paws, push the soil beneath their bodies with their hind legs, then turn around and push the loose soil away with their muzzles and front paws. This tunneling process is reminiscent of a bulldozer. Burrowing activity is greatest during the late summer and fall and decreases markedly by November and December. With the thawing of the soil in mid-March, mound building resumes.

There is probably little predation on Indiana pocket gophers since they are burrowers, but gopher snakes (*Pituophis catenifer*) are thought to prey on them; on at least two occasions we have observed gopher snakes with their heads inserted into gopher mounds.

Selected References. Mohr and Mohr 1936; Thorne 1989; Tuszynski 1971.

Plains pocket gopher mounds

Beavers are large, heavily built animals with a broad, scaly, spatulate (horizontally flattened) tail. They are the largest of North American rodents, some attaining a weight of 32 kg (70 lbs). The hind feet are prominently webbed. The three outer toes on the hind feet have typical claws; the two inner toes possess specialized claws that are used for grooming and combing the fur. The skull is massive and broad and lacks a postorbital process.

Two species of beaver exist today: the New World beaver, *Castor canadensis,* and the Old World beaver, *C. fiber.* There had been a question whether the two were different or not, but they differ both in chromosome number (the diploid number is 40 in *Castor canadensis,* 48 in *C. fiber*) and in cranial morphology. We have also found recently that the New and Old World beavers differ almost completely in their ectoparasitic mite communities. They consist entirely of large numbers (of individuals and species) of separate groups of species of host-specific chirodiscid mites of the genus *Schizocarpus,* with but one linking species in common, *S. mingaudi. Schizocarpus mingaudi,* then, would appear to have occurred alone on the progenitor beaver stocks that gave rise to *Castor canadensis* and *C. fiber.* These data support the recognition of two separate species of beavers.

Beaver
Castor canadensis Kuhl

Distinguishing Features and Measurements: The beaver is a large, dark reddish-brown rodent with a broad, dorsoventrally flattened, scaly tail. The pelage consists of soft, dense underfur and long, coarse guard hairs. The upperparts are usually chestnut brown (the color of the guard hairs), but the underparts are paler brown and lack any reddish tinge. The hind feet are webbed, and the two inner claws on each foot are split and used in grooming the pelage. Each foot has five toes. The ears are small and round.

TL 900–1,200, T 300–400, HF 170–195, Wt. 12–27 kg (up to 60 lbs)

Skull: Length: 119–140 (4.8–5.6").

The large, heavy skull contains large incisors with orange enamel on their anterior surfaces.

Dental Formula:

$$I \ \frac{1}{1} \ \ C \ \frac{0}{0} \ \ P \ \frac{1}{1} \ \ M \ \frac{3}{3} \ = \ \ 20$$

Habitat: Beavers are now abundant in lakes, marshes, streams, and drainage ditches in northern Indiana, and they are common throughout the state. Beavers are now abundant along most of the rivers of the state. They live in burrows in the ground along rivers too large or deep for them to dam. In southern Indiana, beavers have been introduced into some of the strip-mined land, where they have numerous ponds available for den and lodge sites.

Food: Beavers are vegetarians. Bark and twigs form the bulk of their diet. Aspen, cottonwood, and willow are favorite food trees; they are easily found and gnawed because of their widespread occurrence near water and their relatively soft wood. Many aquatic plants, such as cat-tail, arrowhead or duck potato, water lily, sedges, and grasses, along with many other herbaceous plants growing in their habitats, are eaten during spring and summer. Young blackberry canes and corn are also eaten. Bark and twigs are consumed mostly in cold weather. Many tree branches (and sections of trees) are stored under water for winter. They are cut and deposited on the bottom of the pond or river as a large brush pile; the newly cut material is rather heavy when green and most of it sinks to the bottom quite readily when waterlogged. Food piles are stored near the lodge or den and can be reached by the animals after the water has frozen. Food may be carried back inside the lodge, where the bark is eaten, then the peeled stick or tree branch is deposited outside.

Reproduction: Mating is from January through March. One litter is produced per year. Gestation is about 128 days, and the young are born usually between May and July. Litter size varies from one to eight (averaging about three to four). Breeding first occurs in animals about 2.5 years old. Newborn beavers weigh about a pound, and the young remain in the nest for the first month. Young about 6 months old average 14 lbs 6 ounces.

A beaver colony usually consists of two adults with their young from the two previous breeding seasons. When young reach an age of almost 2 years they are driven away by the parents and seek homes of their own. An average colony consists of five to six beavers. The members of a colony are intolerant of individuals from another colony, and family groups tend to be rather isolated. Once a colony is established and water and food conditions remain sufficient to sustain it, it may persist for years.

Range: The beaver was once found throughout Indiana but disappeared from nearly all of the state by 1840, perhaps even earlier. Once extirpated, it was gone for a long time. The Indiana Department of Conservation (now the Department of Natural Resources) obtained small numbers of beavers from Wisconsin and Michigan in 1935 and released them on the Jasper-Pulaski Fish and Wildlife Area (Jasper and Pulaski counties) and on the Kankakee Fish and Wildlife Area (Starke County). Other introductions

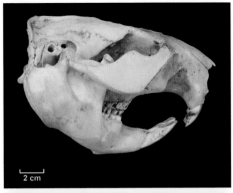

Side view of skull

Ventral view
of skull and
lower jaw

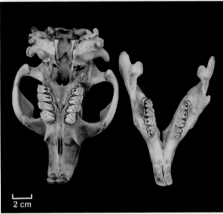

Beaver. *Photo by Larry Lehman*

Beaver run and
plunge hole.
*Photo by
Terry L. Castor*

Beaver lodge.
*Photo by
Terry L. Castor*

Beaver canal.
*Photo by David
Benson*

and transplantings were made (some in southern Indiana), and by 1947 an estimated 5,000 beavers were thought to be living in the state. Beavers were uncommon through the early 1970s, after which they began to increase. By 1982, they had a wide distribution. Currently the beaver is abundant everywhere and often causes problems by cutting trees, causing floods, and so forth.

Habits and Comments: The most important and obvious activity of the beaver is the building of dams, which are constructed primarily of sticks and mud. They may also include rocks, old fence posts, boards, discarded rolls of wire, and other items. One dam contained a discarded door from an automobile. Much dam material consists of sticks cut from brush and small trees. Many beavers in this region inhabit drainage ditches and small creeks, whose banks are frequently kept cleared of large trees by landowners. Large trees are cut by the beavers, however, when available. Beavers had gnawed extensively (but did not fell) a cottonwood tree more than 2' in diameter along the Kankakee River.

Where possible, beavers construct lodges of sticks, mud, and other items. A typical beaver lodge in Indiana is usually a modified bank burrow and has one or two tunnels leading from below water level into a nesting chamber above water level. Nesting chambers are about 2' high and 4–6' in diameter. The lodge is quite variable in size, ranging 5–6' tall and 10–20' in diameter. The size of the house depends upon its age, the size and strength of the bank, and the number of beavers inhabiting it. Three lodges opened by Whitaker contained no nesting material. Inside was a simple clay or dirt floor, with an exit to the water on one side. When lodges are not possible, Indiana beavers make burrows in a bank. Burrows used as dens are usually situated at the edge of the water.

Beaver dam. *Photo by David Berrey*

Small poplar tree felled by a beaver. *Photo by Rita Veal*

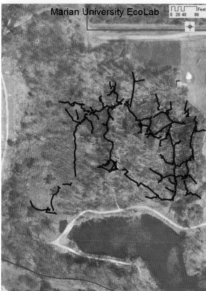

Marian University Ecolab with beaver canals highlighted. *Photo by David Benson*

Above the nest chamber, on top of the bank in which it is constructed, there is often a pile of interlacing sticks and branches plastered with mud. Burrowing into levees upon which roads have been constructed frequently results in the collapse of portions of the road surface, the formation of deep holes, and increased water erosion of the levee.

The beaver is seldom encountered out of water but goes on land to feed and to travel. Most activity takes place at night, although in areas where the animals are not unduly disturbed, they may be seen by day. Beavers are excellent swimmers and can spend considerable time beneath the water. Entrances to their lodges and dens are usually under water. Where beavers enter and leave the water over extended periods, well-marked paths and slides devoid of most vegetation are formed.

Although cottonwood, willow, aspen, and birches are frequently cut, and even sometimes pines, both for food and for the construction of dams, trees of harder wood—oaks and maples—are also used. Beavers keep the dams in good repair, keeping leaks sealed and replacing materials carried away by erosion (or by man). The adult male does much of the repair work. A surprising amount of dam can be constructed or repaired in a single night. Where sufficient water is available for storing winter food and for other activities, the animals do not construct dams.

Startled beavers will often slap their broad tail on the water with a loud smacking sound, then submerge noisily, causing a sound similar to that of a boulder being dropped into the water. This alarm signal is heeded by other beavers in the area. At other times, a swimming beaver or one at the water's edge will silently slip beneath the water with scarcely a ripple. An individual can remain submerged for up to 6 minutes. Swimming speed has been estimated at about 2–2.5 miles per hour. The tail may be used as a rudder or as an aid in propelling the beaver through the water. When a tree is being cut, the beaver's tail is used as support for the upright body.

Beavers contain two kinds of external parasites, a beaver "flea" (actually a host-specific beetle) and tiny host-specific mites of one genus, *Schizocarpus*. These mites cling to individual hairs of the underfur. A number of species and thousands of individuals can be found on one individual beaver, but almost nobody even knows they exist. Indiana beavers have few enemies other than man. Dogs and other predators probably kill young beavers found out of the water.

Selected References. Baker and Hill 2003; Jenkins and Busher 1979; Rue 1964.

FAMILY CRICETIDAE

The Cricetidae includes two subfamilies found in Indiana, the Neotominae or New World rats and mice, and the Arvicolinae or "microtines," the voles and lemmings that occur in both New and Old World.

The Neotominae have rooted teeth, that is, the adult teeth stop growing when mature. The Neotominae generally have cusped molariform teeth except for Neotoma itself (woodrat), which has flat crowned molariform teeth with loops. Rooted teeth can normally be recognized by the bases of the teeth being contracted as they enter the jawbone. The cusps are arranged in 2 longitudinal rows. The genera included in Indiana are *Neotoma* (woodrat), *Reithrodontomys* (harvest mouse), and *Peromyscus* (deer mouse and white-footed mouse).

The Arvicolinae, or voles (including muskrats and bog lemmings), are primarily herbivorous. Plant foods include cellulose, which is difficult to chew and digest. Voles have evolved ever-growing, or "rootless," molariform teeth, that is, they generally grow throughout the life of the animal. Otherwise, they would soon wear down because of the cellulose and the animals would be toothless at an early age. The molariform teeth are flat at the crown with chewing surfaces formed into enamel loops and triangles rather than cusps. The incisor teeth of both Neotominae and Arvicolinae likewise continue to grow, but the front of the teeth wear more slowly than the back because of the enamel, thus the teeth remain sharp.

SUBFAMILY NEOTOMINAE—NEW WORLD RATS AND MICE

Western Harvest Mouse
Reithrodontomys megalotis (Baird)

Distinguishing Features and Measurements: This is a small, long-tailed, short-eared mouse. It is brownish-gray (somewhat grizzled) above and white or whitish below. The sides of the head and body are fulvous. In Indiana, the harvest mouse is most likely to be confused with the house mouse, the white-footed mouse, or the deer mouse. From all three the harvest mouse can be immediately distinguished by the prominent grooves on the front of the upper incisors (see Fig. 26 in key). Adult white-footed mice and deer mice are considerably larger than harvest mice. House mice are variable in color, and some individuals may resemble harvest mice; however, house mice normally do not have a bicolored tail and whitish underparts.

TL 114–146, T 50–69, HF 15–18, Wt. 9.1–21.9

Skull: Length: 19.0–21.4 (0.8–0.9").

Incisors orange with prominent longitudinal groove.

Dental Formula:

$$I \ \frac{1}{1} \quad C \ \frac{0}{0} \quad P \ \frac{0}{0} \quad M \ \frac{3}{3} \ = \ 16$$

Habitat: This is a species normally found in weedy and early grassy fields. Important grasses there are bluegrass, quack grass, timothy, redtop, cheat, foxtail, fescue, Indian grass, and panic-grass. Some other herbaceous plants often included in harvest mouse habitat are red clover, alfalfa, goldenrod, ragweed, ironweed, sunflower, wild carrot, rose, blackberry, giant ragweed, wild parsnip, prickly lettuce, and horseweed. Harvest mice often occur along railroad rights-of-way and roadsides.

Food: In the rye field (see under range), where the early invasion occurred, rye seeds and caterpillars were by far the most important foods. In other habitats, caterpillars and various grass seeds are the most important items.

Reproduction: Breeding activity begins in March and litters may be produced from March to November. Litter size in Indiana averaged 3.8 (range from two to six, but most often three or four).

Range: Harvest mice first entered Indiana about 1969 at or near the Willow Slough Fish and Wildlife Area (Newton County). Here they flourished in a large, unharvested rye field, which served as a population dispersal center. In 1973, a single individual was taken in Jasper County, about 20 miles east of Willow Slough, and in 1974 the species was taken from Benton, Carroll, Tippecanoe, Vermillion, and Warren counties. None were taken north of the Kankakee River or east of the Tippecanoe River in Carroll County, and none east or south of the Wabash River, even with extensive work. Two just east of the Illinois-Indiana state line (1 mile north of Rileysburg, in Vermillion County) represented the southernmost station for the species in Indiana at that time. The species continued its rapid spread, and by 1998 it was known from 18 northwestern Indiana counties: Benton, Cass, Carroll, Clay, Fountain, Fulton, Jasper, Lake, Marshall, Newton, Parke, Pulaski, Starke, Tippecanoe, Vermillion, Vigo, Warren, and White. It has now been taken southeast of the Wabash River in Parke, Clay, and Fountain counties, and north of the Kankakee in Lake County. The approximate 1969, 1975, and 1998 ranges can be seen on the range map (see p. 188).

It is interesting that Evermann and Butler (1894), Hahn (1909), and Lyon (1936) all predicted that the eastern harvest mouse (*Reithrodontomys humulis*) might eventually be discovered in southeastern Indiana; this possibility is not ruled out, although we have been unable to find *R. humulis*.

Habits and Comments: The harvest mouse builds a globular nest in grass or weeds, under bushes, and sometimes above the ground in a bush. The nest is of shredded grass or other vegetation, and the opening on one side leads into a cavity lined with thistledown, milkweed, fine grass, or other soft material.

Harvest mice may be active day or night but are primarily nocturnal. They are good climbers and will climb up grass and other plant stems in search of food. They do not make runways but often use those of other species. Harvest mice are particularly active in the late summer and fall, when they store seeds for winter use. The species does not hibernate, but during cold periods it may remain in the nest. Harvest mice make a series of birdlike squeaks, loudest in the middle and trailing off on both ends, reminiscent of the call of the blackpoll warbler. Owls and probably all other predators feed on harvest mice.

Selected References. Birkenholz 1967; Ford 1977; Leibacher and Whitaker 1998; Verts 1960; Webster and Jones 1982; Whitaker and Mumford 1972b; Whitaker and Sly 1970.

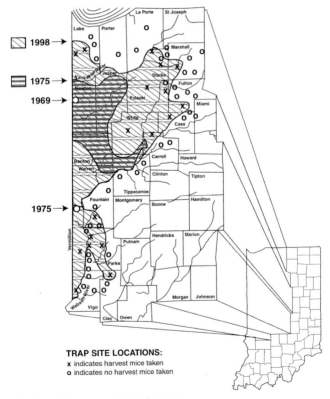

Map from Leibacher and Whitaker 1988

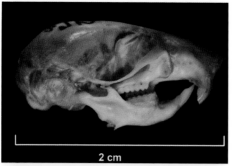

Side view of skull

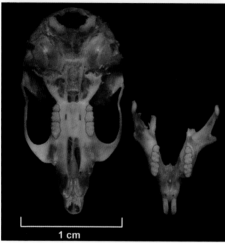

Ventral view of skull and lower jaw

Western harvest mouse

Prairie Deer Mouse
Peromyscus maniculatus bairdii (Wagner)

Distinguishing Features and Measurements: The species of *Peromyscus* in Indiana are *P. maniculatus* and *P. leucopus*. For many years, the species were confused; some earlier authors listed a single species. Both have been commonly called deer mice or white-footed mice. Certain individuals of either species are sometimes quite difficult to identify to species; both may be brownish above and white below and may have white feet. The deer mouse is usually grayer above than the white-footed mouse, but color varies considerably. Juveniles of both species are slate-gray above and white below. Deer mice are smaller and have shorter ears, shorter hind feet, and shorter tails than do white-footed mice. *Peromyscus maniculatus bairdii* has a tail length much less than half its total length and averaging about 50–55 mm; tail length almost never exceeds 65 mm. *Peromyscus leucopus* has a tail length slightly less than half its total length and averaging about 75 mm. The hind foot measurement of *P. maniculatus* is normally 19 mm or less, whereas *P. leucopus* usually has a hind foot 19 mm or longer (even in obvious gray-pelaged juveniles). The deer mouse has shorter ears (about 13 mm) than does the white-footed mouse (16 mm). We have generally not used subspecies names in this volume. This one is used because the prairie deer mouse is so different from other eastern deer mice (they have very long tails—more than half the total length—they do not occur in Indiana).

The skulls of the two species in Indiana are very similar, and we have not found good characters to distinguish between them.

TL 120–165, T 42–69, HF 15–19, Wt. 12–26

Skull: Length: 22.4–24.7 (0.9–1.0").

Dental Formula:

$$I \ \frac{1}{1} \quad C \ \frac{0}{0} \quad P \ \frac{0}{0} \quad M \ \frac{3}{3} \ = \ 16$$

Habitat: The prairie deer mouse is primarily found in cultivated fields in Indiana. Populations appear to remain relatively constant throughout the year. Herbaceous cover is not necessary for deer mice but is necessary for all other species of small rodents in Indiana. Deer mice can inhabit plowed fields, which furnish little or no vegetative cover and are therefore unsuitable for other species. Deer mouse populations were highest in plowed fields from November through April. Essentially no hiding places were available except under the soil, although many of the fields in this category had been planted and contained some vegetation. The deer mouse was probably originally most common in the relatively dry, open fields of the prairie areas of northwestern Indiana and in the isolated, smaller prairies in the western part of the state. It undoubtedly occurred also on the front line of sand dunes along Lake Michigan where vegetation is sparse. Since it is not an inhabitant of wooded areas, it was probably absent (or occurred in isolated openings) in the nine-tenths of Indiana originally covered by forests until the late 1800s. With the removal of most of the forest vegetation by logging around the turn of the last century, and with the steady increase of cultivation, suitable habitat became available and enabled the species to enjoy a much wider geographic distribution. It is not known how rapidly the deer mouse might have immigrated into this newly created habitat, as mammalogists seldom study cultivated field habitats.

The deer mouse is very common in fields plowed in the fall and left barren all winter. One such habitat on a floodplain had been inundated by spring flooding and, when the area was trapped after the water receded, the soil was sunbaked and cracked. In 3 nights, five mice were collected; they were living in the cracks and feeding on seeds accumulated there. The prairie deer mouse is also the most abundant species in early seral stage strip-mined areas, giving way to *P. leucopus* as heavier ground cover and shrubs and trees become established.

Food: Deer mice consume a wide variety of food items, approximately a third each of cultivated crops, wild seeds, and animal foods. Caterpillars were the most important food of 444 prairie deer mice from Indiana, constituting 15% of their food volume. Seeds of wild plants made up another 15%. Soybeans and wheat each constituted about 10% and corn made up 5.6%.

Reproduction: Gestation in the deer mouse is about 25 days. In Indiana, pregnant females have been trapped in each month of the year, and females produce more than one litter per year. Most females appear to bear young in spring and early summer, with the smallest percentage of gravid females taken in midwinter. The number of embryos per female averaged 4.7 and ranged from 2 to 8. The most common number of embryos per female was 4. Four of nine females trapped in January and three of nine caught in February were pregnant. Young are born in nests constructed of various plant materials in sheltered sites. Nests have been found in hollow logs and fence posts and under piles of soybeans lying in the field. Deer mice sometimes appropriate old

birds' nests and dome them over for winter living quarters. The nest forms the foundation, and the mice transport soft materials (such as milkweed fluff or thistledown) and form a warm globular structure nearly 6" in diameter, with an entrance low on one side.

Range: Prairie deer mice occur throughout the state in cultivated or sparse open field habitats.

Habits and Comments: The deer mouse is nocturnal and usually spends the day in burrows. Twelve burrows studied in detail averaged 16'

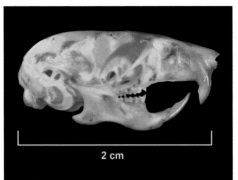

Side view of skull

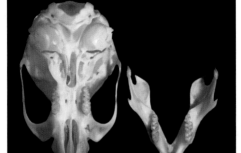

Ventral view
of skull and
lower jaw

Deer mouse with litter. *Photo by Tony Brentlinger*

in length and varied from 5 to 35'; they ranged from 1 to 12" below the ground surface and averaged 4.1" in depth. The deepest point of the burrow was often near the entrance. Usually a single opening (0.75–1.5" in diameter) led to the underground system of tunnels, which was rather complex, with up to 12 branches off the main burrow. The average number of side passages was 6. Three of the burrows contained caches of stored seeds. Eight each terminated in a large chamber; three of the chambers contained nesting materials of grasses, straw, leaves, or paper. The deer mouse is undoubtedly much less arboreal than the white-footed mouse. It is so well adapted for living in habitats devoid of woody vegetation that climbing is probably not very important to its livelihood and survival.

The home range of a deer mouse is probably confined to 0.5–1.5 acres, the larger home ranges tending to be in poorer habitats. Males have larger home ranges than do females. These animals do not move about much.

The deer mouse is a major prey species of nocturnal, predatory mammals and owls.

SELECTED REFERENCES. Blair 1940; Houtcooper 1972; Howard 1949; Whitaker 1966.

Prairie deer mouse. *Photo by Linda K. Castor*

White-footed Mouse

Peromyscus leucopus (Rafinesque)

Distinguishing Features and Measurements: The white-footed mouse is reddish-brown to fawn above and white below, with large ears and large black eyes. The tail is slightly shorter than the combined head and body length and is brownish above and whitish below. Juvenile white-footed mice are uniform gray above and white below. In Indiana, this species is most likely to be confused with the prairie deer mouse, which has a shorter tail, smaller ears, and shorter hind feet. Adult Indiana white-footed mice seldom have a hind foot length less than 19 mm; the hind foot of the deer mouse is usually 16–18 mm long.

TL 147–199, T 62–90, HF 19–23, Wt. 17–33

Skull: Length: 24.1–27.4 (1.0–1.1").

We have been unable to distinguish adequately between the skulls of the two species of *Peromyscus,* although that of the deer mouse averages smaller. Both species of *Peromyscus* can be separated from other Indiana mice by having 2 rows of cusps on the grinding surfaces of the cheek teeth (see Fig. 23 in key) and no grooves on the anterior faces of the incisors.

Dental Formula:

$$I \ \frac{1}{1} \ C \ \frac{0}{0} \ P \ \frac{0}{0} \ M \ \frac{3}{3} \ = \ 16$$

Habitat: The white-footed mouse is primarily a woodland species that occurs occasionally in open areas. It is common in fencerows and even may occur in small numbers in swampy places where land may be flooded for weeks at a time. The species was found on the brush-covered and wooded sand dunes in Porter County but not on the sparsely vegetated dunes along the lake shore. White-footed mice often occur in caves. During a random trapping program conducted by Whitaker in Vigo County, 316 white-footed mice were taken. They were relatively common in eight habitats—river bottom woods, brushy fields, weedy fields, upland woods, brush, grassy fields, winter wheat fields, and cornfields. This species is common in strip-mined areas. The prairie deer mouse is an early inhabitant after stripping and it is replaced by *P. leucopus* as herbaceous vegetation is replaced by woody. The white-footed mouse is the most abundant mammal at the Indiana Dunes National Lakeshore. It is most prevalent in wooded and shrubby habitats but encroaches on most other habitats as well. This species is the mouse usually found in buildings in wooded areas.

Food: The white-footed mouse is primarily a seed eater but also eats other plant material and some animal material. A complete list of the plant species consumed would be quite long, for the mouse has a tremendously varied diet. Some of their foods are acorns; hickory nuts; seeds of redbud, wahoo, bittersweet, sunflower, wild plum, tulip poplar, cocklebur, and giant ragweed; berries of coralberry; and corn.

Three kinds of snails (*Physa, Limnaea, Sphaerium*) number among the foods of white-footed mice. In Mayfield's Cave, *P. leucopus* ate seeds, myriopods, and insects. Multiflora rose hips are readily eaten, and some mice have been found with pokeberry seeds in their cheek pouches. White-footed mice store considerable food for winter use, and large amounts of nuts, seeds, acorns, and other seeds may be found in hollow trees, stumps, branches, beneath rubbish, in buildings, or in other suitable locations. Pits from the fruits of black cherry are eaten in considerable quantities; a quart or so of the opened pits can sometimes be found about the base or in a hollow in a black cherry tree. Beechnuts are an important food, and large numbers are often stored in a hollow limb or other protected place for winter food. Caterpillars and other insect larvae, and also spiders and other arthropods, are heavily eaten as are many other kinds of wild seeds. An interesting food is the seeds of touch-me-not, commonly eaten by this and other species. The endosperm of the seeds is turquoise and often the turquoise color can be seen through the wall of the stomach of the animal before it is opened. Feeding platforms are frequently established on top of old birds' nests, particularly those of the size made by American robins, mockingbirds, gray catbirds, and brown thrashers. Such feeding platforms are usually evident in multiflora rose fencerows, and a cupful of debris left from the feeding of the mice on rose hips may be present in or on a single nest.

Reproduction: The gestation period of *P. leucopus* is about 21–23 days but may be extended in nursing females. In Indiana, the species may breed throughout the year, but breeding is much reduced in winter. Most young are probably born from May to August. Females produce multiple litters, bearing 2–7 embryos per litter. Average litter size is 4.3.

Range: The white-footed mouse occurs throughout the state and is one of the most common Indiana mammals.

Habits and Comments: The white-footed mouse is primarily a nocturnal, woodland-inhabiting species that spends a considerable amount of time on the ground. It is not confined, however, to wooded areas, and at times it is somewhat diurnal. One is most likely to observe these mice moving about in the daytime when nighttime temperatures are near 0°F or colder. Under such conditions, the mice may forage some during the day. This species is a good climber and spends quite a bit of time in bushes and trees. It has been found in a nest at least 20' above the ground in a tree cavity. Nests are constructed in almost any site that affords enough protection. Nests may occur in woodpecker holes or other cavities in

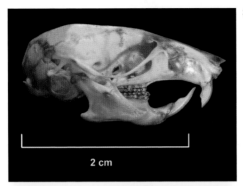

Side view of skull

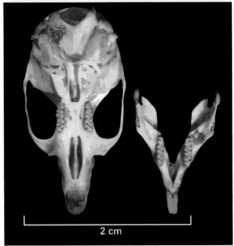

Ventral view of skull and lower jaw

White-footed mouse. *Photo by Roger Barbour*

trees, rotten stumps, buildings, eaves, bird boxes, idle farm machinery, fence posts, discarded tires, rock crevices, and beneath boards, bridges, logs, stones, or rubbish on the ground. The white-footed mouse readily invades houses (both abandoned and occupied) and other buildings, particularly during the colder months, and nests may be observed in almost any nook or cranny in such buildings. It is not unusual to find bird nests that the mice have capped over with soft materials for winter use. Nesting materials include grasses, bits of paper or other soft materials, feathers, hair, milkweed, thistle or cattail down, pieces of leaves, or other items. They may also live in small burrows in the ground, with openings about the base of a tree or stump. The mice also use the burrows of larger mammals (such as the woodchuck). They will sometimes vibrate their tails rapidly when excited.

The usual method of locomotion on the ground appears to be a series of jumps, on all four feet at once, about the length of the mouse's body; some jumps are longer (10–12″). The tracks in such cases appear in groups of four, similar to miniature rabbit tracks, and no tail marks are present with the tracks. Sometimes tracks suggest that the animals have walked, and occasionally tail-drag marks are present. *Peromyscus leucopus* travels along the surface runways made by voles.

SELECTED REFERENCES. King 1968; Lackey et al. 1985; Whitaker 1966.

Juvenile white-footed mouse. *Photo by Linda K. Castor*

Allegheny Woodrat
Neotoma magister (Baird)

Distinguishing Features and Measurements: The woodrat is about the size of the familiar Norway rat but has longer, softer fur, larger ears, and a more heavily haired tail. The feet and underparts are white. The woodrat looks much like a very large white-footed mouse.

TL 360–440, T 156–200, HF 39–45, Wt. 260–450

Skull: Length: 45–56 (1.8–2.2").
  Dental Formula:
  $$I \ \frac{1}{0} \ C \ \frac{0}{0} \ P \ \frac{0}{0} \ M \ \frac{3}{3} \ = \ 16$$

Habitat: In Indiana, the Allegheny woodrat is restricted to limestone escarpments and caves in the heavily forested hills of Harrison and Crawford counties. Red cedar (*Juniperus*) when present appears to be an important tree to the species, which often makes its nest of the shredded bark and makes heavy use of the twigs. However, woodrats are also found at several sites in which juniper does not occur. Where juniper is present, green juniper sprigs are scattered all along runs and throughout caves used by woodrats. Caves used by woodrats are dry and have numerous fissures, crevices, and ledges along their length. Appropriate characteristics for a site to harbor woodrats, therefore, appear to be extensive limestone cliffs with a southern component to their exposure and suitable rock formations for den sites. Abandoned buildings and dry caves not associated with cliffs provide possible alternative habitats.

Food: The woodrat feeds on a wide variety of plant foods. Food is transported to the nest area and stored in fissures. Green vegetation (foliage) accounted for 69.5% of the total volume in stomachs, while fruits and seeds contributed 30.4% of total volume. Nearly identical proportions of foliage and fruits and seeds were found in cutting piles. Fungi (5.0% volume) and unidentified items accounted for the remainder. The major food found in large cutting piles was *Ailanthus altissima* (tree-of-heaven). Foliage of this species made up the majority of volume; however, samaras were also occasionally collected. Fruit of *Phytolacca americana* (pokeweed) was the second most important item by volume. *Juniperus virginiana* (eastern red cedar) accounted for 9.1% of total volume, and only foliage was collected. Although *Eupatorium rugosum* (white snakeroot) occurred in nearly one-third of the cutting piles examined, it contributed only 4.7% of total volume. *Parthenocissus quinquefolia* (Virginia creeper), *Cercis canadensis* (redbud), *Rhamnus carolinana* (Carolina buckthorn), and *Lonicera japonica* (Japanese honeysuckle) represent the remaining important items that accounted for greater than 5.0% of total volume. Cutting piles were generally a good predictor of which plant species were actually eaten. Eight of the top 10 items in stomachs and cutting piles were the same. *Ailanthus,*

Phytolacca, Juniperus, Parthenocissus, Rhamnus, Lonicera, and fungi were all eaten in amounts that approximated the degree to which they were collected.

Reproduction: Gestation is about 33–42 days. Most young are born in spring but may be born through September. Juveniles retain their almost entirely gray pelage for 5–6 weeks after birth.

Range: In 1930, Paul F. Hickie and Thomas Harrison (students at the University of Michigan) conducted a survey of mammals around the perimeter of Indiana. They searched for woodrats in southern Indiana and were successful in collecting the first four individuals from the state, all from Harrison County. The species once occupied a wider distribution in south central Indiana. Recent fossil remains have been found in caves in Harrison, Jennings, Lawrence, Monroe, Orange, and Owen counties. *Neotoma* distribution in the past was possibly concurrent with the limits of Indiana's karst areas. Woodrat bones were associated with bones of now extirpated Indiana mammals, such as the black bear, porcupine, spotted skunk, and elk. These remains show that at some earlier time the eastern woodrat occurred at least 70 miles farther north than Wyandotte Cave, the northernmost locality it is known to inhabit today. The cause of this depopulation is unknown.

By 1985 there was evidence of active woodrats at 20 sites, all in Crawford and Harrison counties, all restricted to the limestone bluffs along the Ohio River from the Little Blue River in Crawford County east to Evan's Landing, Harrison County. Some of these sites are no longer active. Woodrat densities in 1985 averaged 27.5 animals per 1,000 m of cliff and ranged from 8.3 to 71.9 animals per 1,000 m. Variation in densities between sites is probably most closely related to the availability of den sites. The density of juniper (*Juniperus virginiana*), however, was also positively correlated with woodrat densities and may be an important factor influencing population levels, although juniper does not occur at every site. Interestingly, woodrat densities were not strongly correlated with the density of *Ailanthus altissima* (tree-of-heaven), their major food.

Habits and Comments: Woodrats are essentially nocturnal when foraging, but they can often be observed inside caves or deep fissures in escarpments during the day. Woodrat dens are of four basic types: caves or cavelike openings, breakaway or breakdown type, horizontal crevices, and vertical crevices. A high proportion of available caves or cavelike openings and horizontal crevices are generally in use.

Horizontal crevices are typically long, narrow fissures in cliffs that are often well above the cliff base. Vertical crevices are apparently the least suitable openings for den sites, with only 37.5% in use. Both horizontal and vertical crevices commonly have stick piles associated with them. Woodrats move about over the escarpments, leaving tracks in the dust that collects in narrow, protected ledges. They are excellent climbers, and the rough surfaces of rock ledges and cave walls do not hamper them. Besides junipers, they also must climb to obtain other food items, such as wild grape, pokeberries, and the like, that they store in their caves and crevices in the fall. A captive held food in its forefeet and sat on its haunches and ate, much like a squirrel. Food was manipulated expertly with the front feet. The animal even picked up a single apple seed in one front foot, held it with both forepaws, peeled off the outer coat and ate the inside portion. After holding peanut butter in the front feet and eating it, the rat carefully licked and cleaned the front feet.

Woodrats (pack rats of the west) are noted for their habit of gathering all sorts of items, which they transport to a particular site and pile into "middens." One such midden contained the seeds and fruit of black walnut, hickory, coffee tree, wild grape, tulip poplar, buckeye, redbud, ailanthus, oak, pokeweed, corn, persimmon, and sugar maple; other plant materials included leaves of pokeberry, willow, redbud, white oak, sugar maple, chestnut oak, elm, red cedar sprigs, sycamore bark, tendrils from wild grape, and bits of charcoal. Miscellaneous items included fish bones, turtle bones and shell, bits of glass, lead foil, small paint can, small cardboard box, cellophane, cigarette butt, rubber band, .22 cartridge case, shotgun shell, bottle cap, large mammal dropping, plastic buckle, metal buckle, cigarette package, crow feather, metal teaspoon, bits of cloth, grasshopper head, and a snail shell. In the center of this pile of debris was a globular nest composed of grasses and shredded bark. Debris piles containing sticks, bark, bones, feathers, paper and assorted trash are commonly at the entrances to crevice-type den sites, where they probably serve to protect the den from weather and larger predators.

Cutting piles, which serve as food caches, are nearly always distinct from debris piles and contain only items that are potential food sources. These piles most often occur from September to November. Cutting piles observed in fall are nearly always depleted by early spring, indicating that their contents do serve as winter foods.

Captive woodrats would not tolerate other woodrats in the same cage. When placed together, they become aggressive. Standing on their hind legs and propped up by the tail, they spar and joust with the forefeet, constantly grinding their teeth with a soft rasping noise and vibrating the vibrissae at a tremendous rate.

Man and his activities (especially excessive spelunking) may pose some threat to this uncommon mammal. Undoubtedly, predatory birds, mammals, and snakes occur in the woodrat's habitat and may take their toll. The biggest threat to *Neotoma* is from the raccoon nema-

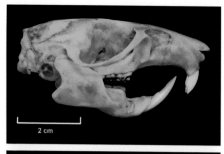

Side view of skull

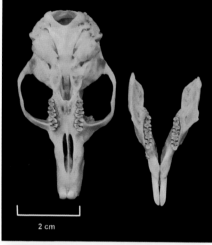

Ventral view
of skull and
lower jaw

Allegheny woodrat
habitat along Ohio
River in Harrison
County

tode, *Baylisascaris procyonis*. The adult worm occurs in the brain and apparently causes little harm to raccoons but is fatal in woodrats and is probably harmful or fatal to many other species, including humans. The eggs are found in the feces and become an increasing threat as the feces dry. The eggs are inhaled. Unfortunately, raccoons often occur along the bluffs where *Neotoma* occurs, and *Neotoma* often collects the feces of other species for deposit in its middens. The raccoon nematode has apparently wiped out the woodrat population in New York.

SELECTED REFERENCES. Cudmore 1985; Hamilton 1953; Hayes and Harrison 1992; Hickie and Harrison 1930; Johnson 2002; Poole 1940; Richards 1972.

Allegheny woodrat. *Photo by Roger Barbour*

Litter of Allegheny woodrats. *Photo by Russell E. Mumford*

Meadow Vole
Microtus pennsylvanicus (Ord)

Distinguishing Features and Measurements: The four species of voles in Indiana are all large-headed, heavy-bodied, short-tailed mice with short legs and have short ears that are mostly hidden by the fur of the head. The meadow vole is the largest of these species and usually has a dull, dark chestnut-colored dorsum and a silvery (sometimes buffy) underside. The back color varies considerably, both seasonally and geographically, so that some individuals (especially immatures) are difficult to distinguish externally from the prairie vole. The meadow vole has a longer tail (from 36 to 45 mm) than the prairie vole (from 28 to 37 mm). The woodland vole (*Microtus pinetorum*) and southern bog lemming (*Synaptomys cooperi*), the other Indiana voles, both have much shorter tails (about the same length as the hind foot).

TL 126–190, T 30–56, HF 17–24, Wt. 24–64

Skull: Length: 20.8–23.4 (0.8–0.9").

The best characteristic for separating the meadow vole from the prairie vole is the number of triangles on the grinding surface of the third upper molar teeth (see Figs. 24 and 25 in key). The meadow vole has at least 3 triangles between the anterior and posterior loops; the prairie vole has only 2.

Dental Formula:

$$I \frac{1}{1} \quad C \frac{0}{0} \quad P \frac{0}{0} \quad M \frac{3}{3} = 16$$

Habitat: The meadow vole is closely associated with moist lush grassy fields and good cover. We have found it in marshes, low meadows, fencerows, damp fallow fields, and along ditches, lake shores, and streams. Individuals have been taken in clover fields, wheat stubble, abandoned gardens, or lawns overgrown with dense grasses. Meadow voles are often captured in summer and fall in low sites that remain completely inundated for long periods in spring. It is seldom in woodlands except along heavily vegetated stream edges or moist areas, but it does occur along woodlot borders and in grassy areas surrounded by woods. Meadow voles occur in the sparse stands of beachgrass growing on pure sand of the foredunes and associated habitats along Lake Michigan. Many were found in a flat, moist depression (panne) behind the foredunes in a pure stand of beachgrass.

Food: Meadow voles eat almost entirely green vegetation, which they chew very finely. The most common food (over 30% of the volume) and the most common plant in study plots for this species was Canada bluegrass. Other plants eaten in large amounts by meadow voles were muhly, tumble-grass, and plantain. Plants eaten were green and succulent. The presence of limited insect material indicates that meadow voles are not entirely herbivorous.

Reproduction: The meadow vole breeds throughout most of the year in Indiana except for January and early February. The gestation period is about 21 days. Females produce numerous litters per year. The number of embryos per female ranges from 1 to 9, with a mean of about 4.5. Breeding occurs mainly from March through October. The species exhibits well-developed 3- to 4-year cyclic peaks in populations. Increasing populations are marked by a longer reproductive season, an acceleration of the breeding rate, and an increased number of young per litter. Increased winter breeding occurs during the increasing phase of the population cycle.

Range: The meadow vole is often abundant in northern Indiana but less common to the south and west. We have examined meadow voles from 77 Indiana counties.

Habits and Comments: Meadow voles are active both day and night but are especially active near dawn and dusk. They do not hibernate. They forage for food along well-established and maintained runways on top of the ground. Such runways are constructed by the voles, are devoid of any vegetation, and are about 1.5" wide. Runways are mostly hidden beneath the grasses and other vegetation but often emerge from such cover (depending upon the density of the ground vegetation) and cross open areas. The voles can move quite swiftly along these runs and no doubt they become familiar with them from constant use. When a meadow vole is disturbed while foraging, it runs rapidly along the runways to an underground burrow or other safe retreat. Sections of grass stems and fecal pellets are scattered along the runways, and at certain sites there are accumulations of droppings. Underground burrows are also constructed and used at all seasons. At certain times of the year in good meadow vole habitat, one can find much evidence of digging and piles of loose soil lying about the burrow entrances. There is a considerable amount of such activity beneath deep snow, as evidenced by the signs remaining after the snow melts away.

Nests of shredded grasses are constructed on the surface of the ground, in underground burrows, or beneath the protection of some object lying on the ground. Nests are somewhat globular and about 6" in diameter; often they can be seen in a clump of grass, but in good cover such nests may be inconspicuous. The opening to the nest is usually from below and is connected with the runways radiating out from the nest.

Meadow voles are good swimmers, at least for short distances, an advantage where they occupy wet places or areas that are flooded tem-

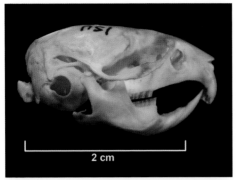

Side view of skull

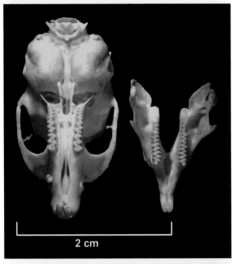

Ventral view
of skull and
lower jaw

Meadow vole cuttings

Order RODENTIA—Rodents or Gnawing Mammals 205

porarily. These voles are capable of standing upright on their hind feet. During the fall and winter, one can sometimes see many individuals moving about in runways during the day. Meadow voles produce several vocalizations, including squeaks, squeals, and a growling sound. They also chatter their teeth quite audibly.

Cuttings left by voles are telltale signs of their presence in an area. Cuttings may be of various lengths, ranging from 1 to 4", and may be strewn along runways or dropped in piles. Meadow voles are preyed upon by numerous avian and mammalian predators, especially owls and hawks, coyotes, foxes, weasels, bobcats, and of course domestic cats.

SELECTED REFERENCES. Bailey 1924; Hamilton 1937; Keller and Krebs 1970; Krebs et al. 1969, 1971; Reich 1981; Zimmerman 1965.

Meadow vole. *Photo by R. Wayne Van Devender*

Prairie Vole
Microtus ochrogaster (Wagner)

Distinguishing Features and Measurements: The prairie vole is usually grayish-brown above, and the mixture of black and brownish-yellow tips of the longer hairs gives the dorsum a salt-and-pepper (grizzled) appearance. It is similar to the meadow vole but has a much shorter tail (28–37 mm) versus 36–45 in the meadow vole, and its belly is usually buffy (ranging from pale buff to ochraceous or fulvous) in contrast to the silvery belly of the meadow vole. The sides are paler than the back, and some individuals have silvery undersides. The pelage of the prairie vole appears coarser and less shiny (more grizzled) than that of the meadow vole. The variation in pelage color both in prairie voles and in meadow voles sometimes renders it difficult to identify a particular individual (especially young) to species without examining the molar teeth.

TL 125–166, T 30–48, HF 18–22, Wt. 30–54

Skull: Length: 24.7–28.9 (1.0–1.2").

The best characteristic for separating the prairie and meadow voles is the number of triangles between the anterior and posterior loops of the third upper molariform teeth: the meadow vole has at least 3, the prairie vole has only 2 (see Figs. 24 and 25 in key).

Dental Formula:

$$\text{I } \frac{1}{1} \text{ C } \frac{0}{0} \text{ P } \frac{0}{0} \text{ M } \frac{3}{3} = 16$$

Habitat: The prairie vole inhabits relatively dry fields, either cultivated (hay, clover, etc.) or noncultivated, that support a cover of grasses or weeds. Overgrown fields with scattered sprouts or a few larger trees are also inhabited by this vole, but it shuns the woods. The largest populations of prairie voles usually occur in fallow fields or hay fields. The meadow vole inhabits mostly moist areas with thick grassy vegetation. The prairie vole inhabits drier areas with much less dense and more varied vegetation.

Food: The meadow and prairie voles both eat nearly 100% green vegetation, but the prairie vole eats a greater variety of herbaceous plants than does the meadow vole, in keeping with the greater variation of plants in its habitat. The most common food of the prairie vole is Canada bluegrass, followed by red clover, lespedeza, tumble-grass, and roots. Curly dock, alfalfa, fleabane, pigweed, and wood-sorrel have low abundance indices but are eaten in larger amounts than would be expected, indicating that these plants are favored by the prairie vole. The prairie vole, like the meadow vole, ate a small amount of insect material (about 5% of the volume), including beetle larvae and caterpillars. The prairie vole feeds on wheat heads when they are just ripening. The stalks are not stiff enough for the mice to climb, and interference with other heads prevents the wheat from falling over when the stalk is cut at its base.

Therefore, the mice raise themselves on their haunches and cut the stalks as high as they can reach; when the cut end falls to the ground, they cut off another section 3 or 4" long and repeat the process until the head is reached.

Reproduction: Gestation is about 21 days. Pups may occur in any month; the greatest number of pregnancies and the highest numbers of young occur in spring and fall. However, there are fewer pregnancies in December–January. Females are more likely to be gravid in winter in southern than in northern Indiana. Embryos ranged from 1 to 7 per female, with a mean of 3.5.

Range: The prairie vole is abundant in Indiana and ranks close behind the house mouse, white-footed mouse, and deer mouse in total numbers. It is definitely more abundant in the southern half of Indiana than in the northern half, but local populations may be periodically high in the latter. It is especially scarce in the northeastern corner of the state. Like the meadow vole, the prairie vole exhibits dramatic cyclic population increases with very high populations one year but with few to be found a year or two later (see discussion under the meadow vole).

Habits and Comments: The habits of the prairie vole are similar to those of the meadow vole. Both construct and maintain conspicuous runways; both leave plant cuttings and droppings along their runways. Their nests appear similar, and they are similar in their diurnal and nocturnal activity patterns. This species is an important prey item for many predators. The prairie vole shares with the Indiana bat the distinction of being one of two species of mammals originally described from Indiana.

Selected References. Jameson 1947; Keller and Krebs 1970; Krebs et al. 1969, 1971; Martin 1956; Stalling 1990; Zimmerman 1965.

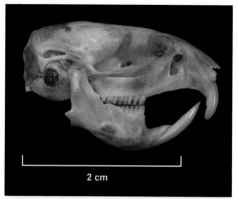

Side view of skull

Ventral view
of skull and
lower jaw

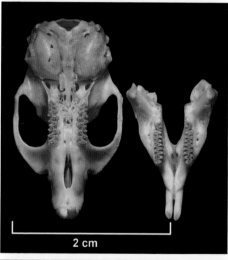

Prairie vole. *Photo by Terry L. Castor*

Woodland Vole
Microtus pinetorum (Le Conte)

Distinguishing Features and Measurements: The woodland vole has glossier, shorter, finer (more molelike or shrewlike) fur and lacks the coarse, long, scattered guard hairs of other Indiana voles. The color above is brownish, usually tinged with reddish or cinnamon; the venter is paler, usually buffy or silvery. Immatures and winter-pelaged adults may be darker and duller. The eyes and ears are small, and the tail is about equal to or less than the length of the hind foot. Among other Indiana microtines, only the southern bog lemming (*Synaptomys cooperi*) has such a short tail, but it can be separated from the woodland vole by its grooved (very light) upper incisors.

TL 109–143, T 14–20, HF 13–18, Wt. 22.7–33.8

Skull: Length: 21.7–25.4 (0.9–1.0").

The skull is almost identical to that of the prairie vole.

Dental Formula:

$$I \quad \frac{1}{1} \quad C \quad \frac{0}{0} \quad P \quad \frac{0}{0} \quad M \quad \frac{3}{3} \quad = \quad 16$$

Habitat: Woodland voles live in a variety of habitats. In Indiana they have been taken in orchards; old corn stubble; pasture; railroad embankments; fencerows; pine plantations; brushy, grassy, and cultivated fields; upland and lowland deciduous forests (including floodplains); upland mixed coniferous and deciduous forests; on lawns, and about the borders of cypress swamps and ponds. However, the woodland vole's major habitat in Indiana is deciduous forest with soft soil and leaf mold that enables the animals to burrow more easily. Despite its scientific and previous common name, this species is seldom found in pine or other evergreen forest. The major species of small mammals found with the woodland vole in forested habitats are the short-tailed shrew and white-footed mouse. The short-tailed shrew and the woodland vole occupy similar niches in woodlands, and both may have their burrows in the same area. Vole burrows are rounded (in cross section) and are larger than shrew burrows, which are somewhat flattened dorsoventrally.

Food: The woodland vole feeds mainly on roots, bulbs, tubers, bark, seeds, nuts, acorns, and insects. Some specific items are young sprouts of white clover, fruit of hawthorn, and the tuberous roots of wild violet. This species stores food for winter. Deposits have been reported that contained a gallon of stored violet tubers; some were stored 18" below the surface of the ground. Stomach contents of 25 woodland voles from Indiana yielded various plant parts (stems, leaves, roots, nuts) constituting 92% of the food, including hickory nuts, beechnuts, and black cherry seeds. The fungus *Endogone* represented 3% and insect material nearly 5% of the identified foods. Fresh, green cuttings of sedge, black maple, and spleenwort were noted in their burrows in October.

Reproduction: Woodland voles produce young from late February or early March through September or October. The gestation is about 20–21 days, and weaning takes place about 17 days after birth. Litter size ranges from two to four. In one case, three females with their litters were found in a single nest. This perhaps accounts for large litters occasionally reported.

Range: This vole is not overly common, although we have usually been able to get specimens without much difficulty when traps were properly set in underground woodland burrows. The species has been reported from 43 counties.

Woodland voles sometimes occur in considerable numbers in deciduous forests. They are probably much more common in southern than in northern Indiana. This species is often caught in pitfall traps for shrews, or one can locate burrows by probing with the fingers into the soft, moist forest earth. Mousetrap-sized holes are then dug into the burrow crosswise, so that a regular snapback mousetrap can be lowered into the burrow with the trap treadle at a level with the surface of the runway; the vole must run over the treadle when running through the tunnel. A piece of bark or cardboard is placed over the hole, being sure that the cover is high enough over the treadle so that the trap can go off.

Habits and Comments: The woodland vole is somewhat colonial. It is active both day and night and perhaps primarily diurnal. Woodland voles forage beneath and among the leaves on the forest floor, especially beneath logs and in deep leaf mold. Much time is spent inside the burrow system, which may be extensive. Along shallow burrows, there are neat, round openings to the surface; there is no soil about these openings. Burrows are usually confined to the softer, loose soils, for woodland voles do not have the powerful digging front feet possessed by moles. Woodland voles push the soil from the burrow with their forefeet, and the excavated soil is then scattered about. Many burrows are just below the ground surface, and the top of the burrow is often pushed up to form a small, low ridge, although the ridges may not be visible until the covering material is scraped aside. Deeper burrows are also constructed, some to a depth of at least 18". Nests are in an enlarged portion of the burrow and are made of fine, dry grass, root fibers, or leaves. They are underground, often under an old stump or log. The woodland vole has fewer natural predators than meadow or prairie voles, since it is a burrower. However, hawks and owls prey on woodland voles, indicating considerable aboveground activity. Seven species of owls, four of hawks, the red fox, gray fox, mink, raccoon, opossum, domestic cat, and rat snake all have been known as predators of woodland voles.

SELECTED REFERENCES. Benton 1955; Hamilton 1938; Pascal 1974; Smolen 1981.

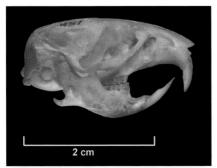

Side view of skull

Ventral view of skull and lower jaw

Woodland vole. *Photo by Roger Barbour*

Muskrat
Ondatra zibethicus (Linnaeus)

Distinguishing Features and Measurements: The muskrat is a vole (Arvicolinae), the largest of the cricetid rodents in Indiana. It is a chunky, dark reddish-brown animal, with a long, essentially naked, scaly, laterally compressed tail. The pelage is dense and shiny, especially in winter, and consists of a thick coat of underfur over which lies a covering of long, glossy guard hairs. The ears and eyes are relatively small for an animal of this size. The feet and tail are dark. The hind feet bear webbed toes and are much larger than the front feet. The anterior faces of the upper incisors are yellowish-orange. Several albinos have been found in Indiana and also some individuals that were uniformly pale tan.

TL 470–631, T 200–273, HF 70–95, Wt. 800–1,525. Males average 1,215 grams and adult females average 1,247 grams.

Skull: Length: 61–69 (2.4–2.8").
Dental Formula:

$$I \frac{1}{1} \quad C \frac{0}{0} \quad P \frac{0}{0} \quad M \frac{3}{3} = 16$$

Habitat: Marshes and other water areas with an abundance of emergent vegetation are the preferred habitats of muskrats, but the species also occurs along streams and ditches and about lakes and ponds, sometimes even in small ponds that may later dry up. Predominant plants at Willow Slough Fish and Wildlife Area (Newton County) in areas with the most productive muskrat populations, in decreasing order, were cattail/bur reed, cattail predominantly, cattail with some bulrush, and duck potato/sedge/water lily (with no cattail). A good stand of cattails and water of sufficient depth are the most important characteristics of the best muskrat habitat.

Food: Muskrats are primarily vegetarian but will eat animal matter, even carrion, under certain conditions. Probably most emergent plants in a muskrat marsh are eaten by the animals, but cattails, bur reed, bulrush, water lilies, pondweeds, smartweeds, duck potato, water plantain, rice cutgrass, hornwort, sedges, grasses, swamp loosestrife, buttonbush, and woolgrass have been specifically mentioned. Other plant foods include red clover, wheat, corn, apples, parsnips, beets, carrots, turnips, and leaves of various tree saplings including willow. The bark or roots are consumed from several of the plants listed above. Two muskrats were observed feeding at the surface on duckweed, *Lemna trisulca,* at Summit Lake, Henry County, late in the afternoon on 5 November 1998. They would swim using a gathering motion to rake in a mass of it. After about four of these motions, they would hold it in their forepaws and gobble it in. One of the muskrats did this for a good 30 minutes, then both entered the same lodge. Muskrats feed on corn that is in the milk stage; sometimes even carrying the corn stalks or ears back to their houses. They may forage up to 150 yards for corn or fallen apples. Animal foods include winter-killed fishes, frogs, crayfishes, and various species of mussels; dead ducks, geese, coots, chickens, and turtles. In winter, muskrats may dive through cracks in the ice to obtain mussels. The animals emerge with a mussel and sit on the edge of the ice on their haunches. They manipulate the shell with their forefeet with much chewing and clawing, usually, but not always, managing to open the shell. They apparently insert their claws or teeth between the valves in such a way as to cut or tear loose the adductor muscle.

Reproduction: Pair formation is initiated mostly by the female, who swims back and forth before the male while uttering squeaking notes. Courtship begins in February and copulation has been observed as early as 10 March. Gestation is about 28–30 days, with first litters in late April produced in dry, warm nests of soft vegetation in houses or burrows. Most young are probably born in May and June, but there are records of gravid females in late fall and even in early winter. Litters range from 3 to 10, averaging about 6. Young at birth are blind, nearly naked, and weigh about 22 grams. Their eyes open at 2 weeks. The young swim about when 3 weeks old but have difficulty diving. At about 4 weeks, they are weaned and on their own at a weight of about 200 grams. The young are driven from the house or burrow and must find new living quarters when a female produces a second litter. Females usually produce two or three litters per season. The young from the last litter may stay with the parents until the next breeding season.

Range: The muskrat is common throughout the state in suitable habitat but is most abundant in northern Indiana, where lakes and marshes are most numerous.

Habits and Comments: The muskrat is mostly nocturnal but also is active by day, especially in spring and fall. It spends most of the daylight hours in its burrows or houses. The houses are the most conspicuous indicators of the muskrat's presence on a marsh. Houses are built in shallow water (1–2') of emergent and submergent vegetation, cattail being a favorite when available. Houses are roughly circular; they average from 4 to 5' in diameter at the water level and extend 2–3' above the water surface. They have walls about 1–1.5' thick. Inside the house is an irregularly shaped chamber above the water level. An underwater entrance leads to this chamber and serves as a plunge hole into which the muskrat dives when danger threatens. Nests are of dry, shredded cattail leaves when available, but bur reed, bulrushes, rice cutgrass, watershield, woolgrass, smartweed,

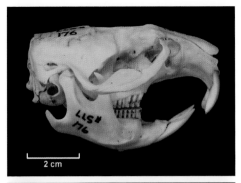
Side view of skull

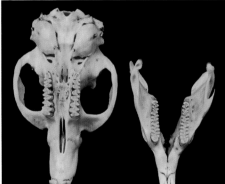
Ventral view of skull and lower jaw

Muskrat. *Photo by Roger Barbour*

hornwort, and other plants also may be used. House sites are often on a stump, in or on some brush, about a tree, along a fence, or on or about some other object. When no such foundation is present, muskrats cut vegetation and make a raft, which sinks to the bottom and serves as an anchor for the rest of the house.

House construction is primarily in spring, late summer, and early fall. Houses are built in one or two nights and do not persist for more than a season unless they are well anchored to some durable object and constantly repaired. Rain, wind, and waves quickly destroy them, and the material from which they are made rots rapidly. In the spring, some new houses are built and others are repaired for rearing of the young. One to 10 animals may occupy a house, but 4–5 is usual. In the breeding season, only one pair is found per house.

In deeper or flowing water, bank burrows are commonly used. The tunnels lead backward and are sloped upward and enlarged into a chamber at the end, where the nest is constructed. A small passage then leads from this chamber to the surface of the ground above. Burrows usually extend 15–20' in a straight line. Where muskrats live for some time, they tend to enter and leave the water repeatedly at certain places, forming "slides." In muddy areas, the footprints, and the drag mark made by the tail, can be seen.

Many muskrats spend their entire lives within a radius of 200 yards of their birthplace, but in late summer and fall, and sometimes in spring, individuals wander and some have been observed more than a mile from water. This prevents overcrowding on the home marsh and is a mechanism for dispersal. Muskrats are quite vulnerable to predation at that time, and many are killed by automobiles.

Muskrats remain active under the ice in winter, taking advantage of air trapped between the ice and the water. They enter and leave the water where the current prevents freezing, where the ice is broken, or where spaces occur in ice enclosing a tree or other object. Muskrats in winter may form feeding structures, called "push-ups," on top of the ice. The animal must first gnaw a hole through the ice from the underside, sometimes at the site of an air bubble. The hole is enlarged so that the muskrat can crawl through it. Then the animal collects masses of submerged vegetation and constructs a small house over the hole, leaving space enough to sit on the edge of the ice inside the shelter to feed. The wet vegetation soon freezes and forms a protective feeding shelter until warmer weather quickly destroys it. At other times, the animals commonly use feeding platforms, small semifloating rafts of cut vegetation resting on bent-over, uncut emergent plants. Such structures are usually roughly 12–15" in diameter.

On warm afternoons muskrats may sun themselves on logs, feeding platforms, or other structures. If disturbed, they plunge into the water and swim to a burrow, or they may remain submerged, coming to the water's surface at brief intervals and showing only their eyes and nose. A swimming muskrat's path can often be traced by a line of air bubbles in its wake. A cornered muskrat may put up a good fight, whether confronted by dog or man. Much fighting takes place in spring at the onset of reproductive activities. Only 10–15% of muskrats reach an age of 1 year; of those that do, some live to their fourth year.

Minks are important predators on muskrats and may enter muskrat houses by making a hole through the side into the central cavity. Dogs are especially destructive in late summer at low water when the houses are more accessible. Raccoons obtain mostly young muskrats by tearing holes in the sides of houses. Heavy rains, winds, and waves and high water may destroy houses and drown the young. Highway kills are numerous, especially where heavily traveled roads border good muskrat habitat. Drainage, however, is the main threat to the species, and severe drought may dry up habitats, causing the animals to become more and more crowded as water recedes; finally, after much friction because of lack of space, the animals may abandon an area completely. Shallow water that freezes to the bottom in winter causes many problems, since muskrats generally do not store food for winter. They may not be able to dig for roots and other foods and may starve if ice persists for long periods.

SELECTED REFERENCES. Brooks 1959; Butler 1885; Willner et al. 1980.

Muskrat house, Vigo County

Southern Bog Lemming
Synaptomys cooperi Baird

Distinguishing Features and Measurements: The southern bog lemming is a small vole with a very short, sparsely furred tail (about the length of the hind foot) and with shallow grooves on the upper incisors. The ears are short and the eyes are small. The upperparts are yellowish-brown to cinnamon brown, grizzled with blackish. The underparts are silvery. This species can be separated from all other Indiana rodents except *Microtus pinetorum* by its short tail and from *M. pinetorum* by its grooved upper incisors.

TL 99–135, T 13–27, HF 15–20, Wt. 20–52

Skull: Length: 24.3–27.1 (1.0–1.1").

This is the only Indiana vole with longitudinally grooved incisors; the grooves are shallow and you must look carefully to see them. Also the angles of the triangles of the molariform teeth are sharply pointed in *Synaptomys;* they are much more rounded in *Microtus.*

Dental Formula:

$$\text{I } \frac{1}{1} \text{ C } \frac{0}{0} \text{ P } \frac{0}{0} \text{ M } \frac{3}{3} = 16$$

Habitat: Despite the vernacular name, *Synaptomys cooperi* is rarely trapped in bogs or other wet areas. Most individuals from Indiana are in grassy fields, especially fields containing bluegrass or little bluestem. A few were taken in wet areas as follows: in an old cranberry bog (Warren County), tamarack area; along the outlet from a pond, where the soil was saturated and water stood in some of the runways; along the river bank at the edge of a tamarack swamp (Lagrange County).

Food: Green plants, especially bluegrass and other grasses, are favored summer foods. Roots of these plants are heavily eaten in winter along with quantities of tuberous roots such as those of wild artichoke stored for winter. Besides green vegetation, one bog lemming contained 90% fungus (*Hymenogaster*); another contained 100% grass seeds. When feeding, *Synaptomys* cuts plant stems into pieces about 3" long. Other voles also produce similar, but usually shorter, cuttings. The animals stand on their hind legs to reach up and cut the grasses and other plants; the plant then drops down and the voles cut off successive sections. Bog lemming runways often contain bright green fecal pellets.

Reproduction: Gestation is about 23 days. Breeding may occur from February or March to December; a lactating

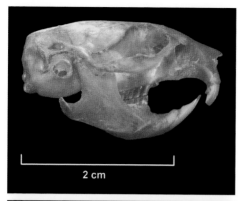
Side view of skull

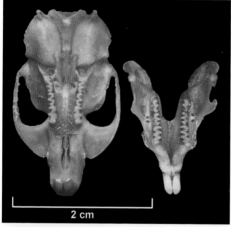
Ventral view of skull and lower jaw

Southern bog lemming. *Photo by R. Wayne Van Devender*

female was taken on 22 January from Benton County. Embryo counts ranged from 2 to 6 and averaged 3.25.

Range: This vole appears to be abundant only in small, local areas, although one must take into account that it is a difficult animal to trap. It seldom is attracted to bait. Some idea of relative abundance of bog lemmings to other voles can be inferred from the analyses of owl pellets. The remains of 13 bog lemmings were found in 145 pellets of the barn owl, 3 in 83 pellets of the long-eared owl, and 1 in 102 pellets of the great horned owl. Comparable figures for prairie voles and meadow voles from the same samples were 121 in 71 barn owl pellets, 95 in 22 long-eared owl pellets, and 63 in 1 great horned owl pellet. The species may be fairly easy to obtain in a locality one year and be impossible to catch there the following year. It is not known if this represents a cyclic population phenomenon or whether the animals move about in search of optimum habitat.

Habits and Comments: Bog lemmings have been trapped during the day and at night, but little is known about this species. It uses the runways constructed by *Microtus* and in some sites makes its own runways in bluegrass. In Jackson County, such runs alternately were beneath the fallen grass and on top of it. The runways were not bare, as is usually the case in *Microtus,* but were lined with living bluegrass. *Microtus* was absent at this site.

During the daytime, bog lemmings often hide beneath objects lying on the ground. Nests are under cover, often in hollow logs or stumps, and composed of fine grasses. Mumford observed a bog lemming that spent several weeks during the fall in a nest under a large sheet of corrugated metal roofing lying on the ground. The nest was nearly globular and composed of dry grasses. Runways radiated out under the roofing from the nest to the surrounding grassy areas.

Bog lemming remains have been identified in the pellets of the barn owl, long-eared owl, and great horned owl, and also in unidentified fox droppings. Several have been found dead along roads, where they may have been left by predators or struck by vehicles.

Selected References. Connor 1959; Linzey 1983.

The Muridae, or Old World rats and mice, include (in our area) the introduced house mouse (*Mus musculus*) and the introduced Norway rat (*Rattus norvegicus*). In the species included, the cheek teeth are rooted and their cusps, or tubercles, are arranged in 3 longitudinal rows.

Norway Rat
Rattus norvegicus (Berkenhout)

Distinguishing Features and Measurements: The Norway rat is a relatively large, well-known rodent, but there is some confusion in Indiana regarding its color variations and distinguishing it from the woodrat. The Norway rat usually has grayish upperparts, more or less grizzled with black. However, some individuals tend to be reddish or more brownish, and the amount of black varies. Some individuals are completely blackish. The underparts are usually gray (sometimes buffy or whitish) and tend to be darkest in those animals with blackish upperparts. The scaly tail is nearly naked and is almost as long as the head and body length combined. The ears and eyes are relatively small. The woodrat looks like a very large *Peromyscus,* has large ears and eyes, a furred tail (gray above, white below). Its color is brownish above and white below in adults, and it occurs only along the Ohio River bluffs in Harrison and Crawford counties.

TL 320–450, T 125–190, HF 30–45, Wt. 200–490

The largest individual we have seen was a captive male, originally trapped in the wild, that weighed 651 grams and measured 489 mm in total length when killed.

Skull: Length: 42–45 (1.7–1.8").

The skull of the Norway rat has 3 rows of cusps on the grinding surfaces of the cheek teeth; the woodrat has 2 rows.

Dental Formula:

$$\text{I } \frac{1}{1} \quad \text{C } \frac{0}{0} \quad \text{P } \frac{0}{0} \quad \text{M } \frac{3}{3} = 16$$

Habitat: Rattus norvegicus is usually associated with man and his activities. Thus, large populations of Norway rats are found in cities (in sewers, about garbage, and in trash dumps), about grain and other food storage facilities, and in and about farm buildings. In earlier years, before sanitary landfill methods were used to dispose of garbage, Norway rat populations at dumps increased rapidly and were periodically kept under control by poisoning. Local residents often visited the dumps to shoot rats, frequently killing dozens in a day. They are also found in and about the borders of cultivated fields, along ditch banks, and in other areas some distance from human habitations. These "feral" populations are much smaller than those associated with more abundant food, cover, and protection.

Food: Norway rats will eat garbage or almost anything edible. Rats from Indiana on and around farms and grain storage areas feed on grain, particularly wheat and corn. This is processed grain, not that left in the field after harvesting. Most other food items are of plant origin. The volume of animal material (mostly flesh) totaled about 8%.

Reproduction: The reproductive rate of the Norway rat is very high, with breeding occurring throughout most of the year. In suitable conditions, this rat can quickly reach a high population level. Gestation is about 21 days. Some females examined had both embryos and placental scars. One female contained 17 embryos; another contained 39 placental scars, which indicates that four separate litters were probably represented. Ten gravid females averaged 8.3 embryos.

Range: There is little in the literature regarding the Norway rat in Indiana, as it is not an animal that people are interested in, except for its destructive habits. The Norway rat is abundant throughout Indiana, but numerical data regarding populations are lacking.

Habits and Comments: This rat is likely to be found living beneath buildings, especially grain storage bins (and corncribs), where it excavates extensive burrow systems and creates a maze of well-used runways. Corncribs are sometimes literally undermined with a network of burrows and tunnels. Runways are often along the base of the building walls and when used enough are barren paths. Burrows are numerous when a thriving colony is extant; they usually have mounds of excavated earth at their entrances. Burrows may be dug to a depth of 18"; they are usually 3–4' long but may reach 6'. The Norway rat is essentially nocturnal, but considerable activity also takes place during the day, particularly at dusk and dawn. The tracks of this species can be found in the mud along streams and ditches, and Norway rats have been caught in muskrat traps set 2" below the surface of the water.

Rats do much gnawing, making holes in walls, at the corner of doors, in foundations, and in other wooden structures. They may enter buildings by enlarging holes through which pipes have been run. Where the animals are numerous, dark stains will be found about holes gnawed through the wood. Rats tend to strew garbage, food refuse, and other materials about, and the plentiful droppings are deposited anywhere except in the nest area.

Norway rats generally forage on the ground but have been known to reach the upper floors (and attics) of buildings. They are good

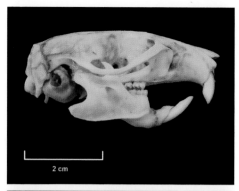
Side view of skull

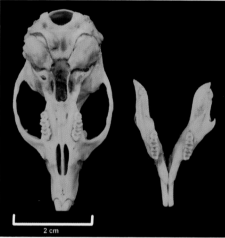
Ventral view of skull and lower jaw

Norway rat. *Photo by R. Wayne Van Devender*

swimmers, which probably enables them to live and travel in sewers, sometimes even getting into water lines. They have been known to surface inside toilet bowls in occupied houses. Adults are wary and are often difficult to trap. The Norway rat is a hardy, adaptable, and aggressive species.

Nests are constructed in a variety of sites, such as at the end of a ground burrow, in a hollow wall of a building, beneath a building or other large object, and in piles of rubbish, boxes, or other items offering suitable protection. Nests are loosely constructed and may consist of any soft materials, such as shredded vegetation, paper, cloth, or insulation.

In general, Norway rats are highly detrimental. In addition to direct food consumption, they spoil and contaminate foodstuffs and grain and cause other types of damage. For example, they chew or destroy stored clothing, furs, carpeting, leather goods, meats, insulation, and other items. Gnawing on wires increases the fire hazard, and gnawing lead water pipes may affect water systems. In dwellings, woodwork, doors, floors, and other wooden parts may be damaged by gnawing. The only benefit that humans derive from this common and widely despised pest is in use of countless specimens of the laboratory white rat (a mutant of this species) that has contributed so much to biological research throughout the world.

Norway rat remains have been identified in the pellets of the barn owl and the great horned owl. No doubt other avian predators prey on this species. Dogs and domestic cats are perhaps the most important predators in Indiana, because most rat populations are in proximity to man and his pets. Other known predators include the badger, gray fox, and black rat snake. Man is certainly the worst enemy of this rat, and constant poisoning campaigns have been waged in attempts to keep rats under control. Immediately after the harvesting of grain crops in the fall, there is an increase in the numbers of rats killed on roads by motor vehicles.

Selected References. Pisano and Storer 1948; Silver 1927; Whitaker 1977.

House Mouse
Mus musculus Linnaeus

Distinguishing Features and Measurements: The house mouse is a gray-ish, medium-sized, long-tailed, long-eared mouse with a nearly naked tail. It tends to be much the same color above and below, but there are many variations and numerous individuals are paler on the underside than above. The house mouse is most likely to be confused with the white-footed mouse, deer mouse, or western harvest mouse. The three latter species have a white or whitish belly, rather than grayish, and all have more hair on the tail than the house mouse. The familiar laboratory white mouse is an albinistic strain of the house mouse.

TL 140–192, T 58–95, HF 17–21, Wt. 15–28

Skull: Length: 20.4–22.5 (0.8–0.9").

The house mouse can also be separated from those listed above by its 3 rows of cusps on the grinding surfaces of the molariform teeth, rather than 2 rows (see Fig. 22 in key). The harvest mouse has deeply grooved upper incisors.

Dental Formula:

$$I \ \frac{1}{1} \quad C \ \frac{0}{0} \quad P \ \frac{0}{0} \quad M \ \frac{3}{3} \ = \ 16$$

Habitat: Most authors writing about the house mouse in Indiana have mentioned its occurrence in buildings, but as early as 1907, Hahn noted that *Mus* was found "in the fields as well as in buildings" along the Kankakee River, and McAtee (1907) observed that this mouse inhabited fields near Bloomington. It is certainly common about rural, suburban, or city buildings and about garbage dumps and other debris-laden habitats. Away from buildings, it is primarily a species of cultivated fields where adequate cover exists. It is abundant in corn-fields with much grassy and weedy vegetation in and between the rows. It perhaps reaches its greatest abundance in winter wheat fields or in wheat fields in the spring and early summer after the wheat has formed dense cover, or in clover or alfalfa fields with dense vegetation. The species is also sometimes abundant in fields allowed to lie fallow for 1–2 years, especially if dense stands of foxtail, pigweed, and other early successional plant species associated with farming operations form good cover. It is essentially an opportunistic migrant, moving into an area when short-term, dense vegetation occurs, but disappearing when the vegetation is removed. Its ideal habitat is in agricultural lands where crops are grown in a relatively short time, then harvested. Habitats with woody vegetation are generally avoided. In the only two noncultivated habitats that the species regularly occupies (weedy field and grassy field), populations are highest from November through February and lowest from March through August. House mice need much ground cover and move into these fields in winter but return to cultivated habitats in summer. Some house mice enter buildings in the fall, but most move to other areas with adequate ground cover. The great fall increase in *Mus* populations in weedy fields and grassy fields is a result of that movement.

Food: Various seeds, especially those of grasses, collectively made up 42% of the diet of house mice from Vigo County, with seeds of foxtail grass (*Setaria*) being the single most important food (20% of the food by volume and appearing in a quarter of the animals). Seeds of cultivated plants—corn, wheat, sorghum, and soybeans—collectively constituted 23%. Animal foods constituted 24% of all foods, with caterpillars being the most important, and the second most important single item overall, accounting for 15% of all food. Important foods in soybean fields were foxtail seeds, caterpillars, and Johnson grass seeds. Soybeans made up only 3.5% of the volume, while soybeans were the major food for the deer mouse in this habitat. In wheat fields, caterpillars and wheat seeds were the major foods; the major food in sorghum fields was sorghum seed. In corn or wheat stubble, food habits of the house mouse and the deer mouse were rather similar, with corn being most important, followed by caterpillars. Corn is available in Indiana fields throughout the year, at least to a degree, but is particularly important in winter, after it has matured and been harvested. At that time there is much loose corn and even whole ears on the ground.

Reproduction: House mice may produce litters throughout much of the year, with cessation in midwinter. Litter size is from 3 to 10, averaging about 6. Smaller litters are produced during early spring (average 4.7) than during the summer and fall (average 6.4), probably relating to the better habitat for house mice during the agricultural productive season.

Range: The house mouse is an introduced Old World species and occurs throughout the state. There is no record of when it came to Indiana, but it may have arrived about the time of the first European settlers. In 1965, the house mouse was the most common small mammal in Indiana. It was found in all agricultural habitats with good herbaceous ground cover. However, it left an area when the crops were harvested or whenever the cover was removed. Today the house mouse may be less abundant, as it is dependent upon good cover, and the recent

widespread herbicide use on cultivated fields has greatly reduced cover.

Habits and Comments: The house mouse is mostly nocturnal. It usually does not make conspicuous runways but uses the runs of other small mammals. It is a good climber, jumper, and swimmer. House mice

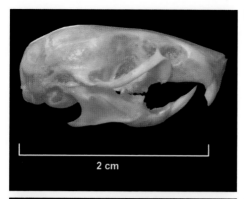

Side view of skull

Ventral view
of skull and
lower jaw

House mouse. *Photo by Roger Barbour*

invade all types of buildings in fall and early winter, but many or most move to other areas with adequate ground cover. Those inside buildings may do extensive damage, through gnawing on paper, cardboard, clothing, or other materials; consuming and spoiling various stored foods; leaving much litter about; and sometimes depositing abundant feces and urine. Also, the characteristic odor of this mouse frequently pervades the atmosphere of buildings where large populations occur. *Mus* is difficult to exclude from buildings, for it can enter very small openings, and it can sometimes be difficult to control. Nests are found in underground burrows, in rubbish, or in buildings, and are usually loose, rather globular masses of grasses, to which have been added feathers, mammal hair, shredded paper, cloth, or other soft materials. The usual sound made by the house mouse is a short, high-pitched squeak.

SELECTED REFERENCES. Evans 1949; Whitaker 1966, 1967a.

FAMILY DIPODIDAE

SUBFAMILY ZAPODINAE—*Jumping Mice*

Representatives of this subfamily are found in the northern portions of the New and Old World. They are characterized by a very large infraorbital foramen, which allows passage of muscles and nerves and, in one of the two North American genera, *Zapus,* by the presence of 4 upper cheek teeth. The woodland jumping mouse, *Napaeozapus,* has only 3. The incisors are compressed and deeply grooved. These animals are mouselike, but are distinguished by an extraordinarily long tail and very long hind feet, which are adapted for leaping.

Jumping mice are found in forests, swamps, and meadows and are often common. They are profound hibernators. These mice were originally described in the family Dipodidae, and then were placed in their own family, the Zapodidae, but work by Stein (1990) and Stenbrot (1992) places them as the subfamily Zapodinae, back in the family Dipodidae.

Meadow Jumping Mouse
Zapus hudsonius (Zimmermann)

Distinguishing Features and Measurements: Medium-sized, yellowish mouse with very long, thin tail, much longer than the body length. Mid-dorsal region yellowish-brown, sides yellowish, underparts white, ears small and rounded. The hind feet are elongated and much larger than the front feet. There are 3 large upper molariform teeth with a small ("peg") tooth anterior to these. Upper incisors are deeply grooved and covered with orange enamel. Infraorbital foramina are large and oval.

TL 180–225, T 105–140, HF 26–32, Wt. 12–25

Skull: Length: 20.8–23.4 (0.8–0.9").

Prominent yellow upper incisors with longitudinal grooves.

Dental Formula:

$$I \ \frac{1}{1} \ C \ \frac{0}{0} \ P \ \frac{1}{0} \ M \ \frac{3}{3} \ = \ 18$$

Habitat: Most often found in old fields or sometimes in woodland where there is much herbaceous ground cover. It is often found in moist situations, but this appears to be related to the lack of disturbance by man and the presence of ground cover, rather than directly to moisture. Sometimes abundant in dense stands of touch-me-not (*Impatiens*).

Food: Seeds are the mainstay of the diet with various kinds, especially grasses, being eaten progressively as they ripen. Seeds of *Impatiens* are heavily eaten when available. *Impatiens* seeds can be easily identified because their endosperm is turquoise in color. This mouse may obtain seeds from certain grasses (notably timothy) by reaching up as far as it can and cutting off the grass stem. It then grasps and pulls the stem down, then repeats the process until the seed head is reached; then it strips the seeds, leaving the rachis and glumes. It will also sometimes climb the grass stem, cutting off the top and bringing this to the ground to eat. Other seeds often eaten are those of chickweed, sheep sorrel, wood sorrel, pigweed, and knotweed. Fruits of strawberry, blackberry, and black cherry are also main foods. Tiny grapelike spores of the fungus *Endogone* make up about 12% of the diet. Caterpillars and other insects are eaten throughout the active season but especially in early spring.

Reproduction: Gestation is about 18 days. Litter size is three to seven young per litter. Young are produced mostly in June, July, and August, in nests of grass in a protected area on the surface or underground.

Range: Occurs throughout the state, but probably more common in the north.

Habits and Comments: Jumping mice may be locally abundant at times. On 9 May 1961, Russ Mumford and one of his Purdue classes saw 19 jumping mice and captured 7 by hand in an area 30 by 200 yards along a narrow, wooded floodplain of a creek in Tippecanoe County. In a small, brushy old field near Terre Haute, it was one of the most abundant small mammals. Many were trapped in stands of *Impatiens* and other heavy herbaceous vegetation along Mill Creek in Parke County. Most active at night, but abroad during the day, especially in spring. A flushed individual will usually make a few jumps of up to 2′ until it locates a safe hiding place. Summer nests are of grasses or leaves on top of or under the ground. *Zapus* makes no runways and leaves little sign of its presence, other than little piles of match-length grass stems and seed heads

Meadow jumping mouse. *Photo by Linda K. Castor*

when feeding on timothy and a few other grasses. It hibernates from mid-October to late April or early May. The latest fall date that *Zapus* has been found in Indiana is 20 November, and the earliest spring date is 4 April. Hibernating nests are usually in a bank or pile of debris. Whitaker found a jumping mouse in hibernation in December, in a nest of oak leaves about 2' below the surface in a cinder pile in Clay County. Another was found on 22 January, in a woodchuck burrow in a levee along the Wabash River. This nest was about 14 cm in diameter and was made entirely of the leaves of the grass *Festuca,* the principal plant on the levee.

SELECTED REFERENCES. Whitaker 1963, 1972a; Whitaker and Mumford 1971.

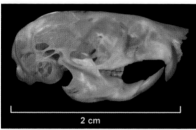
Side view of skull

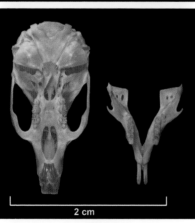
Ventral view of skull and lower jaw

Endogone, an important fungal food of the meadow jumping mouse and other small mammals.
Photo by Mark Oster

Order CARNIVORA—Flesh Eaters

FAMILY CANIDAE

Canis latrans / Coyote

Vulpes vulpes / Red Fox

Urocyon cinereoargenteus / Gray Fox

FAMILY PROCYONIDAE

Procyon lotor / Raccoon

FAMILY MUSTELIDAE

Lontra canadensis / River Otter

Mustela nivalis / Least Weasel

Mustela frenata / Long-tailed Weasel

Mustela vison / Mink

Taxidea taxus / Badger

FAMILY MEPHITIDAE

Mephitis mephitis / Striped Skunk

FAMILY FELIDAE

Lynx rufus / Bobcat

Order Carnivora

Carnivores are native throughout the world, except for Australia. (The dingo, which is actually a dog, is not native to Australia but was presumably brought to the continent long ago by human immigrants.) Today, there are 271 species of carnivores worldwide, in 129 genera and 11 families, including 34 species of pinnipeds (seals, walruses, and such) in 18 genera and 3 families.

Carnivores are characterized by teeth adapted for shearing and cutting. The incisors are small, but the canines are large and pointed and project well beyond the other teeth. Most carnivores also possess a pair of specialized shearing teeth, one in the upper jaw and another in the lower jaw on each side, known as the *carnassial* teeth. Usually there are 5 toes on each foot; these are invariably provided with claws, which are blunt in the dogs and bears but sharp and retractile in the cats.

As their name implies, carnivores are primarily flesh eaters, although many species, such as the raccoons, skunks, and foxes, eat large quantities of vegetation as well. Carnivores are far less abundant than the rodents and lagomorphs, on which most carnivores are largely dependent for sustenance.

We like to think of animals as having homes, as people do. Carnivores often do not. Other than for natal purposes, or for winter lodging (in those species that enter winter lethargy), few carnivores have nests that they use regularly. Rather, most use a nesting site once, or during a brief period when they are exploiting a particular food source, then move on.

Carnivores are often persecuted because they are perceived, rightly or wrongly, to be detrimental to humans, in particular by killing our stock or game animals. They have long been hunted and trapped; man has himself been the predator, the mortal enemy of many of them. But unlike other predators, man continues to hunt certain desired or unwanted species as long as they exist, even to extirpation or extinction. Thus many of the carnivores are extirpated early.

Many carnivores have been important to the fur trade. Recently, however, there has been a great decline in trapping, primarily because of pressures that have been brought to bear against the purchasing of furs. These pressures have come about mostly from the efforts of environmentalists and people concerned for the rights of animals. When growing awareness led to a reticence on the part of the public to buy items containing fur, the bottom fell out of the fur market. This change of attitude has extended beyond the furbearers. It is certainly warranted for some species. Others, such as the black bear, bobcat, and river otter, need complete protection in some areas but not in others. Still others, such as the raccoon and such noncarnivores as the beaver and the white-tailed deer, have often exceeded the carrying capacity of the land and are in need of control over much of their range. Hunting and trapping are good ways to effect control. The management of our animal resources is complicated by social issues. We cannot simply preserve the habitat and leave the animals alone. For example, since we have eliminated the traditional predators of deer in Indiana, the mountain lion and the wolf, a cessation of deer hunting leads to overpopulation of deer. Destruction of habitat then ensues and affects many animal and plant species of the area. Deer need to be controlled, and hunting or controlled shooting is usually the best way to do it.

Five families, embracing 11 species of Carnivora, are represented in Indiana: the dogs (Canidae, 3 species), raccoons (Procyonidae, 1), weasels (Mustelidae, 5), skunks (Mephitidae, 1), and cats (Felidae, 1).

FAMILY CANIDAE

This family in Indiana contains two species of foxes (in two separate genera) and the coyote of the genus *Canis* besides the domestic dog. Canids have 42 teeth, well-developed canines, shearing carnassial teeth (the fourth upper premolar and first lower molar), and crushing surfaces on the teeth behind the carnassials. There are five toes on the forefeet, four on the hind; the claws are blunt and nonretractile.

Coyote
Canis latrans Say

Distinguishing Features and Measurements: Coyotes are doglike with pointed noses and ears and tan to whitish legs and feet. The outsides of the ears are reddish or rusty-colored. The body may be mostly gray, yellowish-gray, or reddish-gray, mixed with varying amounts of black above; the throat and undersides are whitish or grayish. The tail is quite bushy and relatively short; above, it usually is similar in color to the back but may be more grayish with a blackish spot on the dorsal surface near the base. It may have a black tip. The underside of the tail is paler than the dorsal surface.

TL 1,100–1,450, T 290–395, HF 180–220, WT 11–21 kg

Skull: Length: 175–208 (7–8.3").

The coyote, red fox, gray fox, and raccoon all have 6 upper molariform teeth on each side. The raccoon skull is much smaller (short rostrum and rounded braincase) than coyote or fox skulls. The coyote skull is considerably larger than that of either fox. Fox skulls have dorsal crests divided anteriorly; the coyote skull has a single dorsal crest. Coyote skulls are most likely to be confused with skulls of the domestic dog, or with coyote-dog (coydog) hybrids. The distance between the first 2 molariform teeth divided into the length of the molariform toothrow is usually about 3.7 in the coyote, less than 3.0 in dogs, and from 3.1 to 3.6 in hybrids (coydogs). However, coydogs are much less frequent than earlier.

Dental Formula:

$$I \frac{3}{3} \quad C \frac{1}{1} \quad P \frac{4}{4} \quad M \frac{2}{3} = 42$$

Habitat: Waste areas with dense, low vegetation are good coyote habitats in Indiana. Near Lafayette, a family of coyotes lived in a rather extensive brushy series of old gravel pits in the late summer of 1972. Coyotes are also often found in forest. Coyotes often use edge situations, and cornfields are important habitats, especially in fall. Cornfields were used during periods of activity and inactivity, and during the day and night. Coyotes make only light use of soybean and hay fields, because of reduced food and cover there.

Food: Coyotes can subsist on a wide variety of animals (mostly mammals). A considerable amount of food is taken as carrion. Some plant materials are also eaten, including various fruit in summer. The most prevalent items among 47 food items eaten by the coyote in Indiana were small voles and mice, swine, and eastern cottontails together constituting 70.4% of the total volume of stomach contents. Grass occurred in about half. Birds were not uncommon but also were of low volume. Nearly half of all scats collected in fall contained insects, and 39.7% of summer scats held plant remains other than grass. Short-tailed shrews, although common, were almost never eaten, probably because of a smell or taste aversion. A similar aversion possibly exists for house mice.

The coyote captures small prey by pouncing upon it with its feet, but usually kills larger prey by rushing it from the front and slashing the throat, killing with the canine teeth. Coyotes often hunt in groups of three or four. After feeding on a large kill, they may partially cover it for later use. Cottontails are usually the dietary staple when available, but small rodents, especially voles, are important. Numerous complaints of coyotes killing livestock are received, but many of these killings are actually due to dogs. It is difficult to determine after the fact whether a coyote or dog is responsible for damage to livestock, although dog owners and farmers may be quick to blame coyotes. There is no doubt that the coyote is capable of killing poultry and small livestock. Dogs and coyotes or coydogs kill in a similar fashion, and distinguishing between tracks is practically impossible at a kill unless you can find a series of tracks. A coyote puts the hind foot in the front claw print, producing a single line of prints like a cat. A dog produces an alternating series. When swine remains are found in stomachs, the question arises as to whether it was prey or carrion, which can seldom be answered with certainty, but it is usually the result of feeding on carrion.

Reproduction: The height of the breeding season is January and February, with possibly a few adults breeding in December and some juveniles breeding in March. Therefore, pups could be born from March through early May, with whelping probably heaviest in early April. A mated pair remains together for prolonged periods—perhaps even life. Gestation is about 60–63 days. One litter, averaging five to seven young, is produced each year. The young are usually born in underground burrows, sections of which are enlarged to form a chamber about 3' in diameter. Dens are frequently constructed on knolls or other elevated places, probably allowing the adults to detect potential danger more easily.

Range: The coyote originally occurred in northwestern and parts of western Indiana in good numbers. The coyote was never extirpated but persisted despite persecution by settlers. Coyotes began to increase noticeably in the early 1960s and blossomed in the 1970s. Coyotes now occur throughout Indiana, having successfully invaded the hilly, wooded south central portion in recent times. Since the mid-1980s, there have been great increases in populations. Coyotes seldom call when populations are low. We never heard coyotes call in Indiana until the

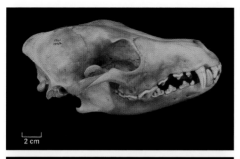
Side view of skull

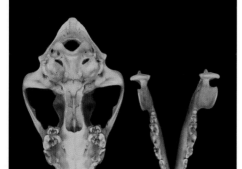
Ventral view
of skull and
lower jaw

Coyote in Eagle Creek Park, Indianapolis. *Photo by Bill Brink*

mid-1980s, but coyotes calling are now commonplace in many parts of Indiana. Our roadkill data clearly indicate that the coyote has greatly increased in number, as well. No coyotes were included among 692 roadkills in 1972–1974, whereas in 2000–2001, 26 of 2,913 roadkills (0.9%) were coyotes. On the fur market, no coyote pelts were taken until 1960, when three were taken. Not until 1971 were coyotes regularly purchased by fur buyers.

Habits and Comments: Coyotes are fully capable of interbreeding with dogs, especially when coyotes are uncommon and they cannot find mates. From the 1960s to the 1980s, there was an increased number of records of coyote-dog hybrids (coydogs). Some of these hybrids were quite large (50 lbs), and many residents mistakenly believed that these animals were gray wolves. Since all degrees of dog or coyote characteristics may occur in any particular hybrid, some interesting and puzzling individuals are sometimes produced. Unlike dogs, male coyotes help care for the young, so a female coyote that breeds with a dog puts herself at a great disadvantage as compared to other female coyotes. Also, coyotes have a specific breeding season, whereas dogs do not. Therefore coyote and dog have to come together during a narrow window of time. Coydogs are thus heavily selected against, and now that coyotes are common, few coydogs are produced. More information is needed, but the coyote may have an adverse effect on other species, particularly rabbits, foxes, and woodchucks. Coyotes are often nocturnal, spending the day bedded down in the cover of a brushy area, fencerow, stubble field, weed field, or cornfield. However, they are often seen during the day, when they will move about. We have often observed them hunting during daylight hours. They will move from patch to patch of good grassy cover where they can capture meadow voles, a behavior also common to red foxes.

Most observations of coyotes are of single animals or small groups, but there have been some reports of larger assemblages. One difficulty in assessing observations of coyotes has been the determination of whether the observer saw a coyote, a dog, or a dog-coyote hybrid. Coyotes usually carry the tail straight but slanting downward.

Dens are usually burrows in the ground. Coyotes may dig their own or modify a burrow system excavated by another mammal, such as a woodchuck. The den may be in a concealed site, such as under a stump, and have two or three entrances. Mounds of excavated soil are frequently found at burrow entrances. Once a den is established, it may be used for several years. Home ranges of five radio-collared coyotes ranged from 4.7 to 10.9 square miles. Three radio-collared coyotes were found 96 miles, 19.8 miles, and 79.8 miles away after leaving their home ranges. Man and the automobile are the major enemies of the coyote in Indiana.

Selected References. Bekoff 1977, 1978; Young and Jackson 1951.

Red Fox
Vulpes vulpes (Linnaeus)

Distinguishing Features and Measurements: The red fox is a bushy-tailed, doglike animal with a pointed muzzle and large, pointed ears. It is usually reddish with the tip of the tail white. The cheeks, throat, underparts, and insides of the ears are white. The "silver fox" is a variation in which the guard hairs are black with frosted or white tips. The "cross fox" shows a darkish band across the shoulders at right angles to the dark middorsal coloration, thus forming a cross.

TL 950–1,050, T 325–410, HF 140–180, Wt. 3.5–7.0 kg

Skull: Length: 134–156 (5.4–6.2").

Skulls of foxes, coyotes, and domestic dogs all have 6 upper and 7 lower molariform teeth. The coyote skull is much larger than those of either species of Indiana fox. The temporal ridges on the red fox skull meet posteriorly to form a V-shaped pattern (see Fig. 29 in key); these same ridges on the gray fox skull meet posteriorly to form a U-shaped pattern (see Fig. 28 in key).

Dental Formula:

$$I \ \frac{3}{3} \quad C \ \frac{1}{1} \quad P \ \frac{4}{4} \quad M \ \frac{2}{3} \ = \ 42$$

Habitat: The usual habitat is open, dry land, such as old fields, pastures, brushy tracts, farmland, and other unforested areas. Red foxes can occur even in rather intensively cultivated areas. They can find sufficient refuge in waste areas or fencerows and along railroads or ditch banks. They may frequently be seen (even in daytime) some distance from cover, in soybean stubble, in winter wheat, or on plowed ground. They make extensive use of forest edges and small woodlands and are able to penetrate into forested areas of Indiana along streams, roads, power lines, trails, cultivated sections, and other more open areas.

Food: The red fox hunts mainly by stealthily stalking its prey. Small mammals and birds are the main prey of foxes, followed by plant foods and insects. Plant foods consist mainly of a variety of berries and other fruits. Insects most often eaten are grasshoppers and beetles. Among the mice eaten are the meadow and woodland voles, the southern bog lemming, and shrews. Voles are eaten about twice as often as mice of the genus *Peromyscus*. We examined the stomach contents of 14 Indiana red foxes and found that the prairie vole occurred most frequently, followed by beetles (Scarabaeidae; Coleoptera), unidentified animal material, cottontail, and short-tailed shrew, in that order. Mice, rabbits, and other animals are often captured, either while resting or while moving about, by foxes pouncing on them. Prey is usually caught with the front feet and is quickly dispatched by biting behind the head. Songbirds are obtained while they are roosting. On three occasions, foxes passed within 10' of roosting bobwhites without disturbing the quail. Foxes captured rabbits in their forms by jumping on them.

Corn, berries, and other miscellaneous food items were eaten from plants or dug out of the snow. Foxes have often been persecuted for their habit of feeding on domestic poultry. Red foxes spend considerable time hunting about the water's edge. In fall and winter they dig about the edges of bales of hay left in the fields, searching for mice and voles.

Reproduction: Male and female red foxes may be seen traveling together in December, and copulation evidently begins during that month. Most young are born in late March or early April. Gestation is about 52 days. One litter per year is produced, usually consisting of three to six young, but up to nine may be produced. Interestingly even at birth most red foxes have the white tail tip. The eyes open at 10–12 days and the female remains in the den with them for the first 10 days, especially in northern areas. Mother and young are fed by the male during this time. Whelping dens are often on a sandy hillside and may be used year after year. They may later even be used by one of the mother fox's daughters. Whelping dens usually have several openings, the largest being about 10" in diameter.

Range: It is unknown when the red fox first appeared in Indiana, but it was introduced into the eastern United States by early settlers for hunting purposes. At present the red fox occurs in relatively low numbers in Indiana, probably because it is not faring well in competition with the coyote.

Habits and Comments: Except during the reproductive season, red foxes do not have permanent dens; rather they bed down at different places on different nights. Daytime beds are located in stubble fields, fallow fields, pastures, dry marsh borders, fencerows, thickets, and other sites providing cover. On sunny days, foxes often lie in the sun. On windy and colder days, they usually bed down on the lee side of a knoll, ditch bank, or gully. Activity does not cease in winter, and tracks of red foxes are commonly seen in the snow. Individual foxes may travel a considerable distance in a single night. Two juveniles equipped with radio transmitters moved 2.6 miles per night in early fall and an adult male moved 5.6 miles per night during January. These same juveniles occupied a common range of 0.64 square miles during the period they were radio-tagged, while the adult male occupied an area of approximately 1 square mile. Foxes often travel along old roads, ditch banks, fencerows, woods trails, railroads, and woodland borders, but they may move long distances over open fields with no cover, even in winter.

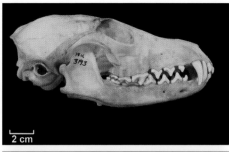

Side view of skull

Ventral view
of skull and
lower jaw

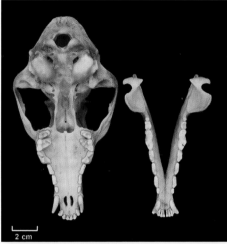

Red fox. *Photo by Roger Barbour*

Red foxes spend some time (especially during the breeding season) in ground burrows. Although foxes can excavate their own dens, they often take over a burrow system constructed by a woodchuck or other mammal and modify it for their own use. Dens have been observed in old fields, along fencerows, on grassy or wooded hillsides, along ditch banks, in pastured woodlots, on sandy knolls, in brushy thickets, in broken drainage tiles, under buildings, in oat fields, and in pastures. Den sites are normally well drained and no nesting material is carried into the den, which usually has at least two entrances. Burrow systems may be 20–25' long. Occupied red fox dens are characterized by a strong odor of fox urine and by the remnants of food items strewn about the entrance.

Foxes use many methods to throw dogs off their scent. These include doubling back along their trail, walking along the top of a rail fence and then jumping far to one side, and taking advantage of the terrain and various obstacles, natural or manmade, that may impede the progress of the pursuing dogs. The red fox has tremendous stamina and will lead dogs on chases that last for hours. Foxes have locations within their territories where they repeatedly urinate on some stick, post, stump, clump of grass, or other object to form scent markings. Such markings signify to other foxes that the particular locality is occupied by a resident fox. The usual call of the red fox is a "barking" sound, somewhat reminiscent of the call of a crow, but the fox also emits other sounds. Unlike most mammals, the red fox's ears are most sensitive to low sounds (about 3.5 kHz) rather than to higher pitches. This enables them to hear gnawing sounds or rustling in the leaves, as they spend much time listening for gnawing or movements of small

Young red fox near entrance to den. *Photo by Mark Stacy*

prey while waiting in ambush. This is why Henry (1986) refers to it as the "catlike canine." Red fox tracks are frequently noted in the soft, loose soil on the tops of large anthills. We do not know why, but they may be scent-marking stations. Red foxes often cache their prey. At five dens in Greene County and four dens in Dubois County were found remains of domestic chicken, cardinal, blue jay, eastern towhee, mourning dove, cottontail, fox squirrel, woodchuck, opossum, striped skunk, eastern mole, short-tailed shrew, *Peromyscus* sp., *Microtus* sp., house mouse, and box turtle.

Since about 1985, foxes appear to have decreased in Indiana, although the decrease shows mostly in the gray fox. Of 692 animals observed during a 1974 roadkill survey, 9 (1.3% of the animals) were foxes, 5 (0.72%) of the total sample of animals being red foxes, whereas in 2000–2001, 13, or 0.45% of 2,913 animals, were red foxes. This was at a time when hunting pressure was low. We think that when the wolf was eradicated in Indiana, the coyote had little competition. However, the coyote did not become abundant until the mid 1980s, partly due to decreased hunting pressure. We also think that increased coyotes have contributed to the decline in foxes, possibly due to competitive pressure for the same niche or den sites. Natural enemies of the red fox in Indiana are few, but hunting, trapping, dogs, and automobiles take their toll.

Selected References. Brooks 1959; Henry 1986; Hoffman and Kirkpatrick 1954; Larivière and Pasitschniak-Arts 1996.

Gray Fox
Urocyon cinereoargenteus (Schreber)

Distinguishing Features and Measurements: The gray fox is grizzled grayish above and on the sides with a whitish belly and throat. It is often confused with the red fox because it has a rather extensive rufous patch on either side of the throat. However, the red fox is entirely red except for white at the tip of its tail. The gray fox has a black mane along the upper surface of the tail, which has a black tip. The feet and legs are rusty-yellowish, similar to the color of the sides of the neck and the backs of the ears. The chin and the sides of the muzzle are black.

TL 875–1,065, T 300–440, HF 125–150, Wt. 119–130

Skull: Length: 119–130 (4.8–5.2").

The skull of the gray fox is most likely to be confused with that of the red fox, as they have the same number of teeth. The well-developed temporal ridges on the gray fox skull meet posteriorly to form a U shape (see Fig. 28 in key); the same ridges on the red fox skull meet posteriorly to form a V shape (see Fig. 29 in key).

Dental Formula:

$$I \ \frac{3}{3} \ \ C \ \frac{1}{1} \ \ P \ \frac{4}{4} \ \ M \ \frac{2}{3} \ = \ 42$$

Habitat: The gray fox prefers brushy and wooded habitats to the open areas that attract red foxes. Their relative abundance in southern Indiana is no doubt favored by the hilly, wooded terrain and the recent development of large areas of brushland on stripped coal lands and abandoned fields.

Food: F. D. Haller (1951) gathered information on winter food habits by following six fox trails in the snow in Greene County. He found evidence of foxes feeding on mice 21 times, songbirds 6, corn 5, pokeberry 1, and cottontail 1. At five gray fox dens with young, he found remains of 3 rabbits, 3 chickens, and a woodchuck. He noted that relatively little food was observed about the entrances, even when litters of young occupied the dens, in contrast to the red fox, which leaves animal parts strewn about its den. The five most important foods of 34 Indiana gray foxes, by percent volume, were corn, cottontail, prairie vole, meadow vole, and birds.

Reproduction: Copulation in gray foxes is mainly in January and February. Gestation is 51 days. There are three to four young per litter.

Range: The gray fox occurs throughout Indiana, but its numbers have decreased greatly, much more than those of the red fox. Four gray foxes occurred

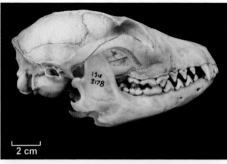

Side view of skull

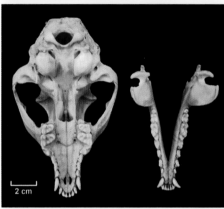

Ventral view
of skull and
lower jaw

Gray fox. *Photo by Roger Barbour*

among 692 roadkills in 1972–1974 (0.58%). In 2000–2001, only four gray foxes were recorded among 2,913 animals (0.14%), as compared to a projected 17 at 1972 rates. We think gray foxes have been adversely affected by the increase in coyotes, probably because of competition for den sites and habitat.

Habits and Comments: Relatively few gray foxes are seen by man. Daytime observations are by no means rare, but this species is mostly nocturnal and spends a considerable part of the day bedded down. Dens are used during the reproductive season, seldom the rest of the year. Using radio telemetry, the home range of an adult male (24 November–15 January) was estimated at 227 acres and that of an adult female (24 May–7 August) at 358 acres. Gray foxes live in burrows that they excavate themselves but also in rocky ledges, caves, and beneath buildings, piles of rocks, or similar structures. There are a few records of dens in the bases of hollow trees. The gray fox has frequently been observed in the low branches of trees, especially trees that lean, and one was seen walking along the top of a rail fence. Although the gray fox appears to spend little time near water, it may wade to cross small creeks.

The bark of the gray fox is similar to that of the red fox, but it has less volume. Another call is a loud, rather high-pitched yowling of about 2 seconds duration, repeated frequently. The call is difficult to describe but reminds one of an animal howling with pain. It is also somewhat similar to the calls given by some monkeys. Gray foxes can sometimes be called within close range by squeaking noises.

Man is the primary enemy of the gray fox, and through hunting, trapping, and poisoning has long waged campaigns aimed at decreasing fox populations.

SELECTED REFERENCES. Fritzell and Haroldson 1982; Haller 1951.

FAMILY PROCYONIDAE

There are about 17 species in seven genera in this remarkably diverse family. Except for the 2 species of pandas in Asia, which some think are not procyonids, all live in the New World. There are 3 species of this family in the United States—the coati, the ringtail, and the raccoon—but the raccoon is the only species found in Indiana.

The raccoon family evolved from the Canidae, the dogs. Most are medium-sized animals with long, ringed tails and pronounced facial markings, although the kinkajou, of Central and South America, is uniformly colored. The carnassial teeth of most carnivores are sharp, for shearing, but those of procyonids have evolved for crushing, as befits their omnivorous habits.

Raccoon
Procyon lotor (Linnaeus)

Distinguishing Features and Measurements: The raccoon is a rather chunky, grayish mammal with a black mask and a relatively long, bushy tail marked with alternate rings of black and pale (often yellowish) fur. The ears are rounded. The hind legs are noticeably longer than the front legs, so that raccoons walk in a rather peculiar position with the rump elevated above the front quarters. Pelage color varies considerably.

TL 700–925, T 220–260, HF 110–125, Wt. 6–20 kg

Skull: Length: 112–125 (4.5–5").

The raccoon skull has 6 upper and 6 lower molariform teeth; it is the only Indiana carnivore with 6 lower molariform teeth. Canids have 6 upper and 7 lower molariforms. Raccoon skulls are shorter (especially the rostrum) than canid skulls, and the posterior portion of the braincase is usually rounded, but low sagittal crests and supraoccipital ridges may be present on older animals.

Dental Formula:

$$I \frac{3}{3} \quad C \frac{1}{1} \quad P \frac{4}{4} \quad M \frac{2}{2} = 40$$

Habitat: Raccoons are most often encountered in wooded areas near water. They travel along small ditches and tiny creeks as well as lakes and the largest rivers. Tracks of this species seem always present in such places. The species also occupies grassland and farmland, where it finds shelter in drainage tiles, woodchuck burrows, or buildings. As Indiana forest areas diminished, and as the marshes and swamps were drained, many thought raccoons would be greatly decreased, but this has not been the case. The raccoon is adaptable and simply learned to live with man even in urban areas. Raccoons often live in attics, sheds, and barns, and it is not unusual to find them living in the largest cities

Food: The raccoon feeds on a great variety of plant and animal foods, including carrion and garbage. It will raid the garden or kill poultry. In spring, animal food is most important, especially crayfish, followed by insects and other invertebrates. In season, raccoons feast heavily on black cherry, grapes, pawpaw, giant ragweed, blackberry, and pokeweed, as evidenced by their seeds in scats. They also eat cultivated fruits and berries, persimmons, fish, snails, eggs, and small birds and mammals. In late summer, they may feed on crickets and grasshoppers. Apples and nuts, especially acorns, are favored fall foods. Sometimes a family of raccoons will cut acorns in the manner of squirrels, then descend to the ground to consume them. Vertebrates are not particularly important, but raccoons will feed on small vertebrates, such as young turtles or muskrats, when available, and they may dig up turtle eggs. Frogs are not eaten as often as one might expect, and salamanders are rarely eaten. Fish are often eaten when encountered in isolated pools, and raccoons will feed on freshwater mussels. Feeding in winter is mostly on acorns and corn, but invertebrates continue to be important. Raccoons have been known to remove the lids of wood duck nesting boxes and eat the eggs, ducklings, and even adults. From stomach contents, the most important foods of 41 Indiana raccoons were corn, earthworms, and mast. Vegetable material accounted for 66% of the total volume, insects 9.2%, other invertebrates 15.1%, and vertebrates 9.4%. In 66 raccoon scats examined by Lehman (1977) during summer and fall on the Jasper-Pulaski Fish and Wildlife Area, frequencies were crayfish, 54%; vegetable matter, 41%; insects, 26%; snails, 18%; corn, 6%; hair, 18%; feathers, 4%. The incidence of corn was low because the study area was mostly marsh, swamp, and woodlands.

The belief persists that raccoons wash their food, and part of the scientific name (lotor) means "washer." Raccoons do handle their food in water, but it is not being washed. When a raccoon captures prey such as a crayfish, it is often held between the front feet and rubbed or rolled about under water. This manipulation serves to kill, disable, or break up the item for easier consumption, rather than to wash it.

Reproduction: Mating occurs from January through March. The female retires to a maternal den, usually a hollow tree, a few days before giving birth, and scratches or chews off wood, thus creating a crude nest. Gestation is about 63 days; Indiana litters are born in April and May. There is one litter per year, of one to nine young (average four or five). Newborns weigh about 2 ounces and are well covered with fur. The eyes open and the face mask and the furred rings of the tail appear at about 3 weeks. Young remain in the den for 10 weeks and are weaned at about 14 weeks. The family forages together, beginning about the eighth to twelfth week, and by the twentieth week the young forage more

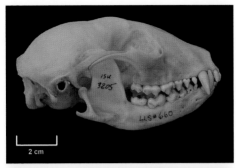
Side view of skull

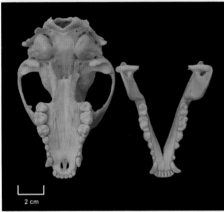
Ventral view
of skull and
lower jaw

Tracks. *Photo by Brianne Walters*

on their own. The young occasionally use a separate den, although the family remains together into late fall or often well into winter, and usually dens together in cold weather. Dispersal is in spring, when the new litter arrives.

Range: Raccoons are abundant throughout the state and are frequently pests. The great abundance is in part due to the collapse of the fur market.

Habits and Comments: The raccoon is solitary for the most part. It is terrestrial, arboreal, and semiaquatic. It typically begins to forage along water after sunset and remains active until daylight. The muddy beds of small streams are often crowded with raccoon tracks in the low water of late summer and fall. The animals visit each pool in search of crayfish, frogs, fish, or other prey. Caves are extensively explored by raccoons; tracks are often seen more than a quarter of a mile inside. Raccoons use trees for escape, denning, and sunning. They often travel in family groups.

Raccoons often sun themselves, especially on warm days in early spring. They can assume numerous positions, sprawled out lengthwise or crosswise over a limb with four legs dangling over the sides, draped through an upright fork, sprawled flat on their backs on a broad limb with four feet sticking up at all angles, or sitting in a reclining position on the limb base and leaning back against the trunk. They may choose similar sites to sleep in daytime. Raccoons will often use the same site to defecate day after day, often a fallen log. The raccoon is an accomplished climber. It descends either tailfirst or headfirst. It is one of relatively few mammals that can descend headfirst, which it does by rotating the hind feet 180 degrees. Raccoons are good swimmers, and though they usually walk, they can run for a considerable distance. Young raccoons produce a variety of vocalizations, including a whimpering, chattering distress call; the female communicates with her young by a purr or a twitter. Adults have a variety of other hisses, barks, screams, growls, and snarls.

Hollow trees are usually the favored dens of raccoons, especially in winter. Dens may be in the main trunk or, more often, in a large limb. When good den trees are not available, raccoons may nest in hollow logs, crevices, under stumps, under buildings, or in attics, chimneys, or garages. The den cavity is often a foot or more in diameter, and no nesting material is added; the raccoon simply uses the rotten wood and other accumulated debris already there for nesting. There may be communal nesting in winter. In summer, raccoons use temporary daytime dens consisting of almost any sort of shelter. They may be on the ground or in a thicket. Summer dens are usually changed almost daily. Communal denning is common in summer among members of a family group. Up to 23 raccoons have been reported in a single den, but a den rarely includes more than one adult male. Raccoons do not hibernate, yet they consume little or no food during winter in northern areas. They depend for energy on stored fat, for they can store a third of their body weight in fat. Raccoons' senses of hearing and smell are excellent. They are colorblind, but their night vision is excellent.

Scats are often deposited on logs or rocks, but they can easily be confused with those of other animals, especially foxes or opossums. The heaps of scats that are occasionally found indicate favored latrine areas, favored perhaps by more than one individual. Raccoons often become a nuisance in campgrounds, city parks, cemeteries, and residential areas. They raid garbage and trash cans, dumping the cans and strewing the contents about. Sick raccoons, when handled, frequently bite people, causing much concern about rabies or other infectious diseases.

Lehman (1984) located 574 daytime rest sites of raccoons using radio-tracking, Sites occurred in buildings 182 times, trees 145 times, ground dens 213 times, and in fields 34 times. Individuals moved from 3,000 to 9,500' per night. Mean home range size was 486 hectares for 5 male raccoons and 264 for 3 females. Data were collected on 692 roadkilled animals in 1972–1974. At that time the animal most often killed was the opossum, comprising 35.2% of the kill. In 2000–2001, the opossum was second, forming 26.3% of the kill, whereas the raccoon was first, at 28%.

We do not recommend keeping raccoons (or other wild animals) as pets. They can be very destructive, but more important, they harbor a nematode that occurs in feces, especially dry feces. This nematode can be harmful or fatal to other animals, including man.

Selected References. Hamilton 1936; Lehman 1977, 1984; Lotze and Anderson 1979; Stains 1956.

Raccoon

FAMILY MUSTELIDAE

There are 56 species of mustelids in 22 genera. The skunks have traditionally been placed in this family, but recently they were established as the skunk family, Mephitidae. The mustelids are variable, but most have short legs, long bodies, nonretractile claws, short heads, medium to long tails, and well-developed anal glands. Mustelids range in size from the least weasel, at about 40 grams, to the giant otter of South America, which can weigh up to 34 kg (75 lbs). This family includes some of the most efficient vertebrate predators; some of the weasels can take prey several times bigger than themselves. Delayed implantation occurs in many of the mustelids, lengthening apparent gestation by up to several months. Mating, which occurs in summer, is followed quickly by fertilization and the development of the embryo. Development, however, temporarily ceases at the blastula stage, the sphere of cells that in due course implants and grows in the uterus. In weasels, the blastula remains free in the uterus for an extended period, usually through the winter, and implantation finally occurs when ensuing gestation will bring the newborn young into the world at the optimum time for their survival. One advantage of delayed implantation is that it conserves the energy necessary for mating during early spring, when energy is at a premium. Its greater advantage, perhaps, lies in allowing the female to become impregnated before attaining full size and before dispersal. In the early weeks of her pregnancy, then, her energy can be devoted to her own further growth and maturation, rather than to rapidly developing offspring.

The genus *Mustela*, including the weasels and mink, is the largest genus of mustelids. Weasels are slender, long-bodied animals with long necks, small heads (not much larger than the neck), and short legs, each leg with five digits. The claws are curved and nonretractile. The ears are short and rounded. All weasels are highly carnivorous, as indicated by their sharply pointed milk teeth and adult teeth and the reduction of their cheek teeth. Only felids, among carnivores, have fewer cheek teeth. Highly carnivorous mammals need to ingest the body organs of their prey and the partly digested vegetation from prey digestive tracts, along with muscle tissue, in order to sustain a balanced diet. The genus *Mustela* is represented in Indiana by two species of weasels and the mink. The mink is larger than weasels and has a much bushier tail.

Reproductive strategies are, of course, important in all species, but they are particularly important in animals like weasels, which are solitary and relatively low in number. In contrast to larger predators, weasels are often preyed upon themselves, so are less likely to be around in their second year. Somewhat different reproductive strategies have evolved in different members of the genus *Mustela* in the eastern United States, depending on their size and frequency of predation. The least weasel is smallest in size, thus likely to suffer the greatest predation rate. This disadvantage is compensated by a rapid growth rate and having two litters in good years, without delayed implantation. Long-tailed weasels, which are intermediate in size and have many predators, have extended periods of delayed implantation. This strategy allows them to mate over a longer period, yet ensures that implantation will occur at the optimum time. It also allows them to become pregnant in their first year. The mink is relatively large, and adult mink, at least, presumably suffer relatively little predation. Its reproductive strategy is similar to that of other larger predators. Female mink do not reach maturity until 1 year of age, and the species exhibits only a brief period of delayed implantation.

Weasels produce three vocalizations: trills, screeches, and squeals. Trills are often produced as weasels investigate their surroundings, or during play, mating, or hunting. The screech, evidently a threat or defensive behavior, is a sudden sound given when the weasel is disturbed and may be coupled with a lunge at an intruder. The squeal is a distress call.

Weasels, like skunks, have anal scent glands. They can discharge their odor when disturbed, and it can be detected for some distance. Weasels that have been observed dragging the body along the ground may have been scent marking, but little is known of the function of these odors in weasels. Apparently the black tail tip of weasels directs the attack of a predator to the black, thereby often sparing the weasel. The black tail tip, were it present in the short-tailed *Mustela nivalis,* would be too close to the body and would thus have no protective effect. There is experimental backing for this hypothesis.

Too often, and for too long, we have persecuted weasels. We should think of them as highly evolved, very interesting animals that are necessary in the balance of nature. Like most predators, they are solitary, which has the advantage of spreading them out over the habitat, thus not putting undue pressure on prey populations and helping to maintain adequate prey for themselves and their offspring. Weasels do need to be near water, since they drink often, though relatively little at a time.

River Otter
Lontra canadensis (Schreber)

Distinguishing Features and Measurements: The river otter is a large, aquatic member of the weasel family with a broad, flattened head; small eyes; small ears; long, stout neck; and a heavy, tapering tail forming just over a third of the total length. The short legs, webbed toes, hairy soles, and thick, dense pelage are also characteristic. The otter is a rich glossy brown, occasionally nearly black. The underparts are lighter, and the lips, cheeks, chin, and throat are pale brown.

TL 900–1,300, T 320–510, HF 110–135, Wt. 12–20 lbs

Skull: Length: 100–115 (4–4.6").
The skull is flattened, the rostrum is short, and the auditory bullae are quite flattened.

Dental Formula:

$$I \ \frac{3}{3} \quad C \ \frac{1}{1} \quad P \ \frac{4}{3} \quad M \ \frac{1}{2} \ = \ 36$$

Habitat: The otter needs much wetland and much aquatic vegetation. It frequents lakes, rivers, streams, ditches, and ponds.

Food: Fish are the main food of otters, but a great variety of other items constitute an important part of the diet. Crustaceans (primarily crayfish), other shellfish, frogs and toads, small mammals (especially voles), birds, and insects are some of the more important nonfish items. Small amounts of plant material, such as blueberries and rose hips, are occasionally eaten. Otters feed most heavily on the more abundant, slower-moving fish species, especially suckers, chubs, daces, darters, and catfish, and also such schooling species as bluegills and sunfish. Otters may capture fish by pursuit or by digging into the sand and lying in wait. Otters may stand on their heads in a pond and root out large frogs from their hibernacula in the mud and dig out soft-shelled turtles from the sand. Otters will sometimes forage on land, especially in winter.

Reproduction: Otters mate shortly after the young are born. Mating can occur at any time from December to May, but peaks in March or April. The male presumably mates with one or more females whose home ranges fall within his. Females in heat may mark at scent stations and haul-outs (trails from water's edge, often scattered with droppings and crayfish parts). Copulation usually takes place in the water but may be on land. For a given female, copulation may recur several times over several days, with the female often caterwauling. Delayed implantation lengthens apparent gestation by 8–9.5 months. The female establishes a natal den shortly before giving birth, and the young are usually born in March or April. The young normally number two to four, occasionally up to six, and they are fairly well developed at birth. They are fully furred, but their ears and eyes are closed, and they have no teeth. They weigh about 275 grams. The eyes open at 35 days, and at 40 days the young are active and playful. They forage with the mother at 10–11 weeks, soon after weaning, and disperse in the fall or winter of their first year, before production of the next litter. Otters reach sexual maturity at 2 years of age, although a few females mate at 15 months. Although able to mate sooner, many males are not successful in establishing territories and breeding until 5–7 years of age.

Range: The river otter originally occurred through nearly all of Canada and the United States except for some of the Southwest. It was once common

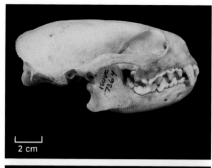

Side view of skull

2 cm

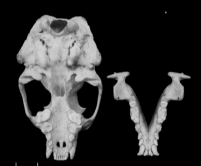

Ventral view
of skull and
lower jaw

2 cm

River otter slide at
Muscatatuck.
Photo by Scott Johnson

throughout Indiana, inhabiting all major watersheds; it was a valuable furbearer to the early settlers. Otters had decreased sharply by the mid-1800s. They were protected beginning in 1921, but this was too late, and the last known native otter was shot at Hovey Lake in 1942. An otter restoration program was initiated in Indiana in 1995 using otters from Louisiana, and the first 25 otters were liberated at the Muscatatuck National Wildlife Refuge in Jackson and Jennings counties on 17 January 1995. This first reintroduction was deemed successful and a total of 12 releases occurred from 1995 to 1999. The otters spread out from these sites and by 2000 had been documented in 31 counties, and by 2007 in 62 counties. It appears that the otter has been successfully reintroduced and may again occur throughout the state before long.

Habits and Comments: The otter is shy and retiring but nonetheless often lives close to humans. It is seldom seen, even though its principal activity is from dawn to mid-morning and again in the evening. It is active throughout the winter. The best-known and most obvious evidence of otters is their slides. The otter slides to the pool or river below, its forelegs tucked under. The slides soon become slick, and several otters of a family may use the same slide. Other signs of otters are haul-outs, bedding sites (depressions on the ground edged with matted leaves or other vegetation), rolling sites (plants flattened along the bank in an area up to 2 square meters, or 20 square feet), scrapes (areas scraped completely clear of vegetation), and scent posts (usually recognized by the disturbance of the ground around them). The tracks of otters are distinctively wide, and often interspersed with the tracks are stretches where the belly drags, frequent short slides, and places where otters have been digging for turtle eggs, mussels, clams, or other items. The otter is a strong, graceful swimmer, moving in an undulating course or swimming with only its head above the surface. It can dive to about 60' and can swim at speeds up to 7 mph for a quarter mile without coming up for air. It can also tread water, projecting its long neck above the water to see. An otter need not travel far in summer, for foraging or hunting areas are usually readily available, but in winter it sometimes has to make long overland journeys to find water to secure the fish that maintain it at this season. In spite of its short legs, the otter moves rapidly on land, and on the ice it often slides. It moves by two to four loping bounds of 15–28", followed by a glide with the abdomen on the ground and the feet trailing behind. The glide may extend for about 5–15' in snow, or up to 22' on ice.

Dens are most often along a bank. A den may be a natural opening or another animal's burrow or lodge (beaver, muskrat, or woodchuck). It may be in some protected place such as among tree roots, under a brush pile, or in a hollow stump or log jam. The entrance to a den may be above or below the surface of the water. The main den may be used for several years. The nest itself may be of grasses, leaves, or aquatic vegetation, and otters will sometimes make a nestlike structure in the aquatic vegetation itself.

Adult otter with four pups in moist-soil unit at Muscatatuck.
Photo by Susan Knowles

Two river otters at Muscatatuck National Fish and Wildlife Refuge.
Photo by Richard Fields

Radio-transmittered otter M23 mating with nontransmittered otter.
Photo by Lara Cerri

Otters are extremely curious and appear to play with one another. They are able to manipulate items with their paws. Their tactile senses, especially those associated with the vibrissae, are well developed. When vibrissae were experimentally removed from European otters, *Lutra lutra,* the animals took much longer to locate items in murky water. Vision is not acute, except under water, although otters can detect movements at great distances. An otter's hearing is good, and its sense of smell probably is as well, since they use scent marking extensively. Otters utter shrill chirps, growls, or hissing barks. Otters occur at perhaps one per 2–2.5 miles of waterway, but dispersing individuals may move 75 miles or more before establishing their own home ranges. Home ranges of males are large, perhaps 9 miles wide, and include the much smaller ranges of one or more females. Both sexes maintain territories within the home ranges and exclude others of the same sex. Territories are marked using the anal scent glands, by depositing scented feces (sprainting) and making scented dirt piles. Humans are the chief enemies of the adult otter, through both direct harvest and habitat destruction.

SELECTED REFERENCES. Johnson and Berkley 1999; Larivière 1998.

River otters at Muscatatuck. *Photo by Bill Brink*

Least Weasel
Mustela nivalis Linnaeus

Distinguishing Features and Measurements: The least weasel (*Mustela nivalis*), the smaller of the two weasels found in Indiana, is the smallest carnivore in the world. It is about 6–8" in total length but has a tail only about an inch long. In summer, the pelage is brown above and white below.

TL 170–210, T 22–44, HF 19–26, Wt. 30–70

Skull: Length: 30–33 (1.2–1.3").

The skull of the least weasel is difficult to distinguish from other *Mustela* skulls except for size. Its small size (less than 34 mm total length) serves to separate *M. nivalis* from the other two Indiana species of the genus. The skulls of *M. frenata* and *M. vison* are 39 mm (1.6") or greater in length.

Dental Formula:

$$I \ \frac{3}{3} \ C \ \frac{1}{1} \ P \ \frac{3}{3} \ M \ \frac{1}{2} \ = \ 34$$

Habitat: The first least weasel collected in the state was captured as it ran from under a corn shock. Others were taken in a burrow beneath a quail coop, in a gravel pit, and two were plowed out of the ground. Several were trapped at Lafayette in weedy bluegrass pastures, where ground squirrel colonies were present. Some have been found in buildings, even in suburban areas. One was seen entering a mole (*Scalopus*) tunnel. Many of the least weasels taken were from mixed grassy/shrubby fields. At the Indiana Dunes National Lakeshore, one came from the young foredunes and one from the black oak-swamp forest.

Food: The major food of this species is probably small mammals, primarily mice. Captive least weasels have been observed killing live mice and rats. Live mice were dispatched by biting behind the right ear. In killing the rats, which weighed more than the weasel, a violent struggle usually took place with the weasel astride the victim's back, gripping with all feet as they rolled and tossed about. The rats were frequently tugged about by the nose before a satisfactory head hold was obtained. Mumford watched a captive female least weasel after a live prairie vole had been placed in her cage. The weasel periodically attacked the vole, with no visible damage to the latter. The vole would resist attack by backing into a corner of the cage, standing up on its back feet and fending off the weasel. The weasel did not seem to be able to see the vole the length of the cage (about 10") but appeared to hunt for it by scent. Four hours after the vole was placed in the cage, it was dead.

Reproduction: Unlike the other two species of the genus *Mustela* in Indiana, *M. nivalis* does not exhibit delayed implantation. Gestation ranged from 34 to 36 days. The number of young per litter varied from 1 to 6 (average 4.7).

Range: It probably is less rare than previously thought. We know of specimens in museums from 35 counties. The southernmost record is from the Muscatatuck National Wildlife Refuge (Jennings County). At Lafayette, Richmond, and Terre Haute, where there has been considerable mammal collecting, 9, 12, and 4 individuals have been obtained, respectively. Many of these had been taken by miscellaneous means (in pits such as swimming pools, or freshly dug post holes or graves, by hand, and dead on the road). We need to learn how to capture this species in order to learn more about its biology.

Habits and Comments: Little is known of the biology of the least weasel. Individuals have been found under a corn shock, dead in a bird feeder, in a can in a garage, beside a woodpile in a suburban yard, in a drain tile beneath a farm road, in a granary, in occupied houses, and beneath a coop housing quail. Nests are in burrows underground and may be composed of grasses or other vegetation plus fur and feathers of prey. Disturbed least weasels discharge a fetid, musky odor from their anal scent glands. Least weasels are active throughout the year and are mainly nocturnal, although they are sometimes observed during the day. We suspect that most live in old fields since *Microtus* seems to be their mainstay. One least weasel was tracked in winter when it was seen during the daytime looking out of its burrow in an old field. Tracks in the snow indicated that the animal had foraged 195' from its den in one direction and had crossed a small, frozen cattail marsh. In the other direction from the den, its tracks led 360'. The path it took meandered about among the cattails, weeds, and clumps of grasses and nowhere followed a straight line. The animal was live-trapped and kept for 6 days. When startled it gave a short, explosive squeak. It slept rolled into a circle, with its head resting on its flank. Most of the daylight hours were spent in a darkened box. Food was usually eaten inside the box.

SELECTED REFERENCES. Heidt 1970; Heidt et al. 1968; Polderboer 1942; Sheffield and King 1994.

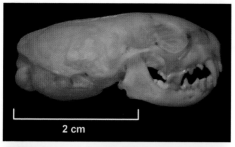
Side view of skull

Ventral view
of skull and
lower jaw

Least weasel. *Photo by Roger Powell*

Long-tailed Weasel
Mustela frenata Lichtenstein

Distinguishing Features and Measurements: Weasels are thin, elongate animals. The long-tailed weasel is much larger than the least weasel and has a much longer tail with a black tip. The least weasel is tiny with an inch-long tail that has no black tip. Both weasels are brown above and white below in summer. Long-tailed weasels vary in the amount of white in the underparts, and some have the white slightly to almost completely replaced with yellowish. In winter, only a few (perhaps 5% or less) of the long-tailed weasels in Indiana change color. The tail tip remains black even when the weasel becomes white.

	males	females
TL	350–440	290–343
T	111–150	85–122
HF	38–50	30–40
Wt.	170–283	83–125

Skull: Length: 35–51 (1.4–2.0").

The skulls of members of the genus *Mustela* are quite similar but separable on the basis of size. In *M. frenata* the total length of the skull is about 44–51 mm in males and about 35–44 mm in females. Males are much larger than females.

Dental Formula:

$$I \frac{3}{3} \quad C \frac{1}{1} \quad P \frac{4}{3} \quad M \frac{1}{2} \quad = \quad 34$$

Habitat: Long-tailed weasels are relatively common but seldom seen. They are found in most wooded or open habitats, but especially where *Microtus* and *Peromyscus* or other rodent prey are plentiful. They occur about limestone escarpments, and they have been taken in traps set in water for mink and muskrat, and in hollow trees and tile drains. They also occur around and in barns and other farm buildings, where they are attracted by rats, mice, and poultry, or even bats.

Food: Weasels do not suck blood, as commonly thought, although they often lap blood from a wound. They feed mostly on small vertebrate animals, eating flesh, bones, feathers, and fur. Although a large number of prey items have been recorded, and the diet of weasels varies with the prey populations available, more than 96% of the food usually consists of small mammals, chiefly rodents. Meadow voles, because of their abundance, are a major food source. Long-tailed weasels successfully stalk and overcome shrews, small birds, and snakes, and do not disdain insects or even earthworms. There are many reports of weasels entering pens or buildings and killing numerous chickens.

Reproduction: Males reach adult body weight in 3–4 months but do not mature and mate until about 1 year. Females mature in 3–4 months, and even during their first year they come into heat and mate in midsummer, June to August. Development of the egg stops at the early blastula (about 15 days), which then remains quiescent in the upper uterus until spring. In spring, implantation occurs and development then proceeds, and a litter of four to eight young is produced in April or May. The average total gestation is 279 days (range 205–314), thus only one litter per year can be produced. Newborns weigh about 3 grams, and approximate standard measurements are total length 56, tail 13, and hind foot 7 mm. They have long, white hair and emit high-pitched vocalizations. At 3 weeks the babies are crawling outside of the nest and feeding on meat. At 5 weeks the eyes open, coloration is nearing that of adults, and the animals are weaned; at this point, they are eating about their own weight in food per day. Only the female brings food to the growing young, which remain with her until midsummer, when they become independent. By 7 weeks the young males are the size of the mother, at about 100 grams; the young females are about 73 grams.

Range: Long-tailed weasels are found throughout the state but are more common in northern than southern Indiana.

Habits and Comments: Long-tailed weasels are active throughout the year. They were once thought to be primarily nocturnal, but they are often out by day. They are generally active when hungry rather than on some daily schedule, and a principal prey, voles, are often active during the day. There are many reports of long-tailed weasels in trees, usually at night. They sometimes climb trees to escape but may also climb trees after prey, taking a vertical leap, then climbing upward by 1 m spirals. A weasel seen killing bats in a barn was running about in the rafters, where the bats were hanging. Long-tailed weasels normally hunt using a zigzag pattern, going from one rodent burrow to another. They run in typical weasel fashion, by a series of bounds with the back humped at each bound, the tail horizontal or raised at 45°. The slender body, short legs, and small head enable foraging weasels to enter small openings and crannies in search of prey. Dens or shelters are in a variety of sites, a shallow earthen burrow, underneath a large stump, or in the bank of a gully. At the end of a tunnel it will build a large nest in which to raise the young. The nest is often composed largely of the fur (and perhaps a few dried muzzles, tails, and feet) of its prey. C. M. Kirkpatrick chased one that had killed many young pheasants in a large outdoor pen. While being shot at and closely pursued, the weasel killed several young pheasants that crossed its path. Aside from tracks (mostly noticed in the snow), the long-tailed weasel appears to leave little visible sign of its presence. Long-tailed weasels produce the three typical weasel vocalizations—trills, screeches, and squeals—and also a "zeep" has been heard during courting behavior.

Weasels subdue mouse-sized rodents by wrapping their bodies around them to pin them, then biting the nape of the neck. Chipmunks and ground squirrels encountered aboveground are killed by a bite to the nape, the bite often severing the vertebral chord. Rabbits, too, are attacked, but rabbits are dangerous even for a large weasel, for they have the potential to kill the weasel. When other prey is available, weasels are less likely to attack rabbits, and probably most of the cottontails they take are young. The weasel feeds on the head and thorax first, often caching food for later use. Weasels in search of food often cover several kilometers in a night, but these journeys may not encompass an area greater than 10–20 hectares (25–50 acres). They hunt in burrows or runways and will burrow under snow.

In good habitat, long-tailed weasels reach a maximum density of about one weasel per 7 acres. The sexes are separate for most of the year. Home ranges of males are much larger and include those of more than one female, but home ranges tend not to overlap within sex. The home range is about 25–60 acres. Home range size and shape are affected by habitat factors, prey availability, and other weasels, and home ranges are smaller in winter. Males may travel about 200 m (655') in their nightly forays, females about 100 m (330'). Domestic dogs capture some long-tailed weasels, some are trapped or hunted by man, and some are killed on roads by vehicles.

SELECTED REFERENCES. Hall 1951; Sheffield and Thomas 1997; Wright 1942, 1947, 1948.

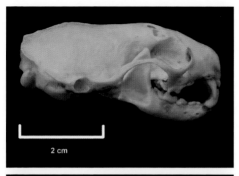

Side view of skull

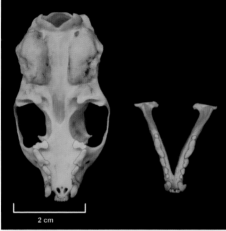

Ventral view
of skull and
lower jaw

2 cm

2 cm

Long-tailed weasel. *Photo by Roger Barbour*

Mink
Mustela vison Schreber

Distinguishing Features and Measurements: Minks are usually a uniform dark brown color above and below. The color on the lower part of the back tends to be darker than that on the forequarters, and part of the tail is sometimes blackish, especially the tip. Pelage color varies from tan, pale brown, and rich brown to blackish. There is often a white chin spot, and some individuals also have small patches of white on the throat, chest, belly, or just anterior to the anus. Although the body proportions of the mink are similar to those of weasels, the mink is larger and has a much bushier tail. Minks do not turn white in winter.

	males	females
TL	550–680	480–530
T	185–224	140–185
HF	62–75	54–65
Wt.	900–1,360	600–900

Skull: Length: male, 63–71 (2.5–2.8"); female 58–65 (2.3–2.6").
Dental Formula:

$$I \quad \frac{3}{3} \quad C \quad \frac{1}{1} \quad P \quad \frac{3}{3} \quad M \quad \frac{1}{2} \quad = \quad 34$$

Habitat: Water is the one essential of any habitat suited to minks, although the animals forage into dry land areas when feeding or seeking mates. The borders of lakes, marshes, and ponds, or the banks of rivers, ditches, and smaller streams and creeks are favorable haunts. Wooded and open areas are both inhabited by minks. The mink is closely associated with the muskrat, and minks sometimes make their dens in muskrat houses. Minks may use muskrat burrows and houses and may feed on muskrats. This association is amply demonstrated by the fact that *Zibethacarus ondatrae,* a host-specific mite of the muskrat, was found on 5 of 12 Indiana minks examined.

Food: Animal foods constitute the diet of the mink. Although most food is obtained in natural habitats, the mink is not above taking poultry. We examined the stomach contents of only five Indiana minks, which contained the following percentage volumes of various foods: muskrat (20%), eastern cottontail (20%), meadow vole (20%), least shrew (16%), eastern mole (10%), unidentified bird (6%), chorus frog (*Pseudacris triseriata*) (4%), snail (2%), vegetation (2%). A mink examined 22 July 1998 from Hendricks County had eaten a 12–16" garter snake, *Thamnophis sirtalis.*

Reproduction: Gestation is thought to be about 40–75 days but is difficult to determine, for delayed implantation occurs. The breeding season in Indiana is probably during March, when males may travel long distances to locate receptive females. Young are born in late April or early May. One litter per year is probably produced; litter size varies from three to six (rarely more).

Range: The mink is common to uncommon throughout the state where suitable habitat occurs. Low fur prices the past several years may have taken some trapping pressure off the mink in Indiana.

Habits and Comments: Minks are excellent swimmers and divers, capable of diving to depths of 15' or more and swimming under water for 100 yards. When foraging along streams, they explore holes, hollow logs and trees, root tangles, piles of brush, and other dark recesses where prey may be found. The mink is mostly nocturnal, but there are numerous daytime observations, both of family groups and of lone individuals.

Minks often move along with a loping gait or by means of a series of 16–18" bounds. Even when disturbed, they may not move swiftly. Males travel more than females, both in search of food and during the mating season. Males often have a hunting circuit of several miles that may take a week to complete; thus each day is spent in a different den. The mink is not a very good climber, but there are records of minks being treed by raccoon dogs at night.

Mink dens are usually ground burrows near the water's edge. They may be constructed by the animal itself or by other mammals (often muskrats). Burrows made by minks are commonly 3–4" in diameter and from 10 to 12' long. Other den sites are hollow trees and logs, tile drains, muskrat houses, and holes under bridge abutments, rocks, and brush piles. Rabbit hunters occasionally flush a mink from daytime retreats in brush piles. Brooks (1959) noted that when muskrat houses were appropriated by minks, the muskrats were usually driven away or killed by the invaders. He cited one instance, however, where a single muskrat house sheltered a mink and a litter of muskrats simultaneously. The nesting chambers of the two species were about 2' apart but not connected. Nests are about 1' in diameter, made of dried grass or leaves and often lined with fur and feathers of its victims. In some habitats, minks leave little visible sign of their presence. Tracks in the mud or snow are the most obvious and common signs.

The mink may discharge the contents of its anal scent glands when disturbed or excited. The secretion from these glands is considered by many to be more disagreeable to humans than the similar discharge of the striped skunk. The mink's secretion seems sweeter than that of the skunk but has a strong, fetid, musky character.

Mink have always been a popular furbearing animal. The prices paid for them have ranged from $4.61 to $20.94 per pelt. Mink prices reached their lowest level at $4.61 in 1970, then began to rise and remained relatively high most years through about 1991, at which time they began to decline. Habitat destruction, especially drainage of wetlands, is the worst enemy of the mink in Indiana.

SELECTED REFERENCES. Larivière 1999.

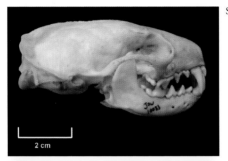

Side view of skull

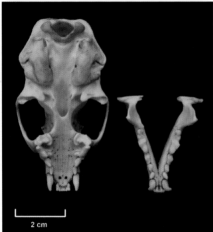

Ventral view of skull and lower jaw

Mink, *below.*
Photo by Larry Lehman

Badger
Taxidea taxus (Schreber)

Distinguishing Features and Measurements: The badger has short legs and tail, a heavy, rather flattened body, and is grayish to grayish-buff in color. The badger's feet are black; the broad front feet have long, strong claws for digging. A narrow white stripe runs from the nose to the shoulders. The face is black and white with a small black patch in front of the ear. The underside is whitish to yellowish.

TL 605–843, T 115–250, HF 85–121, Wt. 6–11 kg

Skull: Length: 110–131 (4.4–5.2").

The skull of *Taxidea taxus* is massive, 80 mm in zygomatic width, with a triangular braincase. The hard palate extends far behind the posterior edge of the last molariform teeth. This is the only Indiana carnivore skull that is more than 100 mm long with 4 upper molariform teeth.

Dental Formula:

$$I \frac{3}{3} \quad C \frac{1}{1} \quad P \frac{3}{3} \quad M \frac{1}{2} = 34$$

Habitat: Badgers generally inhabit grassy areas or grassy areas mixed with various herbaceous species. Their habitat has been described as the following: in a grassy bank of an old gravel pit, and in a dry old field with sparse cover of aster, goldenrod, sweet clover, and other plants on a gravelly moraine of northeastern Indiana. This type of terrain no doubt affords the most favorable habitat for badgers in Indiana and is probably one of the reasons that most of the animals are in this section of the state. Such areas are not conducive to intensive cultivation, and they include abundant cover as well as soils suited to easy digging. Also, chipmunks and thirteen-lined ground squirrels are plentiful. Other habitats from which badgers have been reported include an abandoned gravel pit, hayfields, and railroad rights-of-way.

Food: Badgers obtain much of their food by digging out small rodents, and they feed on other animals as well. Some foods known to have been eaten by badgers from Indiana are Norway rat, woodchuck, cottontail, eastern chipmunk, meadow vole, and prairie vole. One badger's stomach was filled with mulberry.

Reproduction: Badgers have delayed implantation, thus gestation is difficult to determine. Mating peaks in late July and early August and implantation occurs about February. A badger's nest is about 2–2.5' in diameter and is placed in a chamber of the underground burrow system, 2–6' below the ground surface. One litter per year is produced, consisting of one to five young (usually two to three). Young are born in late March or early April. They are furred but blind. Emergence from the den occurs at about 4–5 weeks. The young are weaned in June and disperse at about 10–12 weeks.

Range: A survey for badgers in 1955 had indicated badgers in 33 counties, primarily in the northern third of the state. However, a more recent survey (1997) indicated badgers now occur in at least 83 counties, occupying most of the state. The badger is scarce and remains much more common in the north than in the south.

Habits and Comments: The badger is an accomplished burrower, as suggested by its body form and its powerful front feet that are used for digging. Burrows are large and are usually more broad than high to accommodate the shape of the badger itself. The badger is mostly nocturnal and is therefore difficult to observe. Animals observed during the day are quite wary and usually retreat quickly underground when disturbed. Badgers usually walk slowly, with a waddling gait, but sometimes run with an awkward galloping motion. When threatened they may stand their ground and fight, emitting hisses, snarls, and squeals, and sucking in air noisily. When fighting, badgers may gnash their teeth and raise the long hairs along the back. They also can emit a foul-smelling musk from their anal scent glands, although it is not forcibly ejected. The badger does not hibernate but may remain in its burrow (sometimes plugged) during inclement weather. Like many other carnivores, badgers do not have a "home" in which they live. Other than when they have young, they may move about and use a different den nearly every day. One female used a different den almost every day in summer, used dens for several days at a time in autumn, and used one den all winter. There are many

Badger. *Photographer unknown*

old burrows in areas occupied by badgers, and they often use them. Badgers can dig themselves out of sight in minutes. The natal burrow is more complex than other burrows. There is a rejoining burrow in the main passage that probably allows badgers to pass each other. Burrows can be from 2 to 35 yards long and can be more than 6 yards deep. We know of at least three animals that were found in cities. The strength of a badger is tremendous. Badgers are equipped with a strong skull, large teeth, and long front claws—all formidable weapons of defense. They are more than a match for most dogs. Man is the only enemy of the badger in Indiana. Numerous badgers are killed by motor vehicles, trapped, or shot, and of course human development, incidental trapping, and agricultural practices negatively impact badger populations. Conversely, changes in land-use practices have created habitats more favorable for grassland-dependent species, and their protected status and a decline in trapping have had a positive influence on badgers. Badgers were legal furbearers in Indiana until 1966; the season was closed in 1967.

SELECTED REFERENCES. Berkley and Johnson 1998; Long 1973.

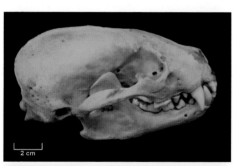

Side view of skull

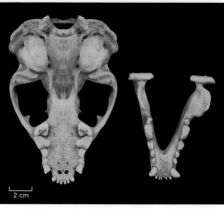

Ventral view of skull and lower jaw

For many years the skunks were placed in the weasel family, Musteli-dae, subfamily Mephitinae. However, Dragoo and Honeycutt (1997), using mitochondrial DNA sequencing data, have shown quite convincingly that the skunks should be placed in their own family, Mephitidae.

Skunks are characterized by their striking black and white patterns, their slow deliberate behavior, and their well-developed scent glands. These glands can spray foul-smelling scent forcefully and rather accurately. Both the color pattern and the behavior serve as a warning to would-be predators to stay away.

The family Mephitidae has nine species in three genera, all in the New World. Two species, the striped skunk, *Mephitis mephitis,* and the eastern spotted skunk, *Spilogale putorius,* occur in the eastern United States. The striped skunk currently occurs in Indiana; the spotted skunk was fairly recently extirpated here.

Striped Skunk
Mephitis mephitis (Schreber)

Distinguishing Features and Measurements: The body and legs of the striped skunk are black. The head is mostly black, usually with a narrow white stripe on the forehead. The back is partly black with a V-shaped white stripe of varying width and length from the nape to the tail and extending down onto the sides. This dorsal white stripe is sometimes absent or represented by small white areas. The long, bushy tail is black and white and may have a white tip. A white skunk was taken at Geneva, Indiana (photo in *Outdoor Indiana* 19:24, 1952), and all-black individuals have been reported (Evermann and Butler 1894). Skunks are variable with regard to the amount of white in the pelage. Skunks have short legs, pointed muzzles, and small ears. Fourteen is the full complement of teats, but some individuals have less.

TL 550–675, T 175–280, HF 60–80, Wt. 1.5–5.0 kg

Skull: Length: 66–82 (2.6–3.3").

This is one of three genera of wild Carnivora in Indiana with 4 upper molariform teeth per side. The others are *Taxidea* and *Mustela* (the domestic cat also has 4). The skunk's skull can immediately be distinguished from the others by its shape. The back of the skull is flat, but its profile over the orbits abruptly angles downward. Also, in the skunk the bony palate ends at the posterior border of the molariform teeth; it extends beyond them in *Mustela* and *Taxidea.*

Dental Formula:

$$I \ \frac{3}{3} \ C \ \frac{1}{1} \ P \ \frac{3}{3} \ M \ \frac{1}{2} \ = \ 34$$

Habitat: Striped skunks occur in a variety of habitats, including fields or woods and along fencerows, streams, and dry ravine banks. Weedy and brushy fields and brushy pastures are attractive to them. They enter caves on occasion.

Food: Insects (adult and larvae) make up much of the food of the striped skunk. Skunks also feed on other animal materials of various kinds, including eggs and poultry. In seven stomachs we found mammal remains (57%) about equally divided among prairie voles, muskrats, short-tailed shrews, and eastern cottontails. Insect remains (42.5%) consisted of grasshoppers, beetles, grubworms (June bug larvae), caterpillars, and crickets. I once observed a skunk at midday in a patch of persimmon trees. Its whole snout was orange from feeding on the fruits.

Reproduction: The gestation period is about 63 days. A single litter is born each year. Copulation probably occurs in late February and early March.

Range: Today, the striped skunk probably occurs throughout the state but may be rare locally. Of 692 mammals observed dead on roads in 1972–1974, 73 were skunks (10.6%), whereas in 2000–2001, only 126 of 2,913 (4.3%) were skunks.

Habits and Comments: The skunk is almost entirely terrestrial, although it is said by some to climb, though infrequently, and to enter water when pursued. It is often observed by day, especially during the late afternoon, but is mostly nocturnal. Females with their litters have been seen traveling during the day. Young follow the females single file. The usual gait of skunks is a waddling, plodding one; at times they may move at a slow trot. When foraging in open areas, they usually keep their noses near the ground as they amble along a trail or fencerow. Their eyesight appears to be poor. Presumably, the striking black-and-white coloration of the skunk serves quite well as a warning to potential predators to stay their distance, and thus skunks need not worry much about running to escape enemies. The ability of the skunk to defend itself by means of a discharge from its anal scent glands is well known. The skunk can eject the musk for distances up to 8′ or more. Even baby skunks have this ability, although there is much less musk and the odor is less disagreeable. When approached, a skunk may waddle away or, if sufficiently disturbed, may lower the head, arch the back, and raise the tail in preparation for spraying. Usually the hair on the back and tail is raised at this time, also. The animal may then stamp or scratch on the ground with its front feet. Continued disturbance may cause the animal to spray the contents of its anal scent glands at the intruder. The material ejected contains a sulphur-alcohol compound, butylmercaptan (chemically, it is trans-2-butene-1-thiol, 3-methyl-1-butanethiol, and trans-2-butenyl-methyl disulfide), which is responsible for the

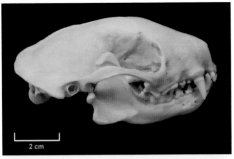

Side view of skull

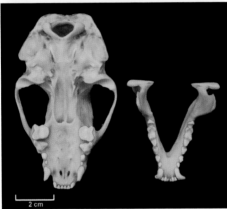

Ventral view of skull and lower jaw

Striped skunk. *Photo by Roger Barbour*

strong odor. The spray may cause coughing, choking, nausea, and even temporary blindness in humans if it enters the eyes. The odor is quite persistent and may be detected for about a mile, depending upon atmospheric conditions.

Skunks usually live in underground burrows, which they may construct themselves, or more often they appear to use burrows dug by woodchucks or other larger mammals. Burrows may have more than a single opening. Grasses are gathered and transported into the den for construction of a nest. Active dens can be detected by the characteristic odor or by the presence of skunk hairs about the entrance. Dens are often under buildings, occupied or not. During very cold periods of winter, skunks may remain inactive in their dens, but they do not hibernate. They accumulate much fat in the fall and are thus able to fast for considerable periods if necessary. It is not unusual to find more than one animal per den in winter; seven were found in one den one February.

Skunks are susceptible to canine distemper, rabies, and encephalitis. In most years from 1963 to 1988, the skunk led all other species in the number of rabies cases diagnosed by the Indiana Department of Health. It appears that the great horned owl is one of the most important natural predators of skunks. Many of the skunks observed in Indiana are those lying dead along roads where they have been killed by vehicles.

Selected References. Verts 1967; Wade-Smith and Verts 1982.

FAMILY FELIDAE

There are 40 species of cats in the world in 14 genera (Wilson and Reeder 2005), but the number of genera has been controversial. We have followed Wilson and Reeder (2005) in using *Felis* for the housecat, *Puma* for the mountain lion, and *Lynx* for the bobcat and lynx. Cats are a relatively uniform group, which has led to much of the controversy as compared to most other mammalian families. Cats occur over much of the world except Australia. They are digitigrade (walk on their toes) and have five toes on the front feet, four on the hind feet, with each toe having a retractable claw. Their skulls are very rounded. Cats and some of the smaller weasels are among the most carnivorous mammals of the order Carnivora, and as such are at the top of the food chain. Cats use vision to locate prey. They are one of few mammals that have color vision, and they have well-developed night vision. Also, they have long sensory vibrissae. Cats are agile, and many, excluding the bobcat, are good climbers.

Bobcat
Lynx rufus (Schreber)

Distinguishing Features and Measurements: The bobcat is a rather long-legged, stubby-tailed, moderate-sized wild cat with large cheek tufts. Pelage color varies but is normally reddish-brown above. It is whitish below with black spots. The pointed ears have inconspicuous hair tufts, and the dorsal tip of the tail is black. Some Indiana residents may mistake feral domestic cats for bobcats, but domestic cats are considerably smaller and normally have long tails.

TL 750–1,100, T 130–180, HF 160–195, Wt. 5–16 kg

Skull: Length: 115–141 (4.6–5.6").

The bobcat skull is short, wide, has a very short rostrum, and is the only Indiana carnivore skull with 3 upper molariform teeth. In Indiana, only the domestic cat skull is likely to be confused with that of a bobcat, but the former is much smaller and has 4 upper molariform teeth.

Dental Formula:

$$I \ \frac{3}{3} \ C \ \frac{1}{1} \ P \ \frac{2}{2} \ M \ \frac{1}{1} \ = \ 28$$

Habitat: Bobcats occur mostly in hilly, well-forested areas, with considerable sections that are rather remote, as occurs where bobcats have done well in Martin, Greene, and Lawrence counties. A second "cluster" of confirmed sightings is in the Warrick and Pike county area of southwest Indiana, where reclaimed strip-mined lands have an interspersion of grasslands, brushy thickets, forested tracts, and agricultural lands. Rock outcrops, rocky ledges, and caves in the unglaciated hill country of south central Indiana create excellent habitat for bobcats, along with wooded bottomlands and timbered slopes, bluffs, brushy country, and swamps, especially where the land is broken up.

Food: Bobcats, like many larger predators, can tolerate extended periods when food is not available, then eat heavily when it is. Bobcats feed by ambushing or stalking their prey, then pouncing. Main prey are mammals ranging from about 1.5 to 12.5 lbs; the cottontail rabbit is its main food. However, it will eat squirrels (including woodchucks), mice and voles, opossums, moles and shrews, raccoons, foxes, and house cats. Even skunks have been recorded as food, along with several species of birds, reptiles, insects, and snails. Deer, especially fawns, are often eaten. Bobcats are capable of killing full-grown deer, though they seldom do except in winter in deep snow, or in times when their principal prey are in short supply. Many of the deer consumed are probably roadkills or have been shot by hunters. Deer or other larger prey are cached and may serve for several days. Caches are covered with snow, leaves, bark, or other available material. Bobcats hunt small prey (mice and squirrels) where prey is abundant, by lying, crouching, or standing motionless, waiting for the prey to approach, before pouncing. They often hunt by crouching in a hunting bed or lookout, changing position so as to view in various directions. The bobcat may then attack after a bit of stalking or by a sudden rush directly from the hunting bed. It hunts larger prey at rest, such as deer, by moving about more frequently. It is most apt to attack deer when it finds them bedded down. After a rush the bobcat will bite violently at the throat, the base of the skull, or the chest.

Reproduction: Most female bobcats breed in their second summer, but a few apparently breed in their first year. Males do not breed until their second year. The mating season commences in February and March, at least in the north. A dominant male may mate several times with a female. Other males may be in attendance, but they remain aloof during matings, although they may mate later. One to six (usually two to four) young are born in spring or early summer, after a gestation of about 62 (range 50–70) days. Some births occur into September, and possibly two litters are occasionally produced. The young are blind, but

well furred and spotted at birth. By the ninth or tenth day, they open their eyes. They start exploring at the end of the fourth week and are weaned when about 2 months old. By their first fall, they weigh about 10 lbs and hunt by themselves, but they remain with the mother until nearly a year old.

Range: The bobcat formerly occurred throughout Indiana, but by 1970 was very rare and was placed on the state endangered list that year. In 1978 the bobcat was thought to be rare or absent in a large part of the midwest including Iowa, Illinois, Indiana, Ohio, and large parts of Michigan and Missouri. The low number was attributed mainly to habitat loss, but sport hunting, trapping, and predator control also played a role. However, the bobcat has staged a big comeback in Indiana since the mid-1980s, at least partly due to the collapse of the fur market. Also much land in southern Indiana has been allowed to revert to brushland. Enough bobcats are now present in the Greene/Martin/Lawrence county area that the Indiana DNR has been able to carry out a radio-tracking study on the species there.

Habits and Comments: The species is shy and retiring and often lives in areas over long periods without being observed. The bobcat is solitary and is basically crepuscular rather than nocturnal. It is generally active from about 3 hours before sunset to midnight and in the last hour before dawn to 3 hours after sunrise. It has a catlike walk, but it can trot or run in bounding leaps of 6–8'. Bobcats climb well, either to take refuge from dogs or to gain a vantage point for hunting or observations. It has no aversion to water. The bobcat modifies its behavior in deep snow, bounding to get through, but often using roads, deer trails, logs, and other places where the snow cover is reduced. Bobcat tracks show only four toes, although there is an elevated fifth toe on both front feet. There are no claw marks since the claws are retractile.

Bobcats are quite vocal at times, uttering screams and growling sounds, some of them similar to those of the domestic cat. They are said to be especially noisy when fighting. However, some of the nocturnal sounds attributed to bobcats in Indiana have been those of raccoons, foxes, and other mammals.

Bobcats employ a natal den, often a cave or a rock shelter if available, and nesting materials (usually vegetation) are carried into the den. They also have auxiliary or shelter dens around the less-visited reaches of their home range. Auxiliary dens may be in brush piles, thickets, rock ledges, hollow logs, stumps, or the roots remaining from uprooted trees. The odor of these dens, and indeed of the cats themselves, is strong.

Bobcats mark home ranges by scent-marking involving urine, feces, and scent from anal glands. They also mark their ranges by scraping and scratches in trees. They will scratch with their front claws as high as they can reach on dry, barkless, standing trees. At times they will cover their feces, at other times not, and they will sometimes prepare a scrape with the hind feet and deposit the feces in the scrape.

Bobcats inhabit fairly well-defined territories or home ranges varying in size depending on sex, season, prey distribution, and abundance. Resident animals spend much of their time in certain favored spots, such as around bluffs and ledges. Other residents are permitted to use these areas, but a dominance hierarchy may be established among the residents. Transients are generally excluded from these favored areas. Home ranges of males in summer are about 0.35 square miles; those of females are less than half that. Winter home ranges are much larger, running about 10–20 square miles. Home ranges of females are much smaller than those of males and generally do not overlap those of other females; two or more may be included in one male home range. Home ranges of males often overlap. Man is the only important enemy of the bobcat in Indiana.

SELECTED REFERENCES. Larivière and Larivière 1997; Pollack 1950, 1951; Rollings 1945; Woolf et al. 2000; Young 1958.

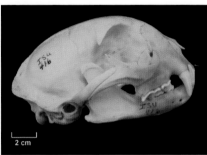

Side view of skull

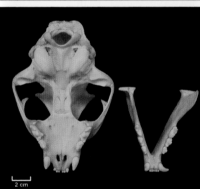

Ventral view of skull and lower jaw

Bobcat. *Photo by Tony Campbell*

Order ARTIODACTYLA—Deer

FAMILY CERVIDAE
Odocoileus virginianus / White-tailed Deer

Order Artiodactyla

The Artiodactyla are the even-toed hoofed mammals and include about 240 species in 10 families, among them the pigs, peccaries, hippopotamuses, deer, giraffes, cows, antelopes and related forms, and camels. Evolution in this group has been toward large size, herbivorous diet, and rapid locomotion. The long bones of the front and hind feet, the metacarpals and metatarsals, have elongated, therefore the ankle and wrist are above the ground and the hooves are formed by the tips of the toes. The two metatarsals and metacarpals have been fused into a "cannon bone," meaning that artiodactyls effectively have an extra segment in the legs. They walk on the tips of their toes. The herbivorous diet presents challenges in that cellulose is difficult to digest, and protein is needed for the amino acids necessary for growth and maintenance of tissues. The teeth and digestive system of artiodactyls show great variation in the way the different groups have solved these problems, such as complicated patterns of grinding surfaces on the teeth. The digestive system may be elongated, the cecum enlarged, and a four-chambered stomach (rumen, reticulum, omasum, and abomasum) has developed in the cow and other ruminants.

FAMILY CERVIDAE

The cervids include 51 species in 19 genera, including the deer, moose, and elk. This family is best characterized by the antlers. Antlers are bony outgrowths from frontal bones, found in males of all cervids. There are no upper incisors in the upper jaw, leaving a diastema. The antlers are shed annually. They begin growth in spring and are covered with "velvet," soft skin including blood vessels and nerves. The blood vessels carry nutrients to the antlers. The antlers mature in fall and are used in fighting or thrashing bushes. Decalcification occurs at the "pedicels" at the base of the antlers after the mating season, and the antlers eventually fall off of their own weight or by catching on brush.

White-tailed Deer
Odocoileus virginianus (Zimmermann)

Distinguishing Features and Measurements: The white-tailed deer requires no extensive description, for it is such a well-known animal. It is the largest wild mammal presently in Indiana. From April to January or sometimes February, males carry antlers; those of young bucks are simple spikes on either side. Antlers on does are extremely rare. The ears are large. The summer pelage is reddish brown above and whitish below. The winter pelage is grayer and more dense than the summer coat. Fawns molt from the second week of September through the first week of October. Newborn fawns are brownish-red above and white below with white spots over the body. These spots disappear when the first winter pelage is acquired in the fall.

TL 5–7 feet, T 10–14 inches, HF 19–21 inches, Wt. 100–300 lbs

Skull: Length: 270–330 (10.8–13.2").

The skull is elongate with no upper incisors or canines but with 6 molariform teeth. The orbit is completely surrounded by a bony ring.

Dental Formula:

$$\text{I} \ \frac{3}{3} \ \text{C} \ \frac{1}{1} \ \text{P} \ \frac{4}{4} \ \text{M} \ \frac{2}{3} \ = \ 42$$

Habitat: The white-tailed deer occupies woodlands, woodland borders, brushy areas, swamps, and agricultural land where there is adequate cover. Probably the best habitat includes a water source, mixed forest, brushy areas, some open land (croplands appear important in many sections of the state), and pine plantations. That deer are present even in counties that are intensively cultivated is an indication of the adaptability of the species, which originally was primarily a forest-inhabiting animal. In parts of the former prairie region, deer frequent vegetation (weeds to trees) along drainage ditches.

Food: White-tailed deer eat a wide variety of vegetable matter. Five vines—Japanese honeysuckle, poison ivy, Virginia creeper, greenbrier, and grape—are important. Deer also eat rye, wheat, green beans, cantaloupe, tomatoes, watermelons, and other cultivated plants. Crop damage by deer in Indiana has been reported on corn, soybeans, orchards, gladiolus, melons, and in Christmas tree plantations. Deer tend to feed rather hurriedly, then retire to a safer site to rest quietly. At this time, some food is regurgitated and chewed again (chewing the cud). On five southern Indiana study sites, key browse species were smooth sumac, dwarf sumac, sassafras, flowering dogwood, and red cedar. In northern areas, key browse species were aspen, staghorn sumac, smooth sumac, red osier dogwood, and soft maple. Salt is attractive to deer in many locations. The animals will travel some distance for salt and will frequent natural salt licks.

Reproduction: The mating season (rut) of deer occurs mostly in October and November. Gestation averages 201 days. Fawn and yearling does breed somewhat later in the year than do adult does. Some fawns breed when they are 6–7 months old. Probably most fawns are born from mid-May to early July. Females breeding for the first time usually produce one fawn per litter; thereafter two per litter is the rule, but triplets are not rare. Over a 10-year period (1957–1966), more than 1,000 does with fawns were observed. Of these, 53% had one fawn, 43% had twins, and 4% had three fawns.

White-tailed
deer, buck.
*Photo by Larry
Lehman*

White-tailed
deer, doe.
*Photo by
Terry L. Castor*

Range: Before Indiana became a state,
the white-tailed deer was probably
fairly common, although there is little
evidence other than brief comments of
early travelers and of authors of county histories. The species was extirpated
by 1900. The last deer was reported in
Knox County in 1893, and deer were
apparently absent from the state from
1893 to 1934. A restocking program
was initiated in 1934, when 35 deer
were released in seven Indiana counties. In 1943, 1944, and 1946, estimated
deer populations were 900, 1,200, and
more than 2,900, but may have actu-

ally been much higher considering the uncounted animals on state and federal lands. Indiana initiated a deer-hunting season in 1951, after a closed period of 58 years. By this time, deer damage to crops was becoming frequent. The white-tailed deer is now found throughout Indiana and is locally common. The heaviest concentrations are in the northern quarter and southern third of the state. Since about the 1970s, the deer has become very abundant and in need of control, especially in state parks.

Habits and Comments: The white-tailed deer is largely nocturnal or crepuscular and spends much of the daytime lying in beds in brush, in tall grass and weeds, or in wooded areas. Several animals may bed within a small area. In warm weather, they may bed down in relatively open sites. Deer beds are rather circular and about 3' in diameter. Their presence in snow is obvious because the snow is packed and partially melted by the heat of the body. In weedy areas, the vegetation is flattened by the weight of the animal. When bedded, white-tailed deer avoid eye contact with one another; they face in the same direction or away from each other, as direct eye contact is an aggressive behavior in deer. At dusk, animals become active as they move away from their protective covers and into open fields, along roadsides, and to other areas of sparse vegetation to feed and drink. It is not unusual to see them active during the day, especially on dark or stormy days. They use pine plantations more in winter than at other seasons, whether snow is on the ground or not. This is possibly an attempt to escape wind.

During rutting season, male deer paw the ground and create barren, somewhat circular patches 3–5' in diameter, called scrapes. Before making scrapes, deer reach up (sometimes standing on their hind legs) and pull down a twig or branch, frequently breaking it. The branch is then allowed to spring back across his forehead. He then paws or "scrapes" the litter from the ground directly below the branch and urinates into it. Scrapes serve as signs that a buck is around, and they may be freshened from time to time. Does are apparently attracted to the scrapes. Scrapes become noticeable in October and their use increases markedly from mid-October to the first week of November.

Deer are strong swimmers and cross even large rivers without difficulty. They readily jump into the water to escape danger and will cross wide expanses of wet marsh. Established "deer trails" are a conspicuous part of good deer habitat. Well-used trails become devoid of vegetation and are often cut deeply into the soil. Such trails are usually 10–12" wide. One can find trails that lead up to a fence, then continue on the opposite side, revealing the deer's ability to jump such obstacles. They sometimes clear fences that are 8–9' tall, although they sometimes crawl under them.

White-tailed deer make several sounds; all but the footstomp are vocalizations. The footstomp is made by the foot striking the ground as an alarm. Young deer give bleating calls. The snort often complements the stomping and is the sound most familiar to people. It is made by

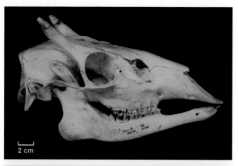
Side view of skull

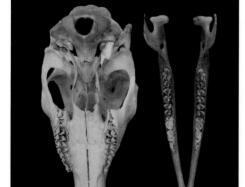
Ventral view of skull and lower jaw

Deer scrape. *Photo by Mary Beth Eberwein*

Deer trail, *above;* deer rub, *below.* *Photos by Mary Beth Eberwein*
White-tailed deer, fawn, *opposite.* *Photo by Brianne Walters*

expelling air through the nostrils with the mouth closed. Adults most frequently "snort" and when disturbed may give this call several times.

Most adult male deer have shed their antlers by early January. Some second-year bucks lose their antlers later, and some have been seen with antlers until early February. Antler growth begins in April but is most rapid from May to July, during which time the antlers reach nearly full development. During fall, when antlers are losing their "velvet" coat, deer often rub the antlers against trees or shrubs. A particular tree or sprout may be used as a rubbing post time after time, until it loses much of its bark and some of its small branches. The rubbing was long thought to facilitate the removal of velvet from the antlers, but it now appears to be a means of marking for communication. The "rubs" are marked with scent from glands on the forehead.

The average distance an individual was observed from its center of activity was 0.4 mile for does and 0.8 mile for fawns. Adult males ranged from 0.6 to 1.2 miles. The life expectancy of male deer for 1967 and 1968 was calculated to be 1.6 years; that of females was 2.4 years. Only a few males lived beyond 10.5 years, but some females reached the age of 14.5 years.

Disease does not appear to play an important role in the health of Indiana deer, although hemorrhagic disease sporadically kills some Indiana deer. Dogs, drowning, motor vehicles, and trains take their toll. Additionally, some deer die from falls or from locked antlers during skirmishes or by getting their antlers caught in fences. One deer was found, dead, wedged tightly in the low crotch of a tree. Poaching has always been a factor in the management of Indiana white-tailed deer and is likely to continue to take a certain percentage of the population annually.

SELECTED REFERENCES. Allen 1955; Kirkpatrick et al. 1976; Smith 1991; Stormer et al. 1974.

English-Metric Measurements Conversion

Converting English Units to Metric Units

Measure	English Unit	Metric Unit
Weight	1 pound	0.45 kilogram
	1 ounce	28.35 grams
Length	1 mile	1.61 kilometers
	1 yard	0.91 meter
	1 foot	30.5 centimeters
	1 inch	2.54 centimeters
Square Measure	1 acre	0.405 hectare

Converting Metric Units to English Units

Measure	Metric Unit	English Unit
Weight	1 kilogram	2.20 pounds
	1 gram	0.04 ounce
Length	1 kilometer	0.62 mile
	1 meter	3.28 feet
	1 centimeter	0.39 inch
Square Measure	1 hectare	2.47 acres
	1 square kilometer	0.39 square mile

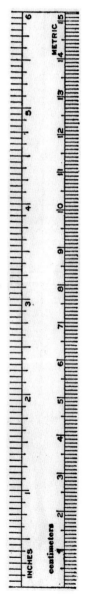

Glossary

abomasum The fourth or last part of the ruminant stomach, the part most similar to the true stomach of other mammals, and where the most absorption takes place. See *ruminant*.

acetabulum Either of the two round openings of the pelvic girdle into which the head of the femur fits.

acre An area of ground surface equal to 0.405 hectare.

aestivation See *estivation*.

albinism An unusual condition in which a genetically induced absence of pigmentation yields an albino, an animal with white hair and pink eyes. Partial albinism results in a spotted animal, with pigmentation completely lacking in some areas. Incomplete albinism results in an animal with reduced pigmentation throughout its body. Cf. *melanism*.

albino See *albinism*.

allantois A saclike outgrowth of the embryonic gut of mammals functioning in excretion, nutrition, and repiration. Cf. *amnion, chorion, placenta*.

allopatric Occurring in different areas or in isolation, ranges not overlapping.

altricial Of the young at birth, being blind, naked, immobile, and entirely dependent on parental care, as is the case with most mammals and many birds. Cf. *precocial*.

amnion The fluid-filled sac enclosing the embryo in mammals. Cf. *allantois, chorion, placenta*.

anal gland A gland associated with the anus of a mammal, particularly the odoriferous gland of a skunk (Mephitidae), or of weasels or other mustelids. Cf. *scent gland*.

analogous Having correspondence in function between anatomical parts of different structure and origin, as, for example, the wings of bees and bats, or horns of cows and rhinoceros.

anestrous Not exhibiting estrus.

annulation A ring about the body, as on the earthworm.

anterior At or toward the front.

anterodorsal Toward the front of the upperparts.

anteroventral Toward the front of the underparts.

anther The pollen-containing structure at the end of the stamen in a flower.

antler The solid, bony growth from the frontal bone of an animal of the deer family, often incorrectly called a "horn." Cf. *horn*.

aquatic Growing or living in or frequenting water. Cf. *terrestrial*.

arboreal Living in or frequenting trees. Cf. *scansorial*.

arthropod Any member of the vast invertebrate phylum Arthropoda, such as an insect, centipede, millipede, sowbug, spider, scorpion, or crustacean.

artiodactyl Any member of the order Artiodactyla, or hoofed mammals (as, for example, the deer or pig), with an even number of functional toes on each foot, and the axis of each limb passing between the third and fourth toes.

Arvicolinae Voles, lemmings, and bog lemmings. Previously the Microtinae. Often called meadow mice.

auditory bulla, or **tympanic bulla** The rounded, thin-walled, bony capsule enclosing the middle and inner ear of most mammals.

baby tooth Any of the first set of teeth of mammals, usually replaced by an adult tooth at an early age.

baculum (pl. bacula) A bone supporting the penis in many bats, rodents, carnivores, and some other mammals. Cf. *os clitoris.*

bay tine An antler tine positioned beyond the brow tine.

bicuspid A tooth, often or usually a molariform tooth, having two cusps.

binomial The basic two-part unit of taxonomic classification, consisting of the generic (genus) name and the trivial name, or epithet, these together constituting the species or specific name, as, for example, *Procyon lotor,* the raccoon.

bipedal Walking on two feet, as, for example, humans and birds. Cf. *quadrupedal.*

brachyodont Having low-crowned teeth, the teeth not as high as they are wide or long. Cf. *hypsodont.*

brow tine The tine closest to the base of an antler. Cf. *bay tine.*

browse To feed on twigs of trees or shrubs. Cf. *graze.*

buff A dull, brownish-yellow color.

bulla (pl. bullae) See *auditory bulla.*

bunodont Having teeth with low, rounded cusps, as in humans and pigs. Cf. *lophodont, myrmecophagous, selenodont, tuberculate.*

caecum (pl. caeca) See *cecum.*

calcar The spurlike, cartilaginous projection on the ankle of a bat that helps to support the interfemoral membrane.

canal An elongate opening through thickened bone, as opposed to a short opening through a thin plate. Cf. *foramen.*

canine One of the teeth, lone, usually elongate, and more or less pointed, that are situated behind the incisors and in front of the molariform teeth of a mammal; the first tooth in the maxillary bone.

canopy The uppermost spreading, branchy layer of a forest.

carcass The dead body of an animal. Cf. *carrion.*

carnassial In many Carnivora, the last upper premolar or the first lower molar; the largest of the molariform teeth that are adapted for shearing rather than tearing or crushing.

carnivore Any flesh-eating animal, especially a mammal belonging to the order Carnivora, presumably a meat eater, but in many cases omnivorous.

carnivorous Feeding on animal foods. Cf. *herbivorous, insectivorous, omnivorous.*

carrion Dead or decaying flesh. Cf. *carcass.*

cartilage A strong, translucent elastic tissue comprising most of the skeleton of embryonic and very young mammals and those of other higher vertebrates, mostly converted to bone in adult animals (but not in sharks).

caterwaul The wailing of mammals during breeding, especially that of cats.

caudal Of, pertaining to, or near the tail or posterior part of the body.

cecum, caecum (pl. ceca, caeca) The blind sac or pouch at which point the large intestine of many mammals begins; the appendix of humans.

cellulose A complex, relatively impervious, carbohydrate material forming the chief substance of plant cell walls; mammals have evolved many adaptations of the teeth and digestive tract to help them break down cellulose.

cervical Of or pertaining to the neck.

character (characteristic) Any of the various traits used to identify, distinguish, or classify organisms, most often, but not limited to, morphological or physical traits.

cheek teeth The premolars and molars, taken together; the molariform teeth.

chigger A larval mite of the acarine family Trombiculidae. Chiggers have three pairs of legs and piercing mouth parts; though small, they are often fairly obvious on hosts, often being highly colored (yellow, orange, red, or white), often solitary but some clustering in the ears or elsewhere on the body. Adult chiggers do not parasitize vertebrates but are the "red spider mites" often found crawling on the ground.

chitin A horny substance secreted by the upper layers of the skin and forming the hard outer covering of insects, crustaceans, and other arthropods.

chorion The highly vascular membrane that envelops the entire embryo, including the *allantois* and *amnion,* forming in mammals, part of the placenta.

class A taxonomic grouping, as, for example, Mammalia, that embraces one or more closely related orders.

classification The systematic arrangement of entities, as, for example, organisms, which are entered into groups or categories corresponding to presumed lines of evolutionary development. Cf. *nomenclature, systematics, taxonomy.*

cline A gradual gradation or *gradient* of characteristics from the individuals of one subspecies to those of another, usually geographic in disposition.

cloaca (pl. cloacae) A chamber at the terminal part of the gut of many vertebrates into which the reproductive, digestive, and urinary systems (and often certain glands) empty and from which waste products (and newborn young) leave the body.

commensalism A situation wherein individuals of two different (often markedly unrelated) species exist in close association, one benefiting from the association, the other not affected. Cf. *mutualism, parasitism, symbiosis.*

common name The non-latinized, colloquial, everyday name for a species or other taxon, as, for example, "red fox." Cf. *scientific name, species name.*

condyle An articular prominence of a bone, for example, the two occipital condyles where the skull articulates with the first cervical vertebra.

condylobasal length of skull Of a mammal, the distance from the anterior end of the premaxillaries to the posterior end of the occipital condyle.

conifer Any of various evergreen trees bearing true cones, as, for example, pines, firs.

conspecific Belonging to the same species, as, for example, individuals of two subspecies of a given species.

convergence The evolutionary tendency of organisms that are not closely related to develop similar adaptations when subjected to similar environmental conditions and constraints.

coprophagy The ingestion, by an animal, of its own undigested feces; also called *reingestion,* or *refection.* Rabbits, for example, feed rapidly on quantities of green vegetation, and the undigested material forms soft green pellets in the intestine. These are then defecated and fed upon in the safety of a burrow or thicket. Later, the typical brownish pellets, as often seen in the field, of digested material are defecated.

cranium The braincase of a vertebrate, consisting of bone in mammals and most other cases.

crepuscular Active during periods of twilight, whether dawn or dusk. Cf. *diurnal, nocturnal.*

cricetid A mouse of the family Cricetidae. New World rats and mice.

crown-rump measurement From crown to rump of developing embryo; it can be measured without removing the embryo from the reproductive tract as the best measurement of size.

cursorial Adapted for running, as, for example, a wolf or hare or deer. Cf. *saltatorial, scansorial.*

cusp A projection or tubercle on the biting surface of a mammalian molar tooth.

cyclic population behavior Of a species, having populations normally and more or less regularly undulating in size, the highs and lows rather consistently attaining about the same levels through intervals of years (often 3 or 4 years per cycle in *Microtus,* 9 or 10 in northern populations of lynx and snowshoe hares).

deciduous Shed at a certain stage of growth (as the teeth of many vertebrates) or annually (as antlers in deer, or the leaves of many plants, typically in the fall). Cf. *evergreen.*

delayed fertilization A condition wherein sperm remain viable in the uterus for an extended period before ovulation and then fertilization occur; for example, in north temperate bats, copulation occurs usually in the fall, fertilization in the spring.

delayed implantation A condition wherein, although fertilization occurs soon after mating and the embryo's development proceeds to the blastula stage, the blastula then remains free in the uterus for an extended period before implanting in the uterine wall; in some carnivores, mating occurs in summer and implantation the following spring.

dental formula See *tooth formula.*

dermal plate One of the external scutes of the armadillo.

dewlap A hanging fold of skin under the neck, such as of the moose.

diastema (pl. diastemata) A distinct space or gap between teeth, occurring as a normal character of various mammal species.

digitigrade Walking on the toes, the heels not touching the ground, as, for example, cats and dogs. Cf. *plantigrade, unguligrade.*

diphyodont Having normally 2 successive sets of teeth, deciduous (or baby) and permanent, as in humans and most other mammals.

diploid Of the body cells of an individual organism, having the normal ($2N$) number of chromosomes, as opposed to the haploid number (N), the number in sex cells (sperms and eggs). See *haploid.*

disjunct Of a population (or populations) of an organism, isolated geographically from the main range of its (their) species.

dispersal Permanent movement of individuals or groups of a population, especially the young, to a new area, often from their birthplace to an area elsewhere. Cf. *emigration, immigration.*

displaced Of an individual animal, being found in, or driven to, a new and unfamiliar location, as from a prior territory or home range.

distal Farther, or farthest, from the main part of the body, as the tip of the tail. Cf. *proximal.*

diurnal Active during daylight hours. Cf. *crepuscular, nocturnal.*

dormancy A deep sleep, but not as deep as that in hibernation or estivation.

dorsal On or pertaining to the back or dorsum.

dorsum The upper surface of a body.

echolocation A process by which an animal orients itself, or identifies the location, character, and perhaps movement of objects, by emitting high-frequency sounds and interpreting the reflected sound waves. Many bats and shrews navigate and locate prey by this method.

ectalental The sideways (rather than up and down) movement of the jaws by rabbits, reflected in the shorter lateral distance between lower toothrows than between upper toothrows.

ectoparasite A parasite that occurs on the outside of the body, such as on the feet or skin, and by definition causes harm to the host.

ectothermic Poikilothermous, cold-blooded. Having a body temperature that approximates that of the environment. Cf. *endothermic.*

effluvium An offensive, invisible exhalation or smell, as, for example, that of the musk of a skunk.

emarginate Having a notched margin or tip, as, for example, the lower part of a bat's ear.

embryo An animal in the early stages of growth and tissue differentiation, prior to assuming the essential form of its kind; often used synonymously with *fetus,* for example, "full-term embryo." Cf. *fetus.*

emigration Leaving one's habitual home range or territory for a life or residence elsewhere. Cf. *dispersal, immigration.*

endangered In danger of more or less imminent extinction with respect to its total, worldwide distribution, or, within a given region, of extirpation. Cf. *threatened.*

endemic Restricted to a particular locality or region, as, for example, kangaroos to Australia.

endoparasite A parasite, such as a trematode, cestode, or nematode, that occurs within the body of an animal and by definition causes harm to the host.

endothermic Homeothermic, warm-blooded. Having a body temperature that is internally regulated, thus remains relatively constant regardless of external temperatures. Cf. *ectothermic.*

environment The total physical and biotic surroundings within the normal range of an organism. Cf. *habitat, niche.*

epipubic bone One of a pair of bones, also called "marsupial bones," extending forward from the anteroventral portion of the pelvic girdle in marsupials and monotremes, serving to support the pouch in which the female carries her young.

epithet See *trivial name.*

estivation A dormancy similar to hibernation in being characterized by greatly slowed metabolic processes but occurring in response to heat or drought during summer. Cf. *hibernation, torpidity.*

estrous Of or pertaining to estrus, or *heat.*

estrus, oestrus See *heat.*

evergreen Of a plant, such as a conifer, not shedding its leaves in an annual cycle. Cf. *deciduous.*

extinction The complete and irrevocable disappearance of all individuals constituting a taxon throughout the worldwide range of that taxon. Cf. *extirpation;* see *endangered, threatened.*

extirpation The extinction of a species within a particular geographic region, as, for example, North America or New England, but not from its total worldwide distribution. Cf. *extinction.*

fallopian tube The small tube between the ovary and the oviduct in female animals, where fertilization often takes place.

family A taxonomic grouping, as, for example, Felidae, that embraces one or more closely related subfamilies and/or genera. The names of animal families end in -idae, those of plant families in -aceae; for convenience, the members of animal families are often called by a modification of the family name, always ending in -id, thus "felid" for a member of the Felidae, or cat family.

fecal Consisting of (usually) waste material originating from the anus. Animals such as rabbits exhibiting coprophagy often produce undigested soft fecal pellets that are then reingested.

feces Animal excrement; *scat.* Cf. *spoor.*

femur The upper bone of the hind leg of mammals and many other vertebrates; the thighbone.

fenestrate Filled with a labyrinth of small openings, as, especially, the rostrum of a hare or rabbit.

feral Wild; said of domestic animals (dogs, cats, pigs, horses) that have reverted to a wild state and are no longer dependent on humans.

fetus An unborn or unhatched vertebrate, after attaining the basic structural plan of its kind. Cf. *embryo.*

fibula The smaller and more slender of the two long bones in the lower part of the hind limb of most vertebrates. Cf. *tibia.*

flehmen The smelling or tasting of the urine of conspecifics for purposes of identification, as often occurs in canids and felids; lip curling in many hoofed mammals.

fluke One of the two lobes of the flattened, taillike appendage of cetaceans and sirenians; also, a trematode parasite.

forage To search for food, such as by browsing or grazing, or, of bats, to search for insects.

foramen (pl. foramina) A small opening or perforation through a thin plate, through which passes nervous tissue, blood vessels, or the like, as in the palate of many vertebrates. Cf. *canal, infraorbital foramen.*

foramen magnum The large opening at the base of the skull in many vertebrates, into which the spinal cord passes.

forb An *herb,* or nonwoody plant, other than grasses or graminiferous plants.

fossa An anatomical pit or depression.

fossorial Adapted for digging and burrowing and spending much time beneath the surface of the ground, as, for example, moles and pocket gophers. Cf. *subterranean, terrestrial.*

friable Easily crumbled or pulverized, as soil.

frontal bone The bone forming the front of the braincase of the mammalian skull, behind (or above) the nasal bones and maxillary bones.

gene A bit of genetic material (DNA) controlling or influencing a particular characteristic in all or various individuals of a population.

gene flow The movement of genetic material from one population of a species to another through interbreeding, or even from one species to another through hybridization.

gene pool The collective genetic material within a closed or contiguous population, or an actually interbreeding unit.

genus A taxonomic grouping, as, for example, *Felis,* that embraces one or more closely related species.

gestation, gestation period The period of development of the embryo in the uterus from conception to birth, in some cases protracted by delayed fertilization or delayed implantation.

gradient The span of change of one or more characters between one group or population of a species and another. Cf. *cline, intergradation.*

gravid Pregnant.

graze To feed on growing herbage or green plant material. Cf. *browse.*

gregarious Living in groups, whether of fixed or variable membership, as, for example, wolves or many of the deer species.

grizzled Gray, or streaked with gray or white.

guano An aggregation of bat or bird feces.

guard hairs The long, usually coarser outer hairs that lie over the shorter underfur of most mammals.

habitat The particular type of environmental circumstance, often highly specific in character, in which individuals or populations of a species of animal typically live, as, for example, forest, swamp, bog, or meadow. Cf. *environment, niche.*

hair See *guard hairs, molt, pelage, underfur.*

hallux The first or preaxial digit of the hind limb of mammals and many other vertebrates; the "big toe."

haploid Of the body cells of an individual organism, having half (N) of the normal number ($2N$) of chromosomes, thus the single set of chromosomes in a gamete (sex cell, whether sperm or egg); haploid sets of chromosomes unite at fertilization to form the diploid or somatic number of the individual. Cf. *diploid.*

harem A group of females herded together, usually by one male.

heat The typically annual period, from hours of duration in some species to weeks in others, during which a female mammal is sexually receptive to a male and reproductively fertile; *estrus,* or oestrus.

hectare An area of ground surface equal to 2.47 acres.

herb A nonwoody plant. Cf. *forb.*

herbaceous Having the character of an herb.

herbivorous Feeding on plant foods. Cf. *carnivorous, insectivorous, omnivorous.*

heterodont Having the teeth differentiated for various functions. Cf. *homodont.*

hibernaculum (pl. hibernacula) A shelter occupied in the winter by a hibernating animal.

hibernation A period of winter inactivity in many animals, in which normal metabolic processes and body temperature are greatly reduced. Cf. *estivation, torpidity, torpor.*

hispid Rough, or covered with stiff hairs.

Holarctic Of, relating to, or being the entire northern region of the lands (and seas) of the Old World and New World, south to but not including the tropics.

home range The area, not defended, that an animal traverses on a day-to-day basis during its normal activities of food gathering, mating, and caring for its young. Cf. *territory.*

homeothermic Endothermic, warm-blooded; having a body temperature that remains relatively constant regardless of external temperatures. See *thermoregulation;* cf. *poikilothermic.*

homing The act of returning to familiar territory after wandering or having been displaced. Cf. *philopatric.*

homodont Having no differentiation of teeth into incisors, canines, and so forth; having all of the teeth essentially similar in both upper and lower jaws. Cf. *heterodont.*

hoof The enlarged, hardened structure on the ends of one or more toes of the ungulate foot, a greatly modified claw, on which the animals run.

horn The bony projection from the head of a bovid, not shed, covered with keratin fiber substance. Cf. *antler.*

humerus The upper bone of the foreleg or arm of mammals and many other invertebrates.

hybrid The offspring of a mating between individuals of two separate but related species, the offspring often infertile; a crossbreed.

hybridization The mating between members of two separate species, the offspring often infertile, for example, a donkey.

hydric Of a soil or habitat, characterized by an abundance of water; of an organism, requiring an abundance of water.

hypogeous Growing underground; said of many fungi.

hypsodont Having high-crowned teeth, the teeth higher than they are wide or long. Cf. *brachyodont*.

Ice Age See *Pleistocene*.

immigration Entering, and becoming established in, an area other than one's prior habitual home range or territory. Cf. *dispersal, emigration*.

implantation The process by which the blastula or blastocyst stage of the developing mammal embryo imbeds in the lining of the uterus.

incisive foramen One of a pair of openings in the anterior portion of the palate, just behind the incisor teeth, in many mammals.

incisor One of the front teeth of most mammals, those ahead of (between) the canines, situated in the premaxillary bones of the upper jaw and in the anterior end of the mandible. Often used for nipping, but incisors are the major cutting and shearing teeth of rodents and lagomorphs.

infraorbital foramen An opening on the side of the rostrum, just anterior to the orbit, passing through the maxillary bone and into the orbit.

inguinal Of or pertaining to the region of the groin.

innate Inborn, as a particular behavior pattern or ability.

insectivoran A mammal of the older order Insectivora. Now Soricomorpha.

insectivore Any insect-eating animal, especially insectivorous bats and anteaters; mammals of the order Soricomorpha (Insectivora) are not nearly as insectivorous as many of the bats. Cf. *insectivoran*.

insectivorous Feeding primarily on insects. Cf. *carnivorous, herbivorous, omnivorous*.

insular Pertaining to, situated on, or living on an island.

interbreeding Breeding between individuals of two different stocks or taxa.

interdigitated Meeting or abutting along a highly irregular front, in the manner of the interlocked fingers of two hands, as, for example, adjacent habitats or populations.

interfemoral membrane The membrane between the hind legs of a bat, usually enclosing the tail; also uropatagium. Cf. *patagium*.

intergradation A gradual change in characteristics or *gradient,* from population to population, in the interim range between two subspecies of a species.

interparietal A small bone, usually triangular, on the posterior part of the top of the skull in mammals.

interpterygoid The opening in the skull above the hard palate. See *palate*.

introduction The intentional or negligent or accidental placing of individuals of a species from one region (e.g., Eurasia) in a region (e.g., North America) where that species had not previously existed, in sufficient numbers and in sufficiently suitable habitat that the species is at least potentially able to establish itself in the wild in the new region. Cf. *reintroduction*.

invertebrate An animal without a spinal column, such as insects, spiders, millipedes, snails, and worms.

keel A ridgelike projection on a bone or cartilage that provides an expanded surface for the attachment of muscles or skin, as, for example, the keel (ridge) on the sternum of a chicken or the calcar of some species of bats.

labial Of the lips; toward the lips from the teeth. Cf. *lingual*.

lactation The production of milk by the mammary glands.

lagomorph Any of an order (Lagomorpha) of gnawing mammals comprising the rabbits, hares, and pikas.

lambdoidal crest The transverse ridge along the posteriodorsal portions of the occipital and parietal bones of the skull.

larva (pl. larvae) A developmental form of many of the higher insects or in mites and ticks, for example, in insects, a grub, maggot, or caterpillar that is fundamentally unlike the adult in appearance and undergoes thorough reorganization at metamorphosis. Larvae of ticks and mites have only three pairs of legs in contrast to the four pairs of adults. Cf. *naiad, nymph*.

lingual Of the tongue; lying near or next to the tongue; on the tongue side of the teeth. Cf. *labial*.

loph A transverse ridge formed on the occlusal surface of a molar tooth.

lophodont Having transverse ridges, said of teeth. Cf. *bunodont, myrmecophagous, selenodont, tuberculate*.

mamma (pl. mammae) See *mammary gland*.

mammary gland One of the two or more milk-producing glands unique to mammals, developing in both sexes but rudimentary in males; the mammae.

mandible The lower, movable jaw of a mammal or other vertebrate.

marsupial bones See *epipubic bone*.

marsupium The pouch of a marsupial, in which are mammae and shelter for the young.

masseter One of the two jaw muscles that raise, thus close, the lower jaw.

mast The accumulation, on the forest floor, of the fruit of various forest trees, such as acorns, beechnuts, and hickory nuts, often serving as food for animals.

maxilla (pl. maxillae) Either of the pair of bones in the upper jaw of vertebrates, closely fused to the skull, that bear the canines and molariform teeth. Cf. *premaxilla*.

maxillary Of or pertaining to the maxilla; or, the *maxilla*.

meiosis The cellular process that results in the number of chromosomes in gamete-producing cells being reduced to one-half, one of each pair of homologous chromosomes passing to each daughter cell. See *mitosis*.

melanism The unusual darkening of coloration in some individuals of some animal species produced by a genetically induced excess of melanin (black) pigment in the skin and/or hair, as manifested, for example, in the black morph of the gray squirrel. Cf. *albinism, morph.*

membrane A thin, soft, pliable sheet of stretched skin, as, for example, on a bat or flying squirrel.

mesic Of a soil or habitat, being of an intermediate moisture condition; flourishing where there is neither an excess nor a paucity of water.

Mesozoic The geologic era extending roughly from 200 to 65 million years ago, the Age of Dinosaurs, in which gymnosperms (conifers) were the dominant plants and toward the end of which the flowering plants and mammals made their appearance.

metabolic rate The rate at which the chemical processes of the body occur, usually measured by the amount of oxygen consumed relative to an animal's mass.

metabolism The sum of the chemical processes in an organism by which energy is provided for vital processes and activities.

metacarpal One of the bones, often elongate and usually five, between the wrist bones (carpals) and the phalanges (finger digits) of the hand or front foot.

metatarsal One of the bones, often elongate and usually five, between the ankle bones (tarsals) and phalanges (toe digits) of the hind foot of a mammal.

microtine A member of the old subfamily Microtinae, the voles and the relatives (now the Arvicolinae).

midden A refuse heap; specifically, a pile of guano, food, or other material, such as the piles of plant materials, bones, and so forth, deposited by woodrats; or, the stored cones or other foods of squirrels.

middle ear A small cavity separated from the outer ear by the eardrum that transmits sound waves from the eardrum to the partition between the middle and inner ears through a chain of tiny bones characteristic of mammals, the malleus, incus, and stapes.

middorsal Situated at the middle of the dorsum.

migration The two-way movement, usually seasonal, often of all or most individuals of an animal species, from one region to another for the purpose of feeding and/or breeding, and the return at a later date.

milk teeth The first set of teeth of mammals, usually replaced by adult teeth at an early age.

mitosis A process in the nucleus of a dividing cell that results in the formation of two new nuclei, each having the same number of chromosomes as the parent nucleus. See *meiosis.*

molar Any of the hindmost teeth of the jaw in most mammals, typically robust and adapted for crushing, that are situated behind the premolars, not developmentally preceded by milk teeth. Cf. *premolar.*

molariform teeth The premolars and molars, taken together; the cheek teeth.

molt The periodic, typically annual or biannual, shedding and replacing of all or much of the hair by a mammal (or of skin or feathers or chitin in other animals). The presence of molting can be determined by examination of the fur from above, revealing the presence of short hairs, pigmented to the base (mature hairs are usually light-colored at the bases). Molt also shows on the underside of the skin where pigment deposition occurs as small dark dots in the new hairs as they are growing. The mature hairs of a "prime" or nonmolting pelt are usually light-colored at the bases (the pigmentation is above skin level), and the skin thus appears pinkish or whitish.

monestrous Having a single estrous cycle (period of heat in the female) per year. Cf. *polyestrous.*

monogamous Having a single mate for life, or at least for one breeding season. Cf. *polyandrous, polygamous.*

monotypic Embracing a single subordinate taxon, as a genus consisting of a single species.

morph A morphological form of an organism different from the typical form for the species, as, for example, the cross fox or the black morph of the gray squirrel.

morphological Of or pertaining to morphology.

morphology The form and structure (anatomy) of an organism or any of its parts; the branch of biology that deals with the form and structure of animals or plants.

mutualism A mutually beneficial, but not necessarily intimate, relationship between individuals of different animal or plant species, as, for example, the burying of acorns, by squirrels, for future consumption; the squirrel consumes many of the acorns, but many others later sprout and become trees, thus benefiting that species of oak. Cf. *commensalism, parasitism, symbiosis.*

mycorrhiza (pl. mycorrhizae) The rootlike structures of a fungus that are in close association with the roots of a tree or other seed plant.

myrmecophagous Of teeth, simple and peglike, lacking enamel, as in the armadillo. Cf. *bunodont, lophodont, selenodont, tuberculate.*

naiad The immature aquatic stage of a mayfly, stonefly, dragonfly, or damselfly; the immature bears some features of the adult but undergoes major changes at metamorphosis. Cf. *larva, nymph.*

nasal bone One of a pair of bones in the front of the mammal skull anterior to the frontal bones.

Neotominae Subfamily of Cricetidae. Includes the New World rats and mice.

niche The typical role or "profession" of an organism within its normal habitat and environment; organisms can carve out niches for themselves in different ways in different habitats, or in different communities in similar habitats. Cf. *environment, habitat.*

nictitating membrane A thin, transparent membrane, present in most mammal species, often called a "third eyelid"; it is drawn over the surface of the eyeball from the inner angle of the eye to the outer angle, thus cleaning the eye.

nocturnal Active during the night. Cf. *crepuscular, diurnal.*

nomenclature The formal international system and procedure of assigning unique and universal New Latin names to taxa of organisms. Cf. *classification, synonym, systematics, taxonomy.*

nominate subspecies The subspecies bearing the same name designation as the species, as, for example, *Sus scrofa scrofa;* the name thus given to the originally described population of a species when, in later years, some other population of that species is distinguished in some way, formally described, and accorded its own, new subspecific epithet; if in due course the newly described subspecies is formally deemed to be superfluous (synonymous), and no other subspecies has been described, the need for the nominate subspecies becomes moot. See *subspecies.*

notch (ear) The lowest notch or indentation of the ear. The length of the ear is measured from this notch to the farthest point on the periphery of the ear.

nymph An immature individual of one of the more primitive orders of insects, as, for example, crickets or grasshoppers (Orthoptera), at any of several successive life stages, each of which more or less closely resembles the adult; or in mites and ticks, the nymph has four pairs of legs like the adult, but it is not yet able to reproduce. Cf. *larva, naiad.*

occipital, occipital bone The bone forming the back or base of the skull, containing the occipital condyles.

occipital condyle One of the two protuberances on the back of the skull that articulates with the first cervical vertebra.

occlusal Of or relating to the grinding surfaces of the teeth.

occlusion The relationship between the opposing surfaces of the teeth of the two jaws when in contact.

ochraceous Having a yellowish-red tint.

oestrous, oestrus See *estrous, heat.*

olfactory Pertaining to the sense of smell.

omasum The third of the four parts of the ruminant stomach, which presses water from the predigested food. See *ruminant.*

omnivorous Feeding typically on both animal and vegetable foods. Cf. *carnivorous, herbivorous, insectivorous.*

orbit The bony eye socket of the skull.

order A taxonomic grouping, as, for example, Carnivora, that embraces one or more closely related families.

os clitoris A tiny bone or cartilage, the homologue of a *baculum,* often found in the female of a species, as, for example, seals and raccoons, the male of which possesses a baculum.

ossified Formed of bone, as opposed to cartilage.

outer ear The outer and visible portion of the ear that collects and directs sound waves toward the eardrum; the pinna. Cf. *middle ear.*

ovulation The eruption, or release, of eggs, or ova, from the ovary, into the fallopian tubes of mammals.

ovum (pl. ova) Egg.

palate The bony roof of the mouth in vertebrates; the palate has two pairs of openings into the skull, the anterior and posterior palatine foramina. Cf. *interpterygoid.*

palatine Of or pertaining to the palate.

palmate Branched from a common point, as the fingers of a hand, or the principal veins of a maple leaf.

parasite An organism that lives on or in, and at the expense of, but generally does not kill, its host. In most cases, it is far smaller than its host and inhabits one or only a few hosts during its lifetime. See *ectoparasite, endoparasite.*

parasitism A situation wherein two individual organisms, usually of markedly unrelated species and markedly different sizes, exist in intimate association, the one (on or within the other) benefiting from the association at the expense of the other. Cf. *commensalism, mutualism, symbiosis.*

parietal Either of the paired bones of the skull between the frontal bones and the occipital bones and forming the posterior portion of the braincase.

parturition, partus The birth of offspring in most mammals; the process by which a fetus separates from the mother's uterine wall and leaves the mother's body.

patagium (pl. patagia) The membrane in flying squirrels and bats that typically stretches down the sides of the body between the forelimbs and hind limbs and in bats in addition usually includes the tail, forming the surface area necessary for gliding (flying squirrels) or flight (bats). Cf. *interfemoral membrane.*

pectoral girdle The bony structure that supports the forelimbs of most vertebrates.

pelage The entire furred coat of a mammal, whether on the living animal or prior to skinning. Cf. *pelt.*

pelt The entire furred coat of a mammal, after its removal from the animal. See *pelage.*

pelvic girdle The bony structure that supports the hind limbs of a vertebrate, including, on each side, a round opening, the acetabulum, into which the head of the femur fits.

phalanx (pl. phalanges) One of the bones of a finger or toe of a vertebrate.

philopatric The tendency or drive of an individual to return to its home area.

phoretic Of or pertaining to phoresis.

phylum A taxonomic grouping, as, for example, Vertebrata, that embraces one or more closely related classes.

pigmentation Coloration in an organism produced by pigment granules, especially melanins (black or brown pigments), but also by anthocyanins (red pigments) or xanthins (yellow pigments).

pinna (pl. pinnae) The external (fleshy) ear of a mammal, lacking in many aquatic and fossorial species; the outer ear.

placenta The assemblage of vascular tissue, formed by the chorion and allantois of the embryo in placental mammals, that provides for the exchange of gases, nutrients, and waste materials between mother and embryo. The opossum (a marsupial mammal) has only a rudimentary placenta. Cf. *allantois, amnion, chorion.*

placental scar One of the discolorations on the wall of the uterus marking former attachments of placentas.

plantar Of or relating to the sole of the foot.

plantigrade Walking on the soles of the feet, the heels touching the ground, as, for example, bears and humans. Cf. *digitigrade, unguligrade.*

Pleistocene The *Ice Age,* or time of extensive glaciation, which lasted roughly from 1 million to 10,000 years ago.

plumbeous Of a leaden-gray color.

poikilothermic Ectothermic, cold-blooded; having a body temperature that varies with that of the environment. Cf. *homeothermic.*

polyandrous Having more than one male mate per female. Cf. *monogamous, polygamous.*

polyestrous Having more than one estrous cycle (period of heat) per year. Cf. *monestrous.*

polygamous Having more than one female mate per male, the male thus having a harem. Cf. *monogamous, polyandrous.*

population A group of interbreeding individuals of a single animal or plant species; a single reproductive unit or gene pool of a species, more or less isolated from other such units. Cf. *subspecies.*

posterior At or toward the rear.

postorbital process A process, or projection, of the frontal bone directly behind the orbit, or eye socket. Cf. *preorbital, suborbital, supraorbital process.*

postpartum estrus, postpartum heat The condition of a female wherein she becomes receptive to mating (and capable of conceiving) soon after giving birth.

precocial Of the young at birth, being fully furred (or feathered), open-eyed, and able to move about immediately, as the young of snowshoe hares, deer, cows, horses, chickens, killdeer, and some other mammals and birds. Cf. *altricial.*

predator An animal that lives, at least in part, by the killing and consuming of other animals, as is characteristic of many mammal species.

prehensile Adapted for grasping by curling or wrapping, as, for example, the tail in the opossum and many New World monkeys.

premaxilla (pl. premaxillae) Either of a pair of bones (the anterior-most) of the upper jaw of vertebrates, between and in front of the maxillae, that bear the incisors. Cf. *maxilla.*

premolar Any of the teeth of a mammal that are situated in front of the molars and behind the canines, developmentally preceded by milk (baby) teeth; in humans, the bicuspids. Cf. *molar.*

preorbital Anterior to the eye. Deer have preorbital glands just forward from the eyes. See *postorbital process.*

prey Any animal seized or hunted by another for food, successfully or not.

primary isolating mechanism Any factor (usually geographic) that separates the members of a species into two or more groups in such a way that interbreeding between the groups can no longer occur; the first of the two essential elements of speciation. Cf. *secondary isolating mechanism, speciation, subspecies.*

promiscuous Mating indiscriminately and perhaps often; said of an individual or a species.

proximal Closer, or closest, to the main part of the body, as the base of the tail. Cf. *distal.*

pupa (pl. pupae) The dormant or inactive stage in the development of insects of species that undergo complete metamorphosis from larva to adult. During the pupal stage, the insect in most cases is enclosed within a protective covering such as an earthen cell, cocoon, or puparium (hardened outer skin).

quadrupedal Having, and moving about on, four feet. Cf. *bipedal.*

quill One of the many hardened, hollow, pointed, and barbed hairs of a porcupine or other species with hardened spine.

radiotelemetry The use of radio transmitters and receivers to track the movements of, or to determine the den locations of, individual animals, the transmitter affixed in one way or another to the animal to be tracked.

radius The anterior, thicker, and shorter of the two bones of the lower foreleg of the forearm of mammals and many other vertebrates. Cf. *ulna.*

reentrant angle Folds into the inner or outer side of teeth, such as of arvicoline rodents.

refection See *coprophagy.*

reingestion See *coprophagy.*

reintroduction The placing of individuals of a species in an area from which the species had previously been extirpated, in sufficient numbers and in sufficiently suitable habitat that the species is at least potentially capable of reestablishing itself in the wild in that area. Cf. *introduction.*

reticulum The second of the four parts of the ruminant stomach, which returns large particles to the rumen for further processing. See *ruminant.*

retractile Capable of being drawn back, or into sheaths, as a cat's claws.

riparian Pertaining to the bank or shore of a river, lake, or stream.

rostrum The preorbital or snout part of the skull of a vertebrate.

rugose Heavily wrinkled; roughened into ridges.

rumen The first of the four parts of the ruminant stomach, a storage organ and a culture chamber for bacteria. See *ruminant.*

ruminant One of the hoofed artiodactyls having a four-parted stomach (the stomach consisting of, in order, the *rumen,* the *reticulum,* the *omasum,* and the *abomasum*).

rut The usually annual period of sexual excitement in the male deer and related mammals.

sagittal crest A raised, median, anteroposterior ridge of bone on the cranium, or braincase, serving as an attachment area for muscles or skin.

saltatorial Adapted for jumping, as a jumping mouse or kangaroo. Cf. *cursorial, scansorial.*

scansorial Having the ability to climb by means of sharp, curved claws, as, for example, tree squirrels and porcupines. Cf. *arboreal, cursorial, saltatorial.*

scapular Pertaining to the region of the shoulder, or scapula.

scat A unit of animal excrement; feces; often diagnostic of species. Cf. *feces, spoor.*

scavenger An organism that feeds habitually on refuse or carrion.

scent gland Any of various glands variously situated on the body of the animal, that produce a scent, or sometimes even an effluvium, employed in different species for different (or unknown) purposes but typically to mark territory, identify individuals, or attract the opposite sex. Cf. *anal gland.*

scientific name The unique, Latin name, of universal application, of a species (or other taxon) of organisms, such as *Mus musculus* for the common house mouse, or Chiroptera for the order embracing bats. The classification of plants is similar but entirely separate from that of animals; therefore the same name can exist for a plant and for an animal. See *species name;* cf. *common name.*

scute An external bony or horny plate, as, for example, those on the dorsum of an armadillo. Also *dermal plate.*

secondary isolating mechanism Any of various divergent adaptations of two or more populations or groups or populations of a species that prohibit resumption of successful interbreeding between the groups, once a primary isolating mechanism (typically geographic in nature) has broken down and the groups are once again in contact. Secondary isolating mechanisms, the second of the two essential components of speciation, may take many forms, as, for example, genetic, ecological, behavioral, temporal, or mechanical. Cf. *primary isolating mechanism, speciation, subspecies.*

selenodont Having teeth in which the enamel of the occlusal surfaces takes the form of successive longitudinal crescents, as in deer. Cf. *bunodont, lophodont, myrmecophagous, tuberculate.*

seminal vesicle A pouchlike structure usually at the base of the penis in mammals that stores seminal fluid (but not sperm) prior to ejaculation.

senescent Showing characteristics of old age.

seral stage One of the various stages in natural succession, as grassland or old-growth forest. See *succession.*

Soricomorpha Current name for part of old order Insectivora. Includes moles and shrews.

spatulate Flattened at the end like a spatula or spoon.

speciation The evolutionary process whereby, over time, two or more species are produced where only one had existed previously, usually following the rise of primary and secondary isolating mechanisms. Primary isolating mechanisms (usually geographic) separate populations or groups of populations of a species, thus cutting off gene flow between them and allowing evolution (biological divergence) to proceed; secondary isolating mechanisms are those factors (genetic, ecological, morphological, ethological) that block resumed interbreeding if and when the primary isolating mechanisms break down. See *primary isolating mechanism, secondary isolating mechanism, species.*

species A group of interbreeding or potentially interbreeding natural populations of organisms that are reproductively isolated from (generally incapable of breeding with) all other organisms or groups of organisms; the basic unit of taxonomy. See *speciation, subspecies.*

species name The currently accepted binomial (two-word) name of a species, consisting of the generic and trivial names, as, for example, *Mus musculus,* or *M. musculus. Mus* is the generic name, *musculus* is the *trivial name,* or *epithet.* Development of the present system of rules, the International Code of Zoological Nomenclature ("the code"), began in 1889, when the first Commission on Zoological Nomenclature met. The code established the tenth edition of Linnaeus' *Systema Naturae* (published in 1758) as the starting point of zoological nomenclature because Linnaeus was the first to apply binomial nomenclature consistently and systematically. The commission meets every 5 years to improve or modify the code as needed and to rule on contested names. Cf. *common name, nominate subspecies.*

spoor The track, trail, or footprint of a wild animal; a manifestation, of whatever sort, of the more or less recent presence (and often identity) of an animal. Cf. *feces, scat.*

standard measurements A set of measurements employed, by general agreement, in the description of an individual mammal or (as an average) of a species or population of a species, given as total length (TL), tail length (T), and hind foot length (HF), always presented in this order.

sternum (pl. sternums, sterna) The bone linking the ribs of a vertebrate along the length of the breast; the breastbone.

subfamily A taxonomic grouping, as, for example, Arvicolinae, that embraces one or more closely related genera within a family. The names of animal subfamilies end in -inae.

submaxillary gland A small gland under the lower jaw of a mammal that supplies saliva to the mouth; in the shrew *Blarina,* the gland contains poison.

subnivean Beneath a ground cover of snow.

suborbital Under the eye. Cf. *postorbital process.*

subspecies One of two or more populations of a species all deemed to be mutually distinct on some basis and given distinct names, as, for example, *Sorex hoyi hoyi,* deemed distinct from *S. h. winnemana;* as used here, a recognizably distinct population or group of populations of a single species, typically having a distinct, separate, and usually more or less disjunct geographic range and, as such, separated from other subspecific populations of that species by a primary isolating mechanism (e.g., a river), thus lacking a clinal gradation to the other subspecies of its species (and perhaps embarked on a process of speciation) but nonetheless potentially capable of interbreeding with other subspecies. (Historically, the problem of precisely defining the concepts *species* and *subspecies,* especially the latter, has been much in debate.) Cf. *nominate subspecies, population, primary isolating mechanism;* see *secondary isolating mechanism, speciation, species, synonym, trivial name.*

subterranean Living or occurring beneath the surface of the ground. Cf. *fossorial, terrestrial.*

succession The gradual, and naturally occurring, replacement of one biotic community by another, such as occurs during the replacement of grassland by shrubland, and eventually by forest. Animal succession follows plant succession. See *seral stage.*

supraorbital process A process, or projection, of the frontal bone above the orbit, or eye socket. Cf. *postorbital, preorbital, suborbital process.*

suspect bats Bats found on the ground, apparently sick, dead, or dying. The percentage of rabies in "suspect bats" (about 5% in Indiana) is much higher than that in bats behaving normally, where this percentage is far less than 1.

swarming (of bats) The gathering of substantial numbers of individuals (of one or more bat species), in late summer and fall, in the air about cave entrances; the function of the behavior is not completely understood but is probably related to mating. (See the account for *Myotis septentrionalis* for further discussion.)

symbiosis The living together in a more or less intimate association or close union of two dissimilar organisms, whether with benefit or harm for either or both or not; often used in the meaning of mutualism or obligate commensalism. See *commensalism, mutualism, parasitism.*

sympatric Occurring in the same range or area without loss of identity from interbreeding.

synonym In nomenclature and taxonomy, one of two or more scientific names deemed, at a given point in time and by a given authority on a group of taxa, to be designating the same species or other taxon, one name recognized by that authority as the accepted name and the others relegated to synonymy. See *nomenclature, subspecies.*

synonymy A list of two or more scientific names all applying to the same species or other taxon, all once thought to be designating distinct taxa but having fallen into synonymy over time (displaced in usage and recognition) as the result of revisions of their subtending group by later specialists, or on the basis of new discoveries or other knowledge.

systematics In the broad sense, the science of classification and nomenclature of organisms. Cf. *classification, nomenclature, taxonomy.* Many consider systematics to be the science of classification and taxonomy to be the process of applying names or nomenclature.

tactile Having, or pertaining to, the sense of touch.

talus A slope formed by rocky debris at the base of a cliff or mountain.

tawny A brownish-yellow color.

taxon (pl. taxa) An indeterminate term for an unnamed form or for a uniquely named and formally defined taxonomic unit, as, for example, one of the various subfamilies, genera, species, or subspecies within the family Muridae; or we can refer to, for example, the taxa of murid rodents. See *classification, nomenclature, systematics, taxonomy.*

taxonomy The formal and orderly classification of plants and animals according to their presumed natural relationships and origins; systematics. Cf. *classification, nomenclature, systematics.*

terete Circular in cross section.

terrestrial Living primarily on the ground, as, for example, a wolf; or growing on the ground, as, for example, a daffodil. Cf. *aquatic, arboreal, fossorial, subterranean.*

territory The portion of its home range that an individual animal routinely defends against members of the same or either sex of its own species, or, sometimes, different species. Cf. *home range.*

thermoregulation The regulation of body temperature in warm-blooded vertebrates (mammals and birds). See *homeothermic*.

threatened At risk of becoming *endangered*.

tibia (pl. tibiae) The larger and more robust of the two bones in the hind limb of most vertebrates. Cf. *fibula*.

tine One of the points on an antler.

tooth formula The itemized distribution of the upper and lower incisors, canines, premolars, and molars of a mammal, such as the dog:

$$ \text{I} \quad \frac{3}{3} \quad \text{C} \quad \frac{1}{1} \quad \text{P} \quad \frac{4}{4} \quad \text{M} \quad \frac{2}{3} \quad = \quad 42 $$

where the "fractions" to the left represent numbers of teeth of each type (incisors first) in the upper and lower jaws of one side of the skull and the number at the right doubles the preceding total, thus counts *all* of the teeth in *both* sides of the skull. Also *dental formula*.

torpidity In mammals, a relatively short-term period of winter inactivity during which the body temperature and rate of metabolism are somewhat reduced. Cf. *estivation, hibernation*.

torpor A deep sleep. Cf. *hibernation*.

track The imprint of successive footprints in soil, snow, or other substrate.

tragus (pl. tragi) The often prominent, sometimes quite long lobe extending vertically from the base of the ear of a bat, the function of which is incompletely known but apparently relates to echolocation.

trivial name The second element of a binomial (species) name, as, for example, *musculus,* of *Mus musculus,* the first element being the genus name. Also called *epithet;* see *subspecies*.

truncate Terminating abruptly, as if the end were cut off.

tubercle A small, rounded projection, such as is found on the crown of a tooth or on the sole of a foot.

tuberculate Primitive type of teeth, low-crowned with 3 cusps. Cf. *bunodont, lophodont, myrmecophagous, selenodont*.

tympanic Pertaining to the ear, especially the middle ear.

tympanic bulla See *auditory bulla*.

ulna The posterior, thinner, and longer of the two bones of the lower foreleg or the forearm of mammals and many other vertebrates. Cf. *radius*.

ultrasonic With respect to sound waves, above the range of human hearing, that is, above about 20,000 Hz (20 kHz).

underfur The thick, soft fur lying beneath the longer and coarser guard hairs of most mammals.

understory The layer of herbs, shrubs, and smaller trees beneath the forest canopy.

unguis A nail, hoof, or claw of a mammal, usually at the end of a digit.

unguligrade Walking in such a manner that only the unguis is in contact with the ground, as, for example, in deer and horses. Cf. *digitigrade, platigrade*.

unicuspid In shrews, one of the 3–5 small teeth between the anterior large 2-cusped upper incisors and the large cheek teeth.

uropatagium (pl. uropatagia) See *interfemoral membrane*.

uterus The internal organ of the female mammal that contains and nourishes the young during development previous to birth.

vacuity An empty space.

vaginal plug A plug formed of congealed seminal fluid that temporarily blocks the vagina and during that time prevents further insemination; found in bats, arvicoline mice, squirrels, and various other mammals.

vascular Of or relating to a channel or system of channels for the conveying of a body fluid, such as the blood of an animal or the sap of a plant.

velvet The soft vascular skin that envelops and nourishes the developing antlers of deer.

venter The underparts of the belly, or abdomen.

ventral On or pertaining to the underside or belly (*venter*).

vertebrate An animal with a backbone, or spinal column; fish, amphibians, reptiles, birds, and mammals.

vesicle A pouchlike or saclike structure that stores seminal fluid (but not sperm). See *seminal vesicle*.

vestige The evolutionary, often degenerate, remnant of an organ or structure that had been functional in ancestral organisms but is no longer in use, as, for example, the human appendix.

vestigial Of the character of, or pertaining to, a vestige.

vibrissa (pl. vibrissae) One of the several stiff facial whiskers or hairs around the nose or mouth of certain mammals, as, for example, felines, and evidently performing a tactile function.

viviparous Said of an animal species (including nearly all mammals and even some sharks) whose developing young become attached to, and receive oxygen and nourishment from, the reproductive tract of the female and are later born alive (not in eggs). Cf. *placenta*.

volant Flying; capable of flight.

xeric Of a soil or habitat, characterized by minimal moisture; of an organism, requiring a very dry situation. Cf. *hydric, mesic*.

yearling A 1-year-old animal, that is, one in its second year.

zygomatic arch The arch of bone forming the lower and outside edge of each orbit, or eye socket, of a vertebrate.

Works Cited

Allen, E. G. 1938. The Habits and Life History of the Eastern Chipmunk, *Tamias striatus lysteri*. N.Y. State Mus. Bull. No. 314: 7–119.

Allen, J. M. 1952. Gray and Fox Squirrel Management in Indiana. Ind. Dept. Conservation. Ind. Pittman-Robertson Bull. No. 1: 1–112.

———, ed. 1955. White-Tailed Deer. Ind. Dept. Conservation. Pittman-Robertson Bull. No. 3: 36–54.

Anthony, E. L. P., and T. H. Kunz. 1977. Feeding Strategies of the Little Brown Bat, *Myotis lucifugus*, in Southern New Hampshire. *Ecology* 58: 775–786.

Arlton, A. V. 1936. An Ecological Study of the Common Mole. *J. Mammal.* 17: 349–371.

Bailey, V. 1924. Breeding, Feeding, and Other Life Habits of Meadow Mice (*Microtus*). *J. Agr. Res.* 27: 523–535.

Baker, B. W., and E. P. Hill. 2003. Beaver. Pp. 288–310 *in* G. A. Feldhamer, B. C. Thompson, and J. A. Chapman, *Wild Mammals of North America: Biology, Management, and Conservation*. Baltimore, Md.: Johns Hopkins University Press.

Barbour, R. W., and W. H. Davis. 1969. *Bats of America*. Lexington: University Press of Kentucky.

Baumgartner, L. L. 1939. Fox Squirrel Dens. *J. Mammal.* 20: 456–465.

Beer, J. R. 1955. Survival and Movements of Banded Big Brown Bats. *J. Mammal.* 36: 242–248.

Beer, J. R., and A. G. Richards. 1956. Hibernation of the Big Brown Bat. *J. Mammal.* 37: 31–41.

Bekoff, M. 1977. *Canis latrans* Say 1823. Mammalian Species No. 79. Amer. Soc. Mamm.

———, ed. 1978. *Coyotes: Biology, Behavior, and Management*. New York: Academic Press.

Benton, A. H. 1955. Observations on the Life History of the Northern Pine Mouse. *J. Mammal.* 36: 52–62.

Berkley, K. A., and S. A. Johnson. 1998. Range Expansion of the Badger (*Taxidea taxus*) in Indiana. *Proc. Ind. Acad. Sci.* 107: 141–150.

Best, T. L., and J. B. Jennings. 1997. *Myotis leibii*. Mammalian Species No. 547. Amer. Soc. Mamm.

Birkenholz, D. E. 1967. The Harvest Mouse (*Reithrodontomys megalotis*) in Central Illinois. *Trans. Ill. Acad. Sci.* 60: 49–53.

Blair, W. F. 1940. A Study of Prairie Deer Mouse Populations in Southern Michigan. *Amer. Midl. Nat.* 24: 273–305.

Blatchley, W. S. 1897. Indiana Caves and Their Fauna. 21st Annual Report, Indiana Department of Geology and Natural Resources. Pp. 121–212.

Boyles, J. G., J. C. Timpone, and W. L. Robbins. 2003. Late-Winter Observations of Red Bats, *Lasiurus borealis*, and Evening Bats, *Nycticeius humeralis*, in Missouri. *Bat Research News* 44: 59–61.

Brack, V., Jr., and R. E. Mumford. 1984. The Distribution of *Pipistrellus subflavus* and the Limit of the Wisconsinan Glaciation: An Interface. *Amer. Midl. Nat.* 112: 397–401.

Brack, V., Jr., R. E. Mumford, and V. R. Holmes. 1984. The Gray Bat (*Myotis grisescens*) in Indiana. *Amer. Midl. Nat.* 111: 205.

Breece, G. A., and J. L. Dusi. 1985. Food Habits and Home Ranges of the Common Long-Nosed armadillo *Dasypus novemcinctus* in Alabama. Pp. 419–427 *in* G. G. Montgomery, ed., *The Evolution and Ecology of Armadillos, Sloths, and Vermilinguas.* Washington, D.C.: Smithsonian Institution Press.

Brooks, D. M. 1959. Fur Animals of Indiana. Ind. Dept. of Conservation. Ind. Pittman-Robertson Bull. No. 4.

Butler, A. W. 1885. Observations on the Muskrat. *American Naturalist* 19: 1044–1055.

Caldwell, R. S., C. K. Smith, and J. O. Whitaker, Jr. 1982. First Records of the Smoky Shrew, *Sorex fumeus,* and the Pygmy Shrew, *Microsorex hoyi,* from Indiana. *Proc. Ind. Acad. Sci.* 91: 606–608.

Chapman, J. A., and G. A. Feldhamer. 1981. *Sylvilagus aquaticus.* Mammalian Species No. 151. Amer. Soc. Mamm.

Chapman, J. A., J. G. Hockman, and M. M. Ojeda. 1980. *Sylvilagus floridanus.* Mammalian Species No. 136. Amer. Soc. Mamm.

Choate, J. R. 1970. Systematics and Zoogeography of Middle American Shrews of the Genus *Cryptotis. Univ. Kans. Publ. Mus. Nat. Hist.* 19: 195–317.

Christian, J. J. 1956. The Natural History of a Summer Aggregation of the Big Brown Bat, *Eptesicus fuscus. Amer. Midl. Nat.* 55: 66–95.

Clark, W. K. 1951. Ecological Life History of the Armadillo in the Eastern Edwards Plateau Region. *Amer. Midl. Nat.* 46: 337–358.

Connor, P. F. 1959. The Bog Lemming *Synaptomys cooperi* in Southern New Jersey. Mich. State Univ. Publ. Mus. Biol. Ser. 1. Pp. 161–248.

Cope, J. B., W. W. Baker, and J. Confer. 1961. Breeding Colonies of Four Species of Bats of Indiana. *Proc. Ind. Acad. Sci.* 70: 262–266.

Cope, J. B., R. E. Mumford, and N. A. Wilson. 1958. Some Observations on a Summer Colony of *Myotis lucifugus. Proc. Ind. Acad. Sci.* 67: 316–321.

Cope, J. B., A. R. Richter, and R. S. Mills. 1974. A Summer Concentration of the Indiana Bat, *Myotis sodalis,* in Wayne County, Indiana. *Proc. Ind. Acad. Sci.* 83: 482–484.

Cowles, H. C. 1899. The Ecological Relations of the Vegetation on the Sand Dunes of Lake Michigan. *Botanical Gazette* 27: 95–117, 167–202, 281–308, 361–391.

Cudmore, W. W. 1985. The Present Distribution and Status of the Eastern Woodrat, *Neotoma floridana,* in Indiana. *Proc. Ind. Acad. Sci.* 94: 621–627.

Cudmore, W. W., and J. O. Whitaker, Jr. 1984. The Distribution of the Smoky Shrew, *Sorex fumeus,* and the Pygmy Shrew, *Microsorex hoyi,* in Indiana with Notes on the Distribution of Other Shrews. *Proc. Ind. Acad. Sci.* 93: 469–474.

Dapson, R. W. 1968. Reproduction and Age Structure in a Population of Short-Tailed Shrews, *Blarina brevicauda. J. Mammal.* 49: 205–214.

Davis, W. B., and L. Joeris. 1945. Notes on the Life History of the Little Short-Tailed Shrew. *J. Mammal.* 26: 136–138.

Davis, W. H., and W. Z. Lidicker, Jr. 1956. Winter Range of the Red Bat, *Lasiurus borealis. J. Mammal.* 37: 280–281.

Davis, W. H., and R. E. Mumford. 1962. Ecological Notes on the Bat *Pipistrellus subflavus. Amer. Midl. Nat.* 68: 394–398.

Decher, J., and J. R. Choate. 1995. *Myotis grisescens.* Mammalian Species No. 510. Amer. Soc. Mamm.

Demaree, H. A., Jr. 1978. Population Ecology and Harvest of the Cottontail Rabbit on the Pigeon River Fish and Wildlife Area 1962–1970. Ind. Dept. Conservation. Pittman-Robertson Bulletin No. 10.

Dolan, P. G., and D. C. Carter. 1977. *Glaucomys volans.* Mammalian Species. No. 78. Amer. Soc. Mamm.

Dragoo, J. W., and R. L. Honeycutt. 1997. Systematics of Mustelid-Like Carnivores. *J. Mammal.* 78: 426–443.

Dunbar, M. B., J. O. Whitaker, Jr., and L. W. Robbins. 2007. Winter Feeding by Bats in Missouri. *Acta Chiropterologica* 9: 305–310.

Eadie, W. R., and W. J. Hamilton, Jr. 1956. Notes on Reproduction in the Star-Nosed Mole. *J. Mammal.* 37: 223–231.

Evans, F. C. 1949. A Population Study of House Mice (*Mus musculus*) following a Period of Local Abundance. *J. Mammal.* 30: 351–363.

Evermann, B. W., and A. W. Butler. 1894. Preliminary List of Indiana Mammals. *Proc. Ind. Acad. Sci.* 3: 124–139.

Fenton, M. B. 1970. Population Studies of *Myotis lucifugus* (Chiroptera: Vespertilionidae) in Ontario. Life Sci. Contributions, Royal Ontario Museum, No. 77: 34.

———. 1977. Variation in the Social Calls of Little Brown Bats (*Myotis lucifugus*). *Canadian J. Zoology* 55: 1151–1157.

Fenton, M. B., and R. M. R. Barclay. 1980. *Myotis lucifugus.* Mammalian Species No. 142. Amer. Soc. Mamm.

Fitch, H. S., P. Goodrum, and C. Newman. 1952. The Armadillo in the Southeastern U.S. *J. Mammal* 33: 21–37.

Fitch, H. S., and L. L. Sandidge. 1953. Ecology of the Opossum on a Natural Area in Northeastern Kansas. *Univ. Kans. Publ. Mus. Nat. Hist.* 7: 305–338.

Fitch, J. H., and K. A. Shump, Jr. 1979. *Myotis keenii.* Mammalian Species No. 121. Amer. Soc. Mamm.

Ford, S. D. 1977. Range, Distribution, and Habitat of the Western Harvest Mouse, *Reithrodontomys megalotis,* in Indiana. *Amer. Midl. Nat.* 98: 422–432.

French, T. W. 1980. Ecological Relationships between the Southeastern Shrew (*Sorex longirostris* Bachman) and the Masked Shrew (*S. cinereus* Kerr) in Vigo County, Indiana. Ph.D. diss., Indiana State Univ.

———. 1984. Dietary Overlap of *Sorex longirostris* and *S. cinereus* in Hardwood Floodplain Habitats in Vigo County, Indiana. *Amer. Midl. Nat.* 111: 41–46.

Fritzell, E. K., and K. J. Haroldson. 1982. *Urocyon cinereoargenteus.* Mammalian Species No. 189. Amer. Soc. Mamm.

Fujita, M. S., and T. H. Kunz. 1984. *Pipistrellus subflavus.* Mammalian Species No. 228. Amer. Soc. Mamm.

George, S. B., J. R. Choate, and H. H. Genoways. 1986. *Blarina brevi-cauda*. Mammalian Species No. 261. Amer. Soc. Mamm.

Gikas, N. S., J. G. Boyles, A. A. Zurcher, and J. O. Whitaker, Jr. The First Record of the Eastern Small-Footed Bat (*Myotis leibii*). Submitted to *Proc. Ind. Acad. Sci.*

Gould, E., W. McShea, and T. Grand. 1993. Function of the Star in the Star-Nosed Mole. *J. Mammal.* 74: 108–116.

Grizzell, R. A., Jr. 1955. A Study of the Southern Woodchuck (*Marmota monax monax*). *Amer. Midl. Nat.* 53: 257–293.

Hahn, W. L. 1907. Notes on the Mammals of the Kankakee Valley. *Proc. U.S. Nat. Mus.* 32: 455–464.

———. 1909. The Mammals of Indiana. 33rd Annual Report Ind. Dept. Geology and Natural Resources. Pp. 417–654, 659–663.

Hall, E. R. 1951. American Weasels. *Univ. Kans. Publ. Mus. Nat. Hist.* 4.

———. 1981. *The Mammals of North America*. New York: Wiley. 2 vols.

Hall, E. R., and K. R. Kelson. 1959. *The Mammals of North America*. New York: Ronald Press Co. 2 vols.

Hall, J. S. 1963. Notes on *Plecotus rafinesquii* in Central Kentucky. *J. Mammal.* 44: 119–120.

Haller, F. D. 1951. Field Studies of the Winter Feeding Habits of Red and Gray Foxes. Ind. Pittman-Robertson Wildlife Research Report 12: 95–100. (Mimeo).

Hamilton, W. J., Jr. 1931. Habits of the Star-Nosed Mole, *Condylura cristata*. *J. Mammal.* 12: 345–355.

———. 1933. The Insect Food of the Big Brown Bat. *J. Mammal.* 14: 155–156.

———. 1934. The Life History of the Rufescent Woodchuck, *Marmota monax rufescens* Howell. *Ann. Carnegie Mus.* 23: 85–178.

———. 1936. The Food and Breeding Habits of the Raccoon. *Ohio J. Sci.* 36: 131–140.

———. 1937. The Biology of Microtine Cycles. *J. Agr. Res.* 54: 779–790.

———. 1938. Life History Notes on the Northern Pine Mouse. *J. Mammal.* 19: 163–170.

———. 1940. The Biology of the Smoky Shrew *Sorex fumeus fumeus* (Miller). *Zoologica* 25: 473–491.

———. 1944. The Biology of the Little Short-Tailed Shrew, *Cryptotis parva*. *J. Mammal.* 25: 1–7.

———. 1953. Reproduction and Young of the Florida Woodrat, *Neotoma f. floridana* (Ord). *J. Mammal.* 34: 180–189.

———. 1958. Life History and Economic Relations of the Opossum (*Didelphis marsupialis virginiana*) in New York State. Cornell Univ. Agr. Exp. Stat. Mem. 354.

Hartman, C. G. 1928. The Breeding Season of the Opossum (*Didelphis virginiana*) and the Rate of Intrauterine and Postnatal Development. *J. Morphol. and Physiol.* 46: 143–215.

Hatt, R. T. 1929. The Red Squirrel: Its Life History and Habits, with Special Reference to the Adirondacks of New York and the Harvard Forest. Bull. New York State College Forestry. Roosevelt Wild Life Annals 2: 1–146.

Hayes, J. P., and R. G. Harrison. 1992. Variation in Mitochondrial DNA and the Biogeographic History of Woodrats (*Neotoma*) of the Eastern United States. *Syste. Biol.* 41: 331–344.

Heidt, G. A. 1970. The Least Weasel *Mustela nivalis* Linnaeus. Developmental Biology in Comparison with Other North American *Mustela*. Publ. Mich. State Univ. Biol. Ser. 4: 227–282.

Heidt, G. A., M. K. Petersen, and G. L. Kirkland, Jr. 1968. Mating Behavior and Development of Least Weasels (*Mustela nivalis*) in Captivity. *J. Mammal.* 49: 413–419.

Henry, J. D. 1986. *Red Fox, the Catlike Canine.* Washington, D.C.: Smithsonian Institution Press.

Hickie, P. F., and T. Harrison. 1930. The Alleghany Wood Rat in Indiana. *Amer. Midl. Nat.* 12: 169–174.

Hoffman, R. A., and C. M. Kirkpatrick. 1954. Red Fox Weights and Reproduction in Tippecanoe County, Indiana. *J. Mammal.* 35: 504–509.

Hoffmeister, D. F., and W. W. Goodpaster. 1963. Observations on a Colony of Big-Eared Bats, *Plecotus rafinesquii. Trans. Ill. Acad. Sci.* 55: 87–89.

Hofmann, J. E. 2005. A Survey for the Nine-Banded Armadillo (*Dasypus novemcinctus*) in Illinois. Center for Biodiversity Technical Report 16: 1–33.

Homoya, M. A. 1985. Map Showing the Natural Regions of Indiana. *Proc. Ind. Acad. Sci.* 94: Plate 1.

Homoya, M. A., D. B. Abrell, J. R. Aldrich, and T. W. Post. 1985. The Natural Regions of Indiana. *Proc. Ind. Acad. Sci.* 94: 245–268.

Hoofer, S. R., R. A. Van Den Bussche, and I. Horáček. 2006. Generic Status of the American Pipistrelles (Vespertilionoidae) with Description of a New Genus. *J. Mammal.* 87: 981–992.

Houtcooper, W. C. 1972. Rodent Seed Supply and Burrows of *Peromyscus* in Cultivated Fields. *Proc. Ind. Acad. Sci.* 81: 384–389.

Howard, W. E. 1949. Dispersal, Amount of Inbreeding, and Longevity in a Local Population of Prairie Deermice on the George Reserve, Southern Michigan. Univ. Mich. Contrib. Lab. Vert. Biol. No. 43.

Humphrey, S. R. 1974. Zoogeography of the Nine-Banded Armadillo (*Dasypus novemcinctus*) in the United States. *Bioscience* 24: 457–462.

Humphrey, S. R., and J. B. Cope. 1968. Records of Migration of the Evening Bat, *Nycticeius humeralis. J. Mammal.* 49: 329.

———. 1970. Population Samples of the Evening Bat, *Nycticeius humeralis. J. Mammal.* 51: 399–401.

———. 1976. Population Ecology of the Little Brown Bat, *Myotis lucifugus,* in Indiana and North-Central Kentucky. Special Publ. No. 4, Amer. Soc. Mamm.

———. 1977. Survival Rates of the Endangered Indiana Bat, *Myotis sodalis. J. Mammal.* 58: 32–36.

Humphrey, S. R., A. R. Richter, and J. B. Cope. 1977. Summer Habitat and Ecology of the Endangered Indiana Bat, *Myotis sodalis. J. Mammal.* 58: 334–346.

Hunt, T. P. 1959. Breeding Habits of the Swamp Rabbit with Notes on Its Life History. *J. Mammal.* 40: 82–91.

Jackson, M. T. 1997. *The Natural Heritage of Indiana.* Bloomington: Indiana University Press. 482 p.

———. 2007. *101 Trees of Indiana: A Field Guide.* Bloomington: Indiana University Press.

Jameson, E. W., Jr. 1947. Natural History of the Prairie Vole (Mammalian Genus *Microtus*). *Univ. Kans. Publ. Mus. Nat. Hist.* 1: 125–151.

Jenkins, S. H., and P. E. Busher. 1979. *Castor canadensis*. Mammalian Species No. 120. Amer. Soc. Mamm.

Johnson, S. A. 2002. Reassessment of the Allegheny Woodrat (*Neotoma magister*) in Indiana. *Proc. Ind. Acad. Sci.* 111: 56–66.

Johnson, S. A., and K. A. Berkley. 1999. Restoring River Otters in Indiana. *Wildlife Society Bulletin* 27: 419–427.

Johnson, S. A., and J. Choromanski-Norris. 1992. Reduction in the Range of the Franklin's Ground Squirrel (*Spermophilus franklinii*). *Amer. Midl. Nat.* 128: 325–331.

Jones, C. 1967. Growth, Development, and Wing Loading in the Evening Bat, *Nycticeius humeralis* (Rafinesque). *J. Mammal.* 48: 1–19.

Jones, C., and R. W. Manning. 1989. *Myotis austroriparius*. Mammalian Species No. 332. Amer. Soc. Mamm.

Jones, C., and R. D. Suttkus. 1975. Notes on the Natural History of *Plecotus rafinesquii*. Occas. Papers Mus. Zool. Louisiana State Univ. No. 47.

Keller, B. L., and C. J. Krebs. 1970. *Microtus* Population Biology, III. Reproductive Changes in Fluctuating Populations of *M. ochrogaster* and *M. pennsylvanicus* in Southern Indiana, 1965–67. *Ecol. Monogr.* 40: 263–294.

King, J. A., ed. 1968. Biology of *Peromyscus* (Rodentia). Spec. Publ. No. 2, Amer. Soc. Mamm.

Kirkpatrick, C. M., C. M. White, T. W. Hoekstra, F. A. Stormer, and H. P. Weeks, Jr. 1976. White-Tailed Deer of U.S. Naval Ammunition Depot Crane. Res. Bull. 932, Purdue Univ. Agr. Exp. Stat.

Koprowski, J. L. 1994a. *Sciurus carolinensis*. Mammalian Species No. 480. Amer. Soc. Mamm.

———. 1994b. *Sciurus niger*. Mammalian Species No. 479. Amer. Soc. Mamm.

Krebs, C. J., B. L. Keller, and J. H. Myers. 1971. *Microtus* Population Densities and Soil Nutrients in Southern Indiana Grasslands. *Ecology* 52: 660–663.

Krebs, C. J., B. L. Keller, and R. H. Tamarin. 1969. *Microtus* Population Biology: Demographic Changes in Fluctuating Populations of *M. ochrogaster* and *M. pennsylvanicus* in Southern Indiana. *Ecology* 50: 587–607.

Kunz, T. H. 1982. *Lasionycteris noctivagans*. Mammalian Species No. 172. Amer. Soc. Mamm.

Kurta, A., and R. H. Baker. 1990. *Eptesicus fuscus*. Mammalian Species No. 356. Amer. Soc. Mamm.

Kurta, A., and J. Kennedy, eds. 2002. *The Indiana Bat: Biology and Management of an Endangered Species*. Austin, Tex.: Bat Conservation International.

Kurta, A., K. J. Williams, and R. Mies. 1996. Ecological, Behavioural and Thermal Observations of a Peripheral Population of Indiana Bats (*Myotis sodalis*). Pp. 102–117, *in* R. M. R. Barclay and R. M. Brigham, eds., *Bats and Forests Symposium*. Victoria, Canada: British Columbia Ministry of Forests.

Kwiecinski, G. G. 1998. *Marmota monax*. Mammalian Species No. 591. Amer. Soc. Mamm.

Lackey, J. A., D. G. Huckaby, and B. G. Ormiston. 1985. *Peromyscus leucopus.* Mammalian Species No. 247. Amer. Soc. Mamm.

Larivière, S. 1998. *Lontra canadensis.* Mammalian Species No. 587. Amer. Soc. Mamm.

———. 1999. *Mustela vison.* Mammalian Species No. 608. Amer. Soc. Mamm.

Larivière, S., and L. R. Larivière. 1997. *Lynx rufus.* Mammalian Species No. 563. Amer. Soc. Mamm.

Larivière, S., and M. Pasitschniak-Arts. 1996. *Vulpes vulpes.* Mammalian Species No. 537. Amer. Soc. Mamm.

LaVal, R. K. 1970. Intraspecific Relationships of Bats of the Species *Myotis austroriparius. J. Mammal.* 51: 542–552.

Layne, J. N. 1954. The Biology of the Red Squirrel, *Tamiasciurus hudsonicus loquax* (Bangs), in Central New York. *Ecol. Monogr.* 24: 227–267.

Lehman, L. E. 1977. Population Ecology of the Raccoon on the Jasper-Pulaski Wildlife Study Area. Bull. No. 9, Ind. Dept. of Nat. Res., Div. Fish and Wildl.

———. 1984. Raccoon Density, Home Range, and Habitat Use on South-Central Indiana Farmland. Ind. Dept. Conservation. Pittman-Robertson Bull. No. 15.

Leibacher, B., and J. O. Whitaker, Jr. 1998. Distribution of the Western Harvest Mouse, *Reithrodontomys megalotis,* in Indiana. *Proc. Ind. Acad. Sci.* 107: 167–170.

Linzey, A. V. 1983. *Synaptomys cooperi.* Mammalian Species No. 210. Amer. Soc. Mamm.

Long, C. A. 1973. *Taxidea taxus.* Mammalian Species No. 26. Amer. Soc. Mamm.

Lotze, L., and S. Anderson. 1979. *Procyon lotor.* Mammalian Species No. 119. Amer. Soc. Mamm.

Lyon, M. W., Jr. 1923. Notes on the Mammals of the Dune Region of Porter County, Indiana. *Proc. Ind. Acad. Sci.* 31: 209–221.

———. 1936. Mammals of Indiana. *Amer. Midl. Nat.* 17: 1–384.

Martin, E. P. 1956. A Population Study of the Prairie Vole (*Microtus ochrogaster*) in Northeastern Kansas. *Univ. Kans. Publ. Mus. Nat. Hist.* 8: 361–416.

Martin, I. M. 1981. Venom of the Short-Tailed Shrew (*Blarina brevicauda*) as an Insect Immobilizing Agent. *J. Mammal.* 62: 189–192.

McAtee, W. L. 1907. A List of Mammals, Reptiles and Batrachians of Monroe County, Indiana. *Proc. Biol. Soc. Washington* 20: 1–16.

McBee, K., and R. J. Baker. 1982. Dasypus novemcinctus. Mammalian Species No. 162. Amer. Soc. Mamm.

McManus, John J. 1974. *Didelphis virginiana.* Mammalian Species No. 40. Amer. Soc. Mamm.

Miller, G. S., Jr., and G. M. Allen. 1928. The American Bats of the Genera *Myotis* and *Pizonyx.* U.S. Nat. Mus., Bull. No. 144.

Mohr, C. O., and W. P. Mohr. 1936. Abundance and Digging Rate of Pocket Gophers, *Geomys bursarius. Ecology* 17: 325–327.

Mumford, R. E. 1953. Status of *Nycticeius humeralis* in Indiana. *J. Mammal.* 34: 121–122.

———. 1969a. Distribution of the Mammals of Indiana. Monograph No. 1, Ind. Acad. Sci.

———. 1969b. The Hoary Bat in Indiana. *Proc. Ind. Acad. Sci.* 78: 497–501.

———. 1973. Natural History of the Red Bat (*Lasiurus borealis*) in Indiana. *Periodicum Biologorum* 75: 155–158.

Mumford, R. E., and L. L. Calvert. 1960. *Myotis sodalis* Evidently Breeding in Indiana. *J. Mammal.* 41: 512.

Mumford, R. E., and J. B. Cope. 1958. Summer Records of *Myotis sodalis* in Indiana. *J. Mammal.* 39: 586–587.

Mumford, R. E., and C. L. Rippy. 1963. The Southeastern Shrew (*Sorex longirostris*) in Indiana. *Proc. Ind. Acad. Sci.* 72: 340–341.

Mumford, R. E., and J. O. Whitaker, Jr. 1982. *Mammals of Indiana.* Bloomington: Indiana University Press.

Ostroff, A. C., and E. J. Finck. 2003. *Spermophilus franklinii.* Mammalian Species No. 724. Amer. Soc. Mamm.

Owen, J. G. 1984. *Sorex fumeus.* Mammalian Species No. 215. Amer. Soc. Mamm.

Pascal, D. D., Jr. 1974. An Ecological Study of the Pine Mouse, *Microtus pinetorum* (Le Conte), in Clark County, Illinois. MS thesis, Indiana State Univ.

Pearson, O. P. 1944. Reproduction in the Shrew (*Blarina brevicauda* Say). *Amer. J. Anatomy* 75: 9–93.

Peterson, K. E., and T. L. Yates. 1980. *Condylura cristata.* Mammalian Species No. 129. Amer. Soc. Mamm.

Pisano, R. G., and T. I. Storer. 1948. Burrows and Feeding of the Norway Rat. *J. Mammal.* 29: 374–383.

Polderboer, E. B. 1942. Habits of the Least Weasel (*Mustela rixosa*) in Northeastern Iowa. *J. Mammal.* 23: 145–147.

Pollack, E. M. 1950. Breeding Habits of the Bobcat in Northeastern United States. *J. Mammal.* 31: 327–330.

———. 1951. Food Habits of the Bobcat in the New England States. *J. Wildl. Mgmt.* 15: 209–213.

Poole, E. L. 1940. A Life History Sketch of the Allegheny Woodrat. *J. Mammal.* 21: 249–270.

Provost, E. E., and C. M. Kirkpatrick. 1952. Observations on the Hoary Bat in Indiana and Illinois. *J. Mammal.* 33: 110–113.

Reich, L. M. 1981. *Microtus pennsylvanicus.* Mammalian Species No. 159. Amer. Soc. Mamm.

Richards, R. L. 1972. The Woodrat in Indiana: Recent Fossils. *Proc. Ind. Acad. Sci.* 81: 370–375.

Richter, A. R., D. A. Seerley, J. B. Cope, and J. H. Keith. 1978. A Newly Discovered Concentration of Hibernating Indiana Bats, *Myotis sodalis,* in Southern Indiana. *J. Mammal.* 59: 191.

Rollings, C. T. 1945. Habits, Foods, and Parasites of the Bobcat in Minnesota. *J. Wildl. Mgmt.* 9: 131–145.

Rue, L. L., III. 1964. *The World of the Beaver.* Philadelphia: Lippincott.

Rysgaard, G. N. 1942. A Study of the Cave Bats of Minnesota with Special Reference to the Large Brown Bat, *Eptesicus fuscus fuscus* (Beauvois). *Amer. Midl. Nat.* 28: 245–267.

Schmeltz, L. L., and J. O. Whitaker, Jr. 1977. Use of Woodchuck Burrows by Woodchucks and Other Mammals. *Trans. Kentucky Acad. Sci.* 38: 79–82.

Sheffield, S. R., and C. M. King. 1994. *Mustela nivalis*. Mammalian Species No. 454. Amer. Soc. Mamm.

Sheffield, S. R., and H. H. Thomas. 1997. *Mustela frenata*. Mammalian Species No. 570. Amer. Soc. Mamm.

Shelford, V. E. 1912a. Ecological Succession. IV. Vegetation and the Control of Animal Communities. *Biological Bulletin* 23: 59–99.

———. 1912b. Ecological Succession. V. Aspects of Physiological Classification. *Biological Bulletin* 23: 331–370.

Shump, K. A., Jr., and A. U. Shump. 1982a. *Lasiurus borealis*. Mammalian Species No. 183. Amer. Soc. Mamm.

———. 1982b. *Lasiurus cinereus*. Mammalian Species No. 185. Amer. Soc. Mamm.

Silver, J. 1927. The Introduction and Spread of House Rats in the United States. *J. Mammal.* 8: 58–59.

Smith, W. P. 1991. *Odocoileus virginianus*. Mammalian Species No. 388. Amer. Soc. Mamm.

Smolen, M. J. 1981. *Microtus pinetorum*. Mammalian Species No. 147. Amer. Soc. Mamm.

Snyder, D. P. 1982. *Tamias striatus*. Mammalian Species No. 168. Amer. Soc. Mamm.

Sollberger, D. E. 1940. Notes on the Life History of the Small Eastern Flying Squirrel. *J. Mammal.* 21: 282–293.

———. 1943. Notes on the Breeding Habits of the Eastern Flying Squirrel (*Glaucomys volans volans*). *J. Mammal.* 24: 163–173.

Stains, H. J. 1956. The Raccoon in Kansas—Natural History, Management, and Economic Importance. Univ. Kans. Mus. Nat. Hist. and State Biol. Surv., Misc. Publ. 10.

Stalling, D. T. 1990. *Microtus ochrogaster*. Mammalian Species No. 355. Amer. Soc. Mamm.

Steel, M. A. 1998. *Tamiasciurus hudsonicus*. Mammalian Species No. 586. Amer. Soc. Mamm.

Stein, B. R. 1990. Limb Myology and Phylogenetic Relationships in the Superfamily Dipodoidea (Birch Mice, Jumping Mice, and Jerboas). *Z. für.Zool. Syst. und Evol.* 28: 299–314.

Stenbrot, G. I. 1992. Cladistic Approach to the Analysis of Phylogenetic Relationships among Dipodoid Rodents (Rodentia, Dipodoidea). [In Russian.] *Sbornik Trudov Zool. Muzeya* MGU 29: 176–201.

Stormer, F. A., T. W. Hoekstra, C. M. White, and C. M. Kirkpatrick. 1974. Assessment of Population Levels of White-Tailed Deer on NAD Crane. Purdue Univ. Agr. Exp. Stat., Research Bull. No. 910.

Streubel, D. P., and J. P. Fitzgerald. 1978. *Spermophilus tridecemlineatus*. Mammalian Species No. 103. Amer. Soc. Mamm.

Terrel, T. L. 1972. The Swamp Rabbit (*Sylvilagus aquaticus*) in Indiana. *Amer. Midl. Nat.* 87: 283–295.

Thomas, D. W., M. Dorais, and J. Bergeron. 1990. Winter Energy Budgets and Cost of Arousals for Hibernating Little Brown Bats, *Myotis lucifugus*. *J. Mammal.* 71: 475–479.

Thomson, C. E. 1982. *Myotis sodalis*. Mammalian Species No. 163. Amer. Soc. Mamm.

Thorne, D. H. 1989. Plains Pocket Gopher Distribution and Nutritional

Status in Indiana. Indiana Department of Natural Resources. Non-game and Endangered Wildlife Program Report No. 36.

Tuszynski, R. C. 1971. The Ecology of the Pocket Gopher (*Geomys bursarius illinoensis*) in Indiana. MS thesis, Purdue Univ.

Tuttle, M. D. 1975. Population Ecology of the Gray Bat (*Myotis grisescens*): Factors Influencing Early Growth and Development. Occas. Papers Mus. Nat. Hist. Univ. Kans. No. 36: 1–24.

———. 1976a. Population Ecology of the Gray Bat (*Myotis grisescens*): Factors Influencing Growth and Survival of Newly Volant Young. *Ecology* 57: 587–595.

———. 1976b. Population Ecology of the Gray Bat (*Myotis grisescens*): Philopatry, Timing and Patterns of Movement, Weight Loss during Migration, and Seasonal Adaptive Strategies. Occas. Papers Mus. Nat. Hist. Univ. Kans. No. 54.

———. 1979. Status, Causes of Decline, and Management of Endangered Gray Bats. *J. Wildl. Mgmt.* 43: 1–17.

Tuttle, M. D., and D. E. Stevenson. 1977. An Analysis of Migration as a Mortality Factor in the Gray Bat Based on Public Recoveries of Banded Bats. *Amer. Midl. Nat.* 97: 235–240.

Van Vleck, D. B. 1965. The Anatomy of the Nasal Rays of *Condylura cristata. J. Mammal.* 46: 248–253.

Veilleux, J. P., J. O. Whitaker, Jr., and S. L. Veilleux. 2003. Tree Roosting Ecology of Reproductive Female Eastern Pipistrelles, *Pipistrellus subflavus,* in Indiana. *J. Mammal.* 84: 1068–1075.

Verts, B. J. 1960. Ecological Notes on *Reithrodontomys megalotis* in Illinois. *Nat. Hist. Misc.* 174: 1–7.

———. 1967. *The Biology of the Striped Skunk.* Urbana: University of Illinois Press.

Wade-Smith, J., and B. J. Verts. 1982. *Mephitis mephitis.* Mammalian Species No. 173. Amer. Soc. Mamm.

Wagner, A. J. 1842. *In* Schreber, J. C. D. Die Saugethiere in Abbildungen nach der Natur mit Beschreibungen. Fortgeset zt von dr. Johann Andreas Wagner. Supplemental 3. abth. Erlangen: Expedition das Schreber'schen saugthier und des Esper'schen Schmetterlingswerkes, 1840–1844.

Watkins, L. C. 1972. *Nycticeius humeralis.* Mammalian Species No. 23. Amer. Soc. Mamm.

Webster, W. D., and J. K. Jones, Jr. 1982. *Reithrodontomys megalotis.* Mammalian Species No. 167. Amer. Soc. Mamm.

Whitaker, J. O., Jr. 1963. A Study of the Meadow Jumping Mouse, *Zapus hudsonius* (Zimmermann), in Central New York. *Ecol. Monogr.* 33: 215–254.

———. 1966. Food *of Mus musculus, Peromyscus maniculatus bairdii* and *Peromyscus leucopus* in Vigo County, Indiana. *J. Mammal.* 47: 473–486.

———. 1967a. Habitat Relationships of Four Species of Mice in Vigo County, Indiana. *Ecology* 48: 867–872.

———. 1967b. Hoary Bat Apparently Hibernating in Indiana. *J. Mammal.* 48: 663.

———. 1972a. *Zapus hudsonius.* Mammalian Species No. 11. Amer. Soc. Mamm.

———. 1972b. Food Habits of Bats from Indiana. *Canadian J. Zoology* 50: 877–883.

———. 1972c. Food and External Parasites of *Spermophilus tridecem-lineatus* in Vigo County, Indiana. *J. Mammal.* 53: 644–648.

———. 1974. *Cryptotis parva.* Mammalian Species No. 43. Amer. Soc. Mamm.

———. 1977. Food and External Parasites of the Norway Rat, *Rattus norvegicus,* in Indiana. *Proc. Ind. Acad. Sci.* 86: 193–198.

———. 1995. Food of the Big Brown Bat, *Eptesicus fuscus,* from Maternity Colonies in Indiana and Illinois. *Amer. Midl. Nat.* 134: 346–360.

———. 1998. Life History and Roost Switching in Six Summer Colonies of Eastern Pipistrelles in Buildings. *J. Mammal.* 79: 651–659.

———. 2004. *Sorex cinereus.* Mammalian Species No. 743. Amer. Soc. Mamm.

Whitaker, J. O., Jr., and B. Abrell. 1986. The Swamp Rabbit, *Sylvilagus aquaticus,* in Indiana, 1984–1985. *Proc. Ind. Acad. Sci.* 95: 563–570.

Whitaker, J. O., Jr., J. B. Cope, D. W. Sparks, V. Brack, Jr., and S. Johnson. 2007. Bats of Indiana. Publication No. 1, ISU Center for North American Bat Research and Conservation. Indiana State University.

Whitaker, J. O., Jr., and W. W. Cudmore. 1987. Food and Ectoparasites of Shrews of South Central Indiana with Emphasis on *Sorex fumeus* and *Sorex hoyi. Proc. Ind. Acad. Sci.* 96: 543–552.

Whitaker, J. O., Jr., H. K. Dannelly, and D. A. Prentice. 2004. Chitinase in Insectivorous Bats. *J. Mammal.* 85: 15–18.

Whitaker, J. O., Jr., and S. L. Gummer. 1992. Hibernation of the Big Brown Bat, *Eptesicus fuscus,* in Buildings. *J. Mammal.* 73: 312–316.

———. 1994. The Status of the Evening Bat, *Nycticeius humeralis,* in Indiana. *Proc. Ind. Acad. Sci.* 102: 283–291.

———. 2000. Population Structure and Dynamics of Big Brown Bats (*Eptesicus fuscus*) Hibernating in Buildings in Indiana. *Amer. Midl. Nat.* 143: 389–396.

———. 2003. Current Status of the Evening Bat, *Nycticeius humeralis,* in Indiana. *Proc. Ind. Acad. Sci.* 112: 55–60.

Whitaker, J. O., Jr., G. S. Jones, and R. J. Goff. 1977. Ectoparasites and Food Habits of the Opossum, *Didelphis virginiana,* in Indiana. *Proc. Ind. Acad. Sci.* 86: 501–507.

Whitaker, J. O., Jr., and R. E. Mumford. 1971. Jumping Mice (Zapodidae) in Indiana. *Proc. Ind. Acad. Sci.* 80: 201–209.

———. 1972a. Food and Ectoparasites of Indiana Shrews. *J. Mammal.* 53: 329–335.

———. 1972b. Ecological Studies of *Reithrodontomys megalotis* in Indiana. *J. Mammal.* 53: 850–860.

———. 2008. *Mammals of Indiana.* Bloomington: Indiana University Press.

Whitaker, J. O., Jr., L. Pruitt, and S. Pruitt. 2001. The Gray Bat, *Myotis grisescens,* in Indiana. *Proc. Ind. Acad. Sci.* 110: 114–122.

Whitaker, J. O., Jr., and L. J. Rissler. 1992a. Seasonal Activity of Bats at Copperhead Cave. *Proc. Ind. Acad. Sci.* 101: 127–134.

———. 1992b. Winter Activity of Bats at a Mine Entrance in Vermillion County, Indiana. *Amer. Midl. Nat.* 127: 52–59.

———. 1993. Do Bats Feed in Winter? *Amer. Midl. Nat.* 129: 200–203.

Whitaker, J. O., Jr., and L. L. Schmeltz. 1974. Food and External Parasites of the Eastern Mole, *Scalopus aquaticus,* from Indiana. *Proc. Ind. Acad. Sci.* 83: 478–481.

Whitaker, J. O., Jr., and G. R. Sly. 1970. First Record of *Reithrodontomys megalotis* in Indiana. *J. Mammal.* 51: 381.

Willner, G. R., G. A. Feldhamer, E. E. Zucker, and J. A. Chapman. 1980. *Ondatra zibethicus.* Mammalian Species No. 141. Amer. Soc. Mamm.

Wilson, D. E., and D. M. Reeder. 2005. *Mammal Species of the World: A Taxonomic and Geographic Reference.* Baltimore, Md.: Johns Hopkins University Press. 2 vols.

Wilson, N. A. 1960. A Northernmost Record of *Plecotus rafinesquii* Lesson (Mammalia, Chiroptera). *Amer. Midl. Nat.* 64: 500.

Winchell, J. M., and T. H. Kunz. 1996. Day-Roosting Activity Budgets of the Eastern Pipistrelle Bat, *Pipistrellus subflavus* (Chiroptera: Vespertilionidae). *Canadian J. Zoology* 74: 431–441.

Woolf, A., C. K. Nielson, and T. G. Kieninger. 2000. Status and Distribution of the Bobcat (*Lynx rufus*) in Illinois. *Trans. Ill. Acad. Sci.* 93: 165–173.

Wright, P. L. 1942. Delayed Implantation in the Long-Tailed Weasel (*Mustela frenata*), the Short-Tailed Weasel (*Mustela cicognani*), and the Marten (*Martes americana*). *Anat. Rec.* 83: 341–353.

———. 1947. The Sexual Cycle of the Male Long-Tailed Weasel (*Mustela frenata*). *J. Mammal.* 28: 343–352.

———. 1948. Breeding Habits of Captive Long-Tailed Weasels (*Mustela frenata*). *Amer. Midl. Nat.* 39: 338–344.

Yates, T. L., and D. J. Schmidley. 1978. *Scalopus aquaticus.* Mammalian Species No. 105. Amer. Soc. Mamm.

Yerger, R. W. 1953. Home Range, Territoriality, and Populations of the Chipmunk in Central New York. *J. Mammal.* 34: 448–458.

Young, S. P. 1958. *The Bobcat of North America. Its History, Life Habits, Economic Status and Control, with List of Currently Recognized Subspecies.* Harrisburg, Pa.: Wildl. Mgmt. Inst. and Stackpole Co.

Young, S. P., and H. H. T. Jackson. 1951. *The Clever Coyote.* Washington, D.C.: Wildl. Mgmt. Inst.

Zimmerman, E. G. 1965. A Comparison of Habitat and Food of Two Species of *Microtus. J. Mammal.* 46: 605–612.

Index